Qualitative Inquiry and the Conservative Challenge

For our students

Qualitative Inquiry and the Conservative Challenge

Norman K. Denzin
Michael D. Giardina

editors

Left Coast Press inc.

Walnut Creek, California

LEFT COAST PRESS, INC.
1630 North Main Street, #400
Walnut Creek, CA 94596
http://www.LCoastPress.com

Left Coast
Press Inc.

ISBN 1-59874-045-8 hardcover
ISBN 1-59874-046-6 paperback

Library of Congress Control Number: 2006925062

Printed in the United States of America

∞™ The paper used in this publication meets the minimum requirements of American National Standard for Information Sciences—Permanence of Paper for Printed Library Materials, ANSI/NISO Z39.48–1992.

Book design and production by Hannah Jennings Design.

06 07 08 09 10   5 4 3 2 1

CONTENTS

Acknowledgments

We thank Mitch Allen at Left Coast Press for his tireless efforts bringing this project to press. His dedication to the aims and objectives of this volume has been exemplary, and we look forward to working with him again in the near future. Extra special thanks to Carole Bernard for her editorial expertise and patience with us throughout the production process, and to Hannah Jennings for her excellent production design.

Many of the chapters contained herein were presented as plenary addresses at the First International Congress of Qualitative Inquiry, held at the University of Illinois, Urbana-Champaign, in May 2005. We thank the Institute of Communications Research, the Department of Advertising, and the College of Communications for institutional support of the conference as well as those campus units who contributed time, funds, and/or volunteers to the effort.

That conference, and by extension this book, would not have materialized in its current form without the continuous work of James Salvo, Grant Kien, Li Xiong, Jia Jia, Aisha Durham, David Monje, and Kevin Dolan, who were invaluable in their organizational expertise and dedication. We also recognize the nearly 1,000 participants who attended the conference to actively seek to mark a tidal shift in the field of qualitative inquiry and engage with many of the questions contained in this volume.

An earlier version of Chapter 2 by Patti Lather appeared as "This Is Your Father's Paradigm: Governmental Intrusion and the Case of Qualitative Research in Education," *Qualitative Inquiry,*

10(4), 15–34; an earlier version of Chapter 3 by Katherine Ryan and Lisa K. Hood appeared as "Guarding the Castle and Opening the Gates," *Qualitative Inquiry, 10*(4), 79–95; an earlier version of Chapter 4 by Janice M. Morse was given as the Keynote Address at the First International Congress of Qualitative Inquiry and appeared as "The Politics of Evidence," *Qualitative Health Research* (March, 2006), 1–10; an earlier version of Chapter 8 by Linda Tuhiwai Smith was given as the Keynote Address at the First International Congress of Qualitative Inquiry.

Introduction
Qualitative Inquiry and the Conservative Challenge

Norman K. Denzin and
Michael D. Giardina
University of Illinois

The distortion of scientific knowledge for partisan political ends must cease if the public is to be properly informed about issues central to its well being, and the nation is to benefit fully from its heavy investment in scientific research and education.

—Union of Concerned Scientists, 2004

The War on Truth[1]

To invoke and paraphrase William Kittredge (1987, p. 87), today in post–9/11 America with Patriot Acts, Homeland Security Administrations, No Child Left Behind Acts, Faith-Based Initiatives, and a president who performs scripts of fear written by others, we are struggling to revise our dominant mythology, to find a new story to inhabit, to find new laws to control our lives— laws designed to preserve a model of a free democratic society based on values learned from a shared mythology. The ground on which we stand has dramatically shifted. The neoconservatives have put into place a new set of myths, performances, narratives, and stories—a new set of laws that threaten to destroy what we mean by freedom and democracy (Giroux, 2004).

Qualitative research exists in a time of global uncertainty. Around the globe, governments are attempting to regulate scientific inquiry by defining what is good science. Conservative regimes are enforcing evidence, or scientifically based, biomedical models of research (SBR). These regulatory activities raise fundamental philosophical, epistemological, political, and pedagogical issues for scholarship and freedom of speech in the academy. *These threats constitute the conservative challenge to qualitative inquiry, the topic of this volume.*[2]

A major epistemological shift is underway to produce what Fine and McClelland (In press) call fundamentalist science. Within this neoconservative regime of truth, evidence is rendered problematic. In fact, it no longer needs to exist.

Consider:

Under the auspices of the 2001 No Child Left Behind Act (NCLB), the Bush administration has stated that traditional scientific methods are inadequate for purposes of educational reform. It has endorsed evidence-based models of inquiry, which many regard as inappropriate to human subject research and nearly impossible to implement in concrete research settings (see Ryan & Hood, this volume). Politically, as Eric Alterman and Mark Green (2004) note, NCLB "brings the federal government into local public policy making to an unprecedented extent and does so via Bush's repeated demands that 'if you receive federal money, we expect you to show results'" (p. 140). These results, or, to use Bush's favorite euphemism, "accountability," are measured in the form of so-called high-stakes testing; that is, "tests whose results are tied to material consequences like funding, graduation, and teachers' pay raises" (Alterman & Green, 2004, p. 143). Under the act, states must test students annually in both reading and math from third through eighth grades and at least once in high school, and they must compile a multitude of performance scores for various groups of students (e.g., racial and ethnic minorities, students with disabilities, low-income students, etc.). Schools that do not show "adequate yearly progress" on their test scores in each subgroup each year for two consecutive years would be labeled as "failing" (see Corn, 2003) and be forced to use their Title I federal funds to provide "supplementary education"—tutoring, extras class, and so forth—to any student who so requests it (see Alterman & Green, 2004; Giardina, 2005, pp. 86–91). Schools that do not meet federal standards cannot get federal funding; such funding, however, can be redirected in the form of vouchers to charter schools or parochial schools that can discriminate.

At the same time, and under the guise of endorsing "intelligent design" (or creationism by another Luntzian name), the administration has quite paradoxically launched a full-scale attack on the logic and methods of modern science. Declaring evolution a suspect theory, Bush has stated, "The verdict is still out on how God created the Earth" (quoted in Duff, 2002), while likewise asserting that intelligent design should be taught equally alongside evolution in the nation's public schools.[3] However, intelligent design "is not a theory, as scientists understand the word, but a well-financed political and religious campaign to muddy science" (Klinkenborg, 2005).[4] The basic proposition—the intervention of a designer, a.k.a. God—cannot be tested. It has no evidence to offer, and its assumptions that humans were divinely created are the same as its conclusions (Klinkenborg, 2005). Rather, by advocating a theistic, faith-based model of science, the far right under Bush is attempting to turn back the clock—to undo or debunk the findings of science—so that it can no longer be used by liberals and progressives to advance the goals of social justice and the Great Society initiatives of the last century.[5]

This same muddying of science is also true of issues pertaining to global warming, which scientists the world over nearly unanimously concur *is* a real and valid threat to the future well-being of the Earth's environment. In fact,

> [t]he general consensus in the field of climate science, reflected in the work on the Intergovernmental Panel on Climate Change [IPCC] (an international body comprised of hundreds of scientists), is that global temperatures are on the rise—and may climb 10 degrees Fahrenheit this century—and that this increase is, to some degree, a result of human-induced emissions of carbon dioxide and other gases. [Corn, 2001, p. 1]

Despite this, Bush remains steadfast that "more studies" are needed to verify that the planet is warming—that the climate is changing in potentially irreversible manners—and that human beings are at least partially to blame for such conditions. Yet, somehow, he rejects the Kyoto Protocol—an international treaty on climate change initially championed by the United States under then-President Bill Clinton—for being "not based upon science."[6] Moreover, as Katherine Mieszkowski (2004) has noted, "Bush's see-no-evil, hear-no-evil stance on global warming is so intractable that even when his own administration's scientists weigh in on the issue, he simply won't hear of it" (p. 1). Such was the case when the National Academy of Sciences released a report commissioned by the Bush administration that stated:

> Greenhouse gases are accumulating in Earth's atmosphere as a result of human activities, causing surface air temperatures and subsurface ocean temperatures to rise. Temperatures are, in fact, rising. The changes observed over the last several decades are likely mostly due to human activities, but we cannot rule out that some significant part of these changes are also a reflection of natural variability. Human-induced warming and associated sea level rises are expected to continue through the 21st century... . The committee generally agrees with the assessment of human-caused climate change presented in the IPCC ... report. [National Academy of Sciences, 2001, p. 1]

Writing in *Crimes against Nature: How George W. Bush and His Corporate Pals Are Plundering the Country and Hijacking Our Democracy* (2004), well-respected environmentalist Robert F. Kennedy, Jr., delivers the knockout blow to Bush's stance on global warming, stating in part: "We've got polar ice caps melting, glaciers disappearing all over the world, ocean levels rising, coral reefs dying. But these people are flat-earthers [*sic*]."

Such an aversion to facts is also evident in the tragic farce known as the "war" in Iraq. That is to say, the public was sold on the belief that weapons of mass destruction existed in an empirical reality. The inspectors would be able to locate the weapons, even though Saddam claimed they did not exist. Indeed, Saddam's lies proved the weapons existed. In the end, the weapons did not need to be found. Their absence meant they existed. We had no choice but to go to war. The media model that scripted Bush's war short-circuited history by manipulating the logic of the hyperreal. It created instant meaning by producing a fictional sense of public opinion that supported the war. Saddam and al Qaeda were connected. Saddam was evil. Al Qaeda is evil. The war was making America safer from terrorists. A total mythological system was in place. A closed system in which lies became truth and truth became that which conformed to the hyperreal. Frightening as it may seem, the subversion of reality that Orson Welles skillfully introduced into modern American media in his 1938 "War of the Worlds" radio broadcast has reached its culmination—as reality itself (Rich, 2005d).

On the whole, then, in areas ranging from education and foreign policy to the environment and health care (as well as a plethora of other areas we have not mentioned, such as stem-cell research, emergency contraception, water and air pollution, missile defense, hurricane preparedness, etc.), the George W. Bush White House has treated facts "as a nuisance, and scientists as an interest group—one that, because it lies outside the governing conservative coalition—need not be indulged" (Hertzberg, 2005, p. 22). Additionally, "[t]here is significant evidence that the scope and scale of the manipulation, suppression, and misrepresentation of science [and evidence] by the Bush administration is unprecedented."

Thus, although they have raised the bar concerning the standards for conducting and evaluating educational research with one hand, for example, they have simultaneously moved to debunk these same standards in other areas with the other hand. This allows them to play politics with knowledge, to have it both ways when it fits their right-wing agenda: modern science cannot get us to where we want to be in our schools, *and* we will use the methods of science to prove the case! In the name of pseudo, fake, or junk science, this callous administration manufactures evidence to support its positions and policies, or debunk that which stands in its way (Union of Concerned Scientists, in Kaplan, 2004, pp. 95, 125): It has appointed unqualified persons to scientific advisory committees; fired whistle-blowing scientists; erased large national data files that contradict official White House policy (Kaplan, 2004, p. 96); and hired fake journalists to promote its educational policies (Rich, 2005a, 2005c).[7]

To be clear, whether in the service of multinational corporations, warring neoconservatives, or the far-right conservative Christian coalition, the White House has used science to its own ends (Lather, this volume; Lincoln and Cannella, 2004b). Such a substitution of propaganda for governing, Frank Rich reminds us, bears a striking resemblance to Potemkin. But the ways in which the world is not a stage are not easy to specify. The dramaturgical politics of the Bush administration is one reason why this is so. Indeed, if, as they demonstrate, everything is always performative, staged, commodified, and dramaturgical, then the dividing line between performer and actor, stage and setting, script and text, performance and reality disappear. As this disappearance occurs, illusion and make-believe prevail. Truthful facts are casualties under such regimes. Misrepresentations are passed off as the truth. They produce misunderstandings. When this happens, the right people are not held accountable for the consequences of their actions. The consequences of misrepresentation can be devastating. The likelihood of future catastrophes is increased, and, as in the case of Iraq, people will die needlessly (Solomon, 2005, p. B-3).

These practices by Bush and the far right to redefine science in pseudo-religious terms must be resisted. They cannot be allowed to take science and its methodologies away from the scientific community. They cannot be allowed to treat science as if it were a handmaiden of religion. The processes that shape national security decision making in a democracy should be transparent and open. They should not be based, as was the Bush administration's decision to go to war, on cherry-picked intelligence; disinformation; secrecy; secret information; secrets that are not secrets; leaked, declassified, and reclassified documents; coded phrases; misrepresentations; distortions; and lies. Evidence should not be doctored (Rich, 2005b, p. 13). Contradictory evidence should be openly discussed, its implications for policy debated. Decisions "should be subjected to a robust process of checks and balance" (Herbert, 2005, p. A23). The hallmark of a free society is its unfettered support of research and inquiry on ethically and politically sensitive, controversial issues. Such research yields trustworthy findings that many, including those in political power, may find objectionable. But a society's respect for critical interpretive inquiry is "based on the common understanding that serious health, economic and social consequences are at stake" (Hillman, 2003), not public relations campaigns waged for partisan political gains and the appeasement of far-right religious zealots.

In light of such revelations, the politics of truth and scientifically based models of research take on increased importance.

Many questions are raised. What is truth? What is evidence? What counts as evidence? How is evidence evaluated? How can evidence—or facts—be "fixed" to fit policy? What kind of evidence-based research should inform this process? How is evidence to be represented? How is evidence to be discounted or judged to be unreliable, false, or incorrect? What is a fact? What is intelligence? What are the different discourses—law, medicine, history, cultural, or performance studies—that define evidence? (Pring, 2004, p. 203).

This volume addresses these questions and more, striking a lightning thrust into the heart of politics, scientism, and methodological fundamentalism that currently dominates the mainstream discourse of "Bush science." It is active in its engagement with and promotion of a qualitative research paradigm that collectively imagines creative and critical responses to these regulatory effects. It is forthright in its belief that the personal is political, and that the political is pedagogical. It shares in experiences, problems, and hopes concerning the conduct of critical, qualitative inquiry in this time of global uncertainty. It advocates that safeguards protecting scientists and the scientific community from censorship, misrepresentation, repression, and politicization must be commonplace. That the values of progressive democracy must be at the forefront when scientific advice is used for policy-making decisions. And that the pragmatic consequences for a radical democracy must be taken into account when scientific recommendations for social action are implemented.

To be sure, this is a gendered project, a project where feminist, postcolonial, queer, and indigenous theorists question the logic of the heterosexual ethnographic narrative. It is a moral, allegorical, and therapeutic project, one in which the researcher's own self is inscribed in the text as a prop to help men and women endure and prevail in the opening years of the twenty-first century. And it is avowed in its commitment to a project of social justice that can help us imagine a radical progressive democracy based on the universal values of love, care, and equality for all humanity.

In these times of national despair, a time when war wages on around us, and where the Bush administration promotes a "faith-based" model of truth, contributors to this volume have answered the call to reject politics as usual in favor of another world that *is* possible. It is time for all concerned scholars and citizens to rally against the misuses of science, information, and evidence by the Bush administration (Mooney, 2005, p. 255). A methodology of the heart, a prophetic, feminist postpragmatism that embraces an ethics of truth grounded in love, care, hope, and forgiveness is needed. When the divisions disappear between reality and its appearances, critical inquiry necessarily becomes disruptive, explicitly pedagogical, and radically democratic. Its topics: fascism, the violent politics of global capitalist culture, the loss of freedom in daily life. Where the hyperreal appears more real than the real, pragmatists and cultural critics require apparatuses of resistance and critique, methodologies and pedagogies of truth, ways of making real realities that envision and enact pedagogies of hope. Such pedagogies offer ways of holding fraudulent political regimes accountable for their actions. We demand that history's actors use models of evidence that answer to these moral truths. We need a new politics of truth. But first, a brief review.

Qualitative Inquiry and the Conservative Challenge

Qualitative inquiry is the name for a "reformist movement that began in the early 1970s in the academy" (Schwandt, 2000, p. 189). The interpretive and critical paradigms, in their multiple forms, are central to this movement. Indeed, this movement encompasses multiple paradigmatic formulations. It also includes complex epistemological and ethical criticisms of traditional social science research. The movement now has its own journals, scientific associations, conferences, annual workshops, and faculty positions. The transformations in the field of qualitative research that were taking place in the early 1990s continued to gain momentum as the decade unfolded. The days of value-free inquiry based on a God's eye view of reality are judged by many to be over.

Today, many agree that all inquiry is moral and political. By century's end, few looked back with skepticism on the narrative turn. Today, we know that men and women write culture differently, and writing itself is not an innocent practice. Experimental, reflexive ways of writing first-person ethnographic texts are now commonplace. Critical personal narratives have become a central feature of counterhegemonic, decolonizing methodologies (Mutua & Swadener, 2004, p. 16). Sociologists, anthropologists, and educators continue to explore new ways of composing ethnography, writing fiction, drama, performance tests, and ethnographic poetry. Social science journals are holding fiction contests. Civic journalism is shaping calls for a civic or public ethnography (especially as seen on blogs across the Internet such dailykos.com, blogforamerica.com, and eurotrib.com), and cultural criticism is now accepted practice.

Not surprisingly, however, this quiet revolution has been met by resistance. The field of qualitative research is defined primarily by a series of essential tensions, contradictions, and hesitations. These tensions—many of them emerging in the last decade—work back and forth between competing definitions and conceptions of the field. These tensions are lodged within and outside the field. In the United States, primary external resistance grows out of neoconservative discourses, including the recent National Research Council (NRC) report (see Feuer, Towne, & Shavelson, 2002), which have appropriated neopositivist, evidence-based epistemologies. Leaders of this movement assert that qualitative research is nonscientific, should not receive federal funds, and is of little value in the social policy arena (see Lincoln & Cannella, 2004b). The methodological conservatism embedded in the educational initiatives of the Bush administration have inscribed narrowly defined governmental regimes of truth. The new "gold standard" for producing knowledge that is worthwhile having is based on quantitative, experimental design studies (Lincoln & Canella, 2004a, p. 7).

This "methodological fundamentalism" (Lincoln & Canella, 2004a, p. 7) returns to a much-discredited model of empirical inquiry. The experimental quantitative model is ill suited to

> examining the complex and dynamic contexts of public education in its many forms, sites, and variations, especially considering the ... subtle social difference produced by gender, race, ethnicity, linguistic status or class. Indeed, multiple kinds of knowledge, produced by multiple epistemologies and methodologies, are not only worth having but also demanded if policy, legislation and practice are to be sensitive to social needs. [Lincoln & Canella, 2004a, p. 7]

Qualitative researchers twist and turn within this politicized space (Lather, chap. 2, this volume).[8]

The SBR initiated by the NRC has created a new and hostile political environment for qualitative research. Drawing from the biomedical field, SBR emphasizes research practices that produce so-called objective, reliable, and generalizable evidence (Ryan & Hood, chap. 3, this volume). Such data, gathered from randomized and nonrandomized experimental trials and quantifiable measurement procedures, are used to test causal hypotheses derived from scientific theory. When possible, data are fitted to complex causal models. Evidence based on these assumptions is presumed to be of maximal value for policy makers, practitioners, and the public (National Research Council, 2001, p. 47; Pring, 2004). Evidence that does not conform to these principles or methodologies is of less value and is not to be encouraged or funded.

Within this paradigm, researchers are encouraged to employ "rigorous, systematic, and objective methodology to obtain reliable and valid knowledge" (Ryan & Hood, 2004, p. 80). The preferred methodology has well-defined causal models using independent and dependent variables. Causal models are examined in the context of randomized controlled experiments that allow for replication and generalization (Ryan & Hood, 2004, p. 81). Elizabeth St. Pierre (2004) reminds us, however, that this "privileging of randomized experimental trials seems to occur in a time warp because educational researchers have acknowledged for decades that there is no single method that can serve as the gold standard for quality science" (p. 133).

Under this framework, qualitative research becomes suspect. There are no well-defined variables or casual models. Observations and measurements are not based on random assignment to experimental groups. Hard evidence is not generated by these methods. At best, case studies, interviews, and ethnographic methods offer descriptive materials that can be tested with experimental methods. The epistemologies of critical race, queer, postcolonial, feminist, indigenous, and postmodern theories are rendered useless, relegated, at most, to the category of scholarship, not science (Ryan & Hood, 2004, p. 81; St. Pierre, 2004, p. 132). Critics of the evidence movement are united on the following points. "Bush science" (Lather, this volume), and its experimental, evidence-based methodologies, represent a racialized masculinist backlash to the proliferation of qualitative inquiry methods over the last two decades. The movement endorses a narrow view of science (Maxwell, 2004), celebrating a "neoclassical experimentalism that is a throwback to the Campbell-Stanley [1963] era and its dogmatic adherence to an exclusive reliance on quantitative methods" (Howe, 2004, p. 42). There is a "nostalgia for a simple and ordered universe of science that never was" (Popkewitz, 2004, p. 62). With its emphasis on only one form of scientific rigor, the NRC ignores the need and value of complex historical, contextual, and political criteria for evaluating inquiry.

Furthermore, neoclassical experimentalists extol evidence-based "medical research as the model for educational research, particularly the random clinical trial" (Howe, 2004, p. 48). But the random clinical trial—dispensing a pill—is quite unlike "dispensing a curriculum" (p. 48), and the "effects" of the educational experiment cannot be easily measured, unlike a "10-point reduction in diastolic blood pressure" (p. 48). Qualitative researchers must learn to think outside the box, critiquing the NRC and its methodological guidelines (Atkinson, 2004). We must apply our critical imaginations to the meaning of such terms as randomized design, causal model, policy studies, and public science (Weinstein, 2004). More deeply, we must resist conservative attempts to discredit qualitative inquiry by placing it back inside the box of positivism.

There is a great deal at stake in these arguments. As St. Pierre (2004, p. 132) observes, the SBR criteria marginalize many forms of qualitative inquiry, including critical race, queer, postcolonial, feminist, indigenous, and decolonizing theories. The demands of SBR raise questions that require serious public discussion. They endorse a narrow view of science and evidence. They celebrate a historical moment when the methods of positivistic science were not being challenged. In valorizing the experimental model, they ignore the many criticisms of experimentalism, developed over four decades ago, involving the inability to adequately treat rival causal factors associated with internal and external validity as well as the limitations of naive realism; the erasure of the value-fact-theory distinction; the death of the disinterested observer who has a God's eye view of objective reality; the reliance on an ethics of deception; and a refusal to consider either the contexts of knowledge production or the researcher-subject relationship (Campbell & Stanley, 1963; Howe, 2004; Lincoln & Guba, 2000).

These limitations of the SBR model involve the politics of truth. They intersect with the ways in which a given political regime fixes facts and intelligence to fit ideology. What is true or false is determined, in part, by the criteria that are used to judge good and bad evidence.

SBR and the War on Truth

There are at least three versions of SBR. SBR One is the model outlined by the National Research Council (2002). SBR Two is a simulacra of SBR One. It was the model used by the Bush administration when it sold the unilateral intervention and war in Iraq to the world. This model produces simulacra of the truth. SBR Three (below) rejects SBR One and Two, and articulates a politics and methodology of truth based on a decolonizing, critical pedagogy, and a feminist, prophetic ethical pragmatism (Denzin, 1996, 2003, In press; Siegfried, 1996; West, 1989, 1991).

SBR One, with its focus on objectively verifiable evidence, was not in play when the Bush administration decided to go to war. Instead, it used SBR Two, which allowed it to act as if it was gathering objective, reliable, generalizable evidence. But it was not doing this. The intent, instead, was to gather evidence that appeared to have these characteristics. Under the Bush regime, a fact or piece of evidence is true if it meets three criteria: (1) it has the appearance of being factual; (2) it is patriotic; and (3) it supports a political action that advances the White House's far-right neoconservative agenda.

Evidence that contradicts that agenda is treated as flawed and/or biased. The Bush administration wanted to assert its will in the Middle East. It fabricated a set of facts, using its version of SBR One—SBR Two—to justify that activity. Challenges to the war were unpatriotic and discredited because they undercut the administration's desire to protect Americans from violent terrorists who oppose our political system. An unnamed senior advisor to President Bush described this troubling relationship between performance and reality when he contrasted the "'reality-based community'—people who believe that solutions emerge from ... judicious study of discernible reality" (quoted in Suskind, 2004, p. 51), with his own world-view:

> That's not the way the world really works anymore. We're an empire now, and when we act, we create our own reality. And while you are studying that reality we'll act again creating other new realities, which you can study too... . We're history's actors ... and you, all of you, will be left to just study what we do. [p. 51]

How do we respond to a statement such as this? Whose history are they creating? And for what ends? Who gave them this power? Who is holding them responsible for the consequences of their historical actions? If they do not like the effects of one reality, they create a new one, to which we must respond, living out the consequences of their experiments in reality construction.

SBR Three: Critical Pedagogy, Ethics, and Prophetic Pragmatism

Against the above-mentioned developments, what does it mean to assert that journalists and social scientists can only write about the realities created by history's actors? What does it mean to state that journalists and social scientists write the first drafts of history? In effect, what is truth? For this, we turn to the postpragmatists (see Denzin, 1996, for a review; see also Seigfried, 1996). For the postpragmatist feminist, there is no neutral standpoint, no objective God's eye view of the world. The meaning of a concept, line of action, or representation lies in the practical, political, moral, and social consequences it produces for an actor or collectivity. The meanings of these consequences are not given objectively. They are established through social interaction and the politics of representation. All representations are historically situated, shaped by the intersecting contingencies of power, gender, race, and class (Collins, 1991; Seigfried, 1996, p. 269).

An Afrocentric, feminist ethical framework (Collins, 1991,

1998) mediates the pragmatic theory of meaning. Patricia Hill Collins (1991) offers four criteria—primacy of lived experience, dialogue, an ethics of care, an ethics of responsibility—for interpreting truth and knowledge claims. This framework privileges lived experience, emotion, empathy, and values rooted in personal expressiveness (Edwards & Mauthner, 2002, p. 25). The moral inquirer—whether a politician or a social scientist—builds a collaborative, reciprocal, trusting, mutually accountable relationship with those studied. This feminist ethical framework is care- and justice based. It seeks to contextualize shared values and norms. It privileges the sacredness of life, human dignity, nonviolence, care, solidarity, love, community, empowerment, and civic transformation. It demands of any action that it positively contribute to a politics of resistance, hope, and freedom (Denzin, 2003, p. 258).

For the prophetic postpragmatists, there are no absolute truths, no absolute principles, no faith-based beliefs in what is true or false. At the level of politics and ideology, the postpragmatist, following Cornel West (1989, p. 234, 1991, p. 36), acts as a critical moral agent, one whose political goal is the creation of greater individual freedom in the broader social order. Paraphrasing West (1991, pp. 35–36), prophetic pragmatists as moral agents understand that the consequences of their interventions into the world are exclusively political, judged always in terms of their contributions to a politics of liberation, love, caring, and freedom. Following Collins (1991), Pelias (2004, p. 163), and Freire (1999), the moral inquirer enacts a politics of love and care, an ethic of hope and forgiveness.

Materially, actions are judged in terms of moral consequences and the meanings people bring to them. Consequences are not self-evident. They are socially constructed through the politics of representation. The concept of truth is thus replaced with a consequential theory of meaning. Experience, folded through what Stuart Hall (1996, p. 473) calls the politics of representation, becomes the site of meaning and truth. Facts about the world are treated as facticities, as lived experiences. The pragmatist examines the effects, or consequences of any line of action on existing structures of domination. The pragmatist asks, that is, what are the moral and ethical consequences of these effects for lived human experience? If people are being oppressed, denied freedom, or dying because of these effects, then the action, of course, is morally indefensible. We hope to counter this trend.

The Chapters

The chapters that follow are divided into three parts: The Politics of Evidence, Decolonizing Methodologies, and Contesting Regulation. Contributors in Part One interrogate the concept of evidence, review the history of genres in qualitative inquiry, and examine the effects and forms of governmental intrusion in the United States, Australia, and Great Britain on human subject research. George Kamberelis and Greg Dimitriadis ("Chronotopes of Human Science Inquiry") open this section by calling for a language of human science inquiry (chronotopes) that stretches across disciplines (education, sociology anthropology, language studies), epistemologies (positivism, pospositivism, hermeneutics, poststructualism), and methodologies. By isolating four chronotopes, they underscore the complexity and tensions that currently define the field of qualitative inquiry.

Patti Lather ("Government Intrusion and the Case of Qualitative Research in Education") follows, mobilizing three counterdiscourses to critique the federal government's incursion into legislating SBR standards for research connected to No Child Left Behind legislation. Her use of Foucauldian policy analysis, feminism a la Luce Irigaray, and postcolonialism a la Stuart Hall views the scientism of SBR as a racialized masculinist backlash against the past quarter-century of qualitative inquiry.

Katherine E. Ryan and Lisa K. Hood ("Guarding the Castle and Opening the Gates") use the metaphor of guarding the castle to discuss how the educational community has attempted to counteract the effects of SBR on educational research. Drawing on actual field examples, they show just how hard it is to implement SBR experimental criteria in school settings. They propose the use of both qualitative and quantitative methods in the study of systemic issues, while calling for the creation of a space for public dialogue and public engagement of these issues.

Janice M. Morse ("The Politics of Evidence") likewise criticizes the evidence-based or SBR movement by showing its negative effects in the field of medical research. She criticizes its narrow view of evidence and its myopic vision of health. She calls for a new ethic of inquiry, what she calls the ultimate ethic—the ability to learn from past mistakes so as to maximize the positive effects of research on human beings.

Ernest House ("Methodological Fundamentalism and the Quest for Control/s") presents a valuable reading of the history of methodological fundamentalism in the evaluation field. He then moves to the present, showing how the SBR demands of the Bush administration are compatible with other fundamentalist biblical beliefs.

Chapters 6 and 7 look outside the United States, focusing in particular on the research climates of Australia and the United Kingdom. First, Julianne Cheek ("The Challenge of Tailor-Made Research Quality") shows how the rise in the audit culture in Australia has increased the government's desire to ensure value for money in terms of research investment. The Australian government has introduced a Research Qualitative Framework (RQF) designed to assess the quality and impact of funded Australian research. Cheek criticizes this framework and encourages qualitative researchers to actively resist the RQF. She exposes the conservative challenge and the forms of backlash that are embedded in it. She concludes by raising six questions that all qualitative researchers might consider as they confront this increasingly hostile political environment.

Harry Torrance's chapter ("Research Quality and Research Governance in the UK") then moves the discussion to Great Britain, noting that, as in Australia, and the United States, another version of SBR is taking place. This new orthodoxy seeks to discipline qualitative research by also redefining and regulating the meanings of evidence, quality, science, quality assurance, and quality control. He argues that current discourse about method in the United Kingdom is about *control*, not quality, which is wholly unacceptable.

Part Two of the volume begins with Linda Tuhiwai Smith's chapter ("Choosing the Margins"), which discusses research in/ on indigenous communities, the assembly of those who have witnessed, been excluded from, and have survived modernity and imperialism. She further examines the implications for indigenous researchers as they struggle to produce research knowledge that documents social justice, recovers subjugated knowledges, helps create voices of the silenced to speak, and challenges racism, colonialism, and oppression. Such indigenous research activity offers genuine utopian hope for creating and living in a more just and humane social world.

This is followed by Radhika Viruru and Gaile S. Cannella's chapter, which serves as a postcolonial critique of the ethnographic interview. Asking such questions as how does one move beyond the binary of the question/answer to new ways of communication that do not perpetuate unequal power relationships, they locate postcolonialism/postcolonial critique not as a "theory" but rather as a disposition, a "location from which to adopt an activist position that pursues social transformation" so that "scholarship can be reconceptualized." They then examine the performative language of interviews (spoken, silent, and resistant), and offer suggestions for dealing with the multiple tensions, intentions, and desires of the interviewer and interviewee.

Also focusing on language are Yvonna S. Lincoln and Elsa M. González y González. Their chapter, "Decolonizing Qualitative Research," focuses on the conducting and reporting of cross-cultural qualitative data, specifically as organized around bilingual data, non-Western traditions, multiple perspectives, multilingual and bilingual texts, and technical issues related to accessibility. These five major arenas, they argue, offer possibilities for decolonizing and "locally useful" forms of research that "reach out in democratic and liberatory ways" to foster the goals of social justice.

Remaining with the theme of decolonizing research among indigenous communities, Carolyne J. White ("Humble and Humbling Research") offers a series of narrative collages interlaced with critical discussion of recent trends in indigenous research practices, specifically relating to issues of political and ethical concerns on the part of the "researcher." Traversing personal, political, cultural, theoretical, and geographic landscapes and borderlands, she performs multivocal texts of her engagements with community-based forms of education, the Hopi Teachers for

Hopi Schools Program, and her own personal journey through the academy. Her piece stands as a passionate exposition of the power of language and performance to intervene into the material realities of students and research participants in radically democratic terms.

Part Three opens with Cynthia B. Dillard and Adrienne D. Dixson's exploration of the epistemological and spiritual meanings of "goodness" of science from Black feminist perspectives. Underwritten by a tripartite African-based cosmology of spirituality, community, and praxis, the authors put forth an understanding of an "endarkened feminist epistemology" centered on reciprocity and relationships between researcher and researched, and between "or knowing and the production of knowledge." Poetic verse, dialogue, and narrative accounts are interwoven into their discussion, raising further questions about the "goodness" of our academic work and lives.

Cameron R. McCarthy ("Writing Race into the Twenty-First Century") continues this section with a deeply felt personal reflection on hybridity, difference, and the "postcolonial experience." Working through his own biography as a postcolonial intellectual, he explores the "uses of culture" as he seeks out new understandings of race in locations ranging from literature, art, film, and other works of the imagination. He similarly points to the interconnections, continuities, and cultural translations ongoing in the (post)modern world, troubling the stability of terms such as "race," "identity," and "culture," and arguing for curriculum reform in the area of race relations that "is founded on the principle of the heterogeneous basis of all knowledge."

Section Three closes with H. L. (Bud) Goodall's chapter on qualitative inquiry and the war on terror, which calls qualitative researchers to engage with and find better ways to fight such a war. Writing from his own biography, Goodall contends that it is our moral imperative to act immediately to "combine the tools of academic critique with practical political action." No longer can we remain the mandarin class of ivory-tower intellectuals pontificating on matters of state to a small circle of like-minded academics; rather, we must insert ourselves into a practical discussion held on the ground level of everyday interactions.

Concluding Remarks

In this historical moment, where the hyperreal appears more real than the real, pragmatists and cultural critics require apparatuses of resistance and critique, methodologies and pedagogies of truth, and ways of making real realities that envision and enact pedagogies of hope. Such pedagogies offer ways of holding fraudulent political regimes accountable for their actions. This volume represents one such attempt to do just that. Our colleagues have answered the call to intervene into the material realities of our age—to be present to the scene, as Lauren Berlant suggests. We thank them for their passion and invite you to join us as we struggle—together—to affect change in these times of epistemological uncertainty.

Notes

1. The arguments in this chapter are drawn in part from Denzin, 2003, 2005, 2006; Denzin & Giardina, 2006; Giardina, 2005, 2006.

2. Many of the chapters that follow were presented as plenary or keynote addresses at the First International Congress of Qualitative Research, held at the University of Illinois, May 5–7, 2005. The theme of the congress was qualitative inquiry and the pursuit of social justice in a time of global uncertainty. The International Association of Qualitative Inquiry (IAQI) was also founded at this congress. One purpose of IAQI is to provide a forum and platform for scholars around the world to speak out against these conservative forces. The editors were the director and co-associate director of the congress. For more information on this new association and its newsletter, see http://www.c4qi.org/iaqi/home.html

3. Indeed, a defeated amendment to the No Child Left Behind legislation asserted that creationism should be taught in schools: "Where biological evolution is taught, the curriculum should help students to understand why this subject generates so much continuing controversy" (Wilgoren, 2005, p. 14). The only controversy, however, is generated by fundamentalist adherents to intelligent design.

4. Many Vatican officials—including the pope—have gone so far as to state publicly that intelligent design is not science. To give but one example, Fiorenzo

Facchini (quoted in Thavis, 2006), a professor of evolutionary biology at the University of Bologna, wrote for the official Vatican newspaper, *L'Osservatore Romano*, that: "[intelligent design] isn't how science is done. If the model proposed by Darwin is deemed insufficient, one should look for another, but it's not correct from a methodological point of view to take oneself away from the scientific field pretending to do science." He similarly stated that intelligent design "doesn't belong to science and the pretext that it be taught as a scientific theory alongside Darwin's explanation is unjustified."

5. Attacks on conventional science, including biology and evolutionary theory, are pivotal to the goals of far-right Christian fundamentalists, who were waging a war on science even before the 2000 election (Kaplan, 2004; Mooney, 2005).

6. The Kyoto Protocol is an amendment to the United Nations Framework Convention on Climate Change (UNFCCC), the objective of which is the "stabilization of greenhouse gas concentrations in the atmosphere at a level that would prevent dangerous anthropogenic interference with the climate system."

7. Against this trend, leading scientists, including more than sixty Nobel Prize winners, have all spoken out against these abuses of science under the Bush regime (Kaplan, 2004, pp. 95, 104, 113).

8. Clearly, the tensions and contradictions that characterize the field do not exist within a unified arena. The issues and concerns of qualitative researchers in nursing and health care, for example, are decidedly different from those of researchers in cultural anthropology, where statistical and evidence-based models of inquiry are of less importance. The questions that indigenous scholars deal with are often different from those of interest to critical theorists in educational research. Nor do the international disciplinary networks of qualitative researchers necessarily cross one another, speak to one another, or read one another.

References

Alterman, E., & Green, M. (2004). *The book on Bush: How George W. Bush (mis)leads America*. New York: Viking.

Atkinson, E. (2004). Thinking outside the box: An exercise in heresy. *Qualitative Inquiry, 10*(1), 111–129.

Campbell, D., & Stanley, J. (1963). *Experimental and quasi-experimental design*. Chicago: Rand McNally.

Collins, P. H. (1991). *Black feminist thought*. New York: Routledge.

Collins, P. H. (1998). *Fighting words: Black women & the search for justice.* Minneapolis: University of Minnesota Press.

Corn, D. (2001). George W. Bush. The un-science guy. *AlterNet.* Available at http://www.alternet.org/story/11054/, accessed June 19, 2001.

Corn, D. (2003). *The lies of George W. Bush: Mastering the politics of deception.* New York: Crown Publishers.

Denzin, N. K. (1996). Post-pragmatism. *Symbolic Interaction, 19*(1), 61–75.

Denzin, N. K. (2003). *Performance ethnography: Critical pedagogy and the politics of culture.* Thousand Oaks, CA: Sage.

Denzin, N. K. (In press). The secret Downing St. Memo and the politics of evidence: A performance text. *Cultural Studies/Critical Methodologies.*

Denzin, N. K., & Giardina, M. D. (2006). Introduction: Cultural studies after 9/11. In N. K. Denzin & M. D. Giardina (Eds.), *Contesting empire, globalizing dissent: Cultural studies after 9/11* (pp. 1–21). Boulder, CO: Paradigm.

Duff, M. (2002). Evolution challenged in US schools. *BBC News Online.* Available at http://news.bbc.co.uk/2/hi/americas/1866476.stm, accessed March 5, 2006.

Edwards, R., & Mauthner, M. (2002). Ethics and feminist research: Theory and practice. In M. Mauthner, M. Birch, J. Jessop, & T. Miller (Eds.), *Ethics in qualitative research* (pp. 14–31). London: Sage.

Feuer, M. J., Towne, L., & Shavelson, R. J. (2002). Scientific culture and educational research. *Educational Researcher, 31*(8), 4–14.

Fine, M., & McClelland, S. L. (In press). The unholy marriage of science and public policy: The case of abstinence education. *Cultural Studies/Critical Methodologies.*

Freire, P. (1999[1992]). *Pedagogy of hope* (Robert R. Barr, Trans.). New York: Continuum.

Giardina, M. D. (2005). *Sporting pedagogies: Performing culture & identity in the global arena.* New York: Peter Lang.

Giardina, M. D. (2006). *From soccer moms to NASCAR dads: Sport, culture, and politics in a nation divided.* Boulder, CO: Paradigm.

Giroux, H. (2004). Beyond belief: Religious fundamentalism and cultural politics in the age of George W. Bush. *Cultural Studies/Critical Methodologies, 4*(4), 415–425.

Hall, S. (1996). What is this 'Black' in Black popular culture? In D. Morley & K.-H. Chen (Eds.), *Stuart Hall: Critical dialogues in cultural studies* (pp. 465–475). London: Routledge.

Herbert, B. (2005). How scary is this? *New York Times,* October 20, A23.

Hertzberg, H. (2005). Bush Science. *The New Yorker,* August 22, A21–22.

Hillman, S. T. (2003). *NIH funded research and the peer-review process.* American Sociological Association Press Release, November 3.

Howe, K. R. (2004). A critique of experimentalism. *Qualitative Inquiry, 10*(1), 42–61.

Kaplan, E. (2004). *With God on their side: How Christian fundamentalists trampled science, policy, and democracy in George Bush's White House.* New York: The New Press.

Kennedy, Jr., R. F. (2004). *Crimes against nature: How George W. Bush and his corporate pals are plundering the country and hijacking our democracy.* New York: HarperCollins.

Kittredge, W. (1987). *Owning it all.* San Francisco, CA: Murray House.

Klinkenborg, V. (2005). Grasping the depth of time as a first step in understanding evolution. *New York Times*, August 23, A22.

Lincoln, Y. S., & Cannella. G. S. (2004a). Dangerous discourses methodological conservatism and governmental regimes of truth. *Qualitative Inquiry, 10*(1), 5–14.

Lincoln, Y. S, & Cannella, G. S. (2004b). Qualitative research, power, and the radical right. *Qualitative Inquiry, 10*(2), 175–201.

Lincoln, Y. S., & Guba, E. (2000). Paradigmatic controversies, contradictions, and emerging confluences. In N. K. Denzin & Y. S. Lincoln (Eds.), *Handbook of qualitative research* (2nd ed., pp. 163–188). Thousand Oaks, CA: Sage.

Maxwell, J. A. (2004). Re-emergent scientism, postmodernism, and dialogue across differences. *Qualitative Inquiry, 10*(1), 35–41.

Mieszkowski, K. (2004). Bush: Global warming is just hot air. Salon.com. Available online at http://www.salon.com/tech/feature/2004/09/10/bush/index_np.html

Mooney, C. (2005). *The Republican war on science.* New York: Basic Books.

Mutua, K., & Swadner, B. B. (2004). Introduction. In K. Mutua & B. B. Swadener (Eds.), *Decolonizing research in cross-cultural contexts: Critical personal narratives* (pp. 1–23). Albany: SUNY Press.

National Academy of Sciences. (2001). *Climate change science: An analysis of some key questions.* Washington, DC: National Academy Press.

National Research Council. 2001. *Scientific research in education.* Washington, DC: National Academy Press.

Pelias, R. (2004). *Methodology of the heart.* Walnut Creek, CA: AltaMira.

Popkewitz, T. S. (2004). Is the National Research Council Committee's report on scientific research in education scientific? On trusting the manifesto. *Qualitative Inquiry, 10*(1), 62–78.

Pring, R. (2004). Conclusion: Evidence-based policy and practice. In G. Thomas & R. Pring (Eds.), *Evidence-based practice in education* (pp. 201–212). New York: Open University Press.

Rich, F. (2005a). Enron: Patron saint of Bush's fake news. *New York Times*, March 20, Section 2, pp. 1, 8.

Rich, F. (2005b). Karl and Scooter's excellent adventure. *New York Times*, October 23, A13.

Rich, F. (2005c). The White House stages its "Daily Show." *New York Times*, February 20, Section 2, pp. 1, 20.

Rich, F. (2005d). Two top guns shoot blanks. *New York Times*, June 19, A12.

Ryan, K. E., & Hood, L. K. (2004). Guarding the castle and opening the gates. *Qualitative Inquiry, 10*(1), 79–95.

Schwandt, T. (2000). Three epistemological stances for qualitative inquiry. In N. K. Denzin & Y. S. Lincoln (Eds.), *Handbook of qualitative research* (2nd ed., pp. 189–213). Thousand Oaks, CA: Sage.

Seigfried, C. H. (1996). *Pragmatism and feminism: Reweaving the social fabric.* Chicago: University of Chicago Press.

Solomon, J. (2005). Truth watch: Failed levees had already been fortified. *The News Gazette*, September 15, B3.

St. Pierre, E. A. (2004). Refusing alternatives: A science of contestation. *Qualitative Inquiry, 10*(1), 130–139.

Suskind, R. (2004). Faith, certainty and the presidency of George W. Bush. *New York Times Magazine*, October 17, Section 6, pp. 44–51, 64, 102, 106.

Thavis, J. (2006). Intelligent design not science, says Vatican newspaper. *Catholic News Service*, January 17. Available online at www.catholicnews.com/data/stories/cns/0600273.htm

Union of Concerned Scientists. (2004). Restoring scientific integrity in policymaking. Available online at http://www.ucsusa.org/scientific_integrity/interference/scientists-signon-statement.html

Weinstein, M. (2004). Randomized design and the myth of certain knowledge: Guinea pig narratives and cultural critique. *Qualitative Inquiry, 10*(2), 246–260.

West, C. (1989). *The American evasion of philosophy: A genealogy of pragmatism.* Madison: University of Wisconsin Press.

West, C. (1991). Theory, pragmatisms and politics. In J. Arac & B. Johnson (Eds.), *Consequences of theory* (pp. 22–38). Baltimore: Johns Hopkins University Press.

Wilgoren, J. (2005). Politicized scholars put evolution on the defensive. *New York Times*, August 21, Section 1, pp. 1, 14.

Part One
The Politics of Evidence

Chapter 1 | Chronotopes of Human Science Inquiry

George Kamberelis
University of Albany
Greg Dimitriadis
University of Buffalo

In this chapter, we hope to add to a growing "complicated conversation" (Pinar, 2004) about qualitative research methods. We argue for a language that can work across and through multiple approaches in sophisticated and nuanced ways, in ways that can open a more nuanced discussion that might enable truly inter- and multimethodological approaches. Specifically, we offer an account of what we see to be the prevalent *chronotopes* of inquiry that ground and inform most qualitative research (and the social sciences generally). Our task is akin to the one undertaken by Birdwhistell (1977) in response to his students' queries about whether Margaret Mead and Gregory Bateson had a methodology. These queries led Birdwhistell to argue that theory-method complexes, which he termed "logics-of-inquiry," guide all research.

Our task is also similar to Strike's (1974) construct of "expressive potential." Strike argued that all research endeavors are governed by an expressive potential that delimits the objects worthy of investigation, the research questions that may be asked, the units of analysis that are relevant, the analyses that may be conducted, the claims that may be made about the objects of investigation, and the forms of explanation that may be invoked. We argue here for a new language that can be used to talk across a range of disciplinary and methodological approaches, from ethnography to genealogy and rhizomatics. In working toward such a language, we highlight both the possibilities and dangers of this moment of meta-disciplinary coalescence. Informed by this, we close by offering a new metaphor for the qualitative researcher—that of the genealogist.

Why Chronotopes?

Although similar to "logics-of-inquiry" or "expressive potentials," the construct of chronotopes of inquiry also extends these constructs in important ways. To the best of our knowledge, Bakhtin (1981) borrowed the term "chronotope," which literally means "time-space," from Einstein and applied it to the study of language and literature For Bakhtin, chronotopes do not simply link particular times and spaces with specific cultural events. Instead, they delineate or construct sedimentations of concrete, motivated social situations or figured worlds (Holland et al., 1998) replete with typified plots, themes, agents, forms of agency, scenes, objects, affective dispositions, kinds of intentionality, ideologies, value orientations, and so on. In this regard, chronotopes are like "x-rays of the forces at work in the culture system from which they spring" (Bakhtin, 1981, pp. 425–426).

Chronotopes are normalizing frames that render the world as "just the way things are" by celebrating the prosaic regularities that make any given world, day after day, recognizable and predictable for the people who live in it (Morson & Emerson, 1990, p. 87). They connote specific ways to understand context and the actions, agents, events, and practices that constitute those contexts. Bakhtin was clear about the fact that chronotopes are not a priori structures but durable structuring structures (e.g., Bourdieu, 1990; Giddens, 1979) constituted within concrete histories of human activity across time and space. Among the ways in which he illustrated this idea was to show how the public square in ancient Greece or the family at the height of the Roman Empire were constitutively related to specific modes of rhetorical and literary activity common to those time-spaces.

Chronotopes are a lot like what cultural studies scholars (e.g., Grossberg, 1992; Hall, 1992; Hebdidge, 1979; Willis, 1977) refer to as cultural formations—historically formed/informed and socially distributed modes of engagement with particular sets of practices for particular reasons. Chronotopes describe the lines of force that locate, distribute, and connect specific sets of practices, effects, goals, and groups of actors. Such articulations not only involve selections and configurations from among the available practices, but also a distribution of the chronotopes themselves within and across social time and space. To understand and describe a chronotope requires a reconstruction of its context—the dispersed yet structured field of objects, practices, agents, and so on by which the specific articulation reproduces itself across time and space. Chronotopic assertions are thus "strategems" of genealogy. All chronotopes have their own "common cultural sense," "sensibilities," "tastes," "logics," and so on. These dimensions of being become embodied in the people who work within a chronotope such that they become part of the chronotope itself. What seems natural, proper, and obvious to individuals becomes aligned with what is the "common cultural sense" within the chronotope. For our purposes, then, *chronotopes of qualitative inquiry index durable historical realities that constitute what is common, natural, and expected by collectives of social scientists who conduct particular kinds of qualitative research.*

Although other scholars might argue for slightly fewer or slightly more, we focus on four primary chronotopes of inquiry currently operating in powerful and pervasive ways within the contemporary scene of educational research, especially in relation to literacy studies. We settled on the following "names" for the chronotopes that we believe most commonly ground qualitative inquiry within education and literacy studies:

(1) Objectivism and Representation

(2) Reading and Interpretation

(3) Skepticism, Conscientization, and Praxis

(4) Power/Knowledge and Defamiliarization

All four chronotopes engage with the Enlightenment project, but in different ways—some more resonantly and some more dissonantly. Each chronotope embodies a different set of assumptions about the world, knowledge, the human subject, language, and meaning. Each also embodies or indexes a particular set of approaches/methods for framing and conducting research. Finally, in different ways and to different degrees, each has exerted considerable power in sustaining and reproducing particular logics of inquiry within our field and within the larger world of the social sciences. We propose this loosely coupled taxonomy simply as a heuristic for understanding some of the different ways in which qualitative inquiry is typically framed and how different frameworks predispose researchers to embrace different epistemologies, theories, approaches, and strategies.

Chronotope I:
Objectivism and Representation

Perhaps the roots of this chronotope extend back to early critiques of "correspondence theories of truth" and a "logics of verification" that inhabited representational approaches to research in anthropology and philosophy (e.g., Clifford & Marcus, 1986; Rorty, 1979). "Correspondence theories of truth" posit the possibility of directly and unproblematically mapping symbolic representations onto the facts in the world in a one-to-one fashion. Approaches driven by "correspondence theories of truth" derive from Descartes's dualism of mind and body and have become all but synonymous with the scientific method. This dualism renders the individual human subject as radically separate from the external world but able to know this world through reflection and thought. A variety of methods and research tools have been developed within the chronotope of objectivism and representation. These methods and tools are predicated on the inviolability of the mind-body binary. Language is construed as a neutral medium for accurately *representing* observed relations in the external world.

A considerable amount of the qualitative research that is conducted in the field of language and literacy, for example, fits comfortably within the chronotope of objectivism and representation. E. D. Hirsch's (1987) work on cultural literacy is one example. Within a cultural literacy framework, it is assumed that there is a neutral canon of key cultural knowledge that all students should know. It is also assumed that this body of knowledge exists outside of the individual subject and can be learned, usually through direct instruction and study. This neutral body of knowledge is transmitted to individual subjects through the neutral medium of Standard English. Finally, Hirsch asserts that if students lack a particular and prescribed set of cultural knowledge, they will be unable to read and write adequately and to function productively in society. The cultural knowledge that Hirsch has in mind is presumed to be "common culture," not elite culture, even though it derives primarily from canonical works within a white, European American, middle- to upper-class heterosexist tradition.

Knowledge here is considered to be entirely separate from power relations or any other dimensions of context. A radical separation of subject and object is assumed. Language and literacy practices are assumed to be neutral vehicles for representing equally neutral facts. The real world and talking or writing about the real world are held radically separate. The idea that language and literacy might be able to shape and constitute thought, practice, or circulation of power is eclipsed. Such a construal renders language and literacy practices as little more than conduits or vehicles for preexistent thoughts or conditions, and it occludes the idea that such practices have ontological substance and constitutive power themselves. Questions about whether our relations with and within the world are at least partially constituted by language and literacy practices become unimportant. Little, if any, conceptual room is allocated for political praxis or social change through language and literacy practices because fact and value are believed to be independent of each other. Instead, language and literacy practices are evaluated according to their relative *effectiveness* in representing a priori cognitive or communicative entities or events. Positing effectiveness as a primary (or sole) evaluative criterion galvanizes the tendency to view language and literacy as little more than simple conduits for communicating established perspectives or existing sets of conditions, and it eclipses processes of imagining the constitutive roles that these practices might play in the construction of knowledges, identities, and fields of social practice.

Accepting the separation of subject and object or language and world as "given" or "natural" positions the field of language and literacy studies as a second-order field of inquiry that is de facto subservient to more legitimate fields and dependent on their theories and methods for its existence. It is not surprising, then, that many of the constructs and methods deployed within research on language and literacy conducted within the chronotope of objectivism and representation derive from other disciplines such as psychology (e.g., schema, motivation), sociology (e.g., symbolic interactionism, conversation analysis), anthropology (e.g., speech event, participant observation) or literary studies (e.g., reader response, genre studies). By drawing heavily on conceptual frameworks developed in other fields (especially psychology), research agendas often focus not on actual language and literacy practices but on internal or hidden *variables* such as readers' motivations (e.g., Turner, 1995) or writers' intentions (e.g., Flower & Hayes, 1981). When language and literacy research are located within the chronotope of objectivism and representation, one wonders exactly what language and literacy practices are involved and where they can be found. Are the reasons for practices always to be found outside of the practices themselves—in some hidden or deep structures or an Oz behind the curtain? Is nothing important evident in the surface of things? As we move through the discussions of all four chronotopes, we will show how actual, observable practices have become increasingly important as legitimate resources for explaining the nature and functions of language and literacy activities. And their increasing legitimation as both data and interpretive/explanatory resources has presented serious challenges to canonical ways of thinking about qualitative research practice.

Chronotope II: Reading and Interpretation

Not all approaches to research conducted within a modernist framework adhere to positivist epistemologies and their attendant assumptions. One framework that is modernist but not positivist is what we call the chronotope of reading and interpretation. Grounded in social constructionist epistemologies, this chronotope is not predicated on a complete rejection of Enlightenment perspectives on knowledge, rationality, and truth, but it does rearticulate these perspectives to render knowledge, truth, and rationality as relative (or perspectival) rather than absolute. Such a move rescues these constructs from the hegemonic clutches of scientism and instrumental reasoning without jettisoning these perspectives altogether. Knowledge, reason, and truth are no longer conceived as the representational mirroring (through language and other semiotic media) of an already existing world. Instead, knowledge, reason, and truth are believed to be constructed through the symbolic acts of human beings in relation to the world and to others (e.g., Heidegger, 1962; Rorty, 1979). Concomitantly, science is no longer about verification within a correspondence theory of truth but about human interaction, communication, dialogue, and reasoned argument.

Modernism, then, embraces not only scientistic modes of reason grounded in objectivist epistemologies but also modes of reason that are linguistically (or semiotically) mediated and grounded in the experience of "being-in-the-world." As we noted earlier, chronotopes are fluid, leaky, and flexible, and it is possible to have both objectivist-modernist articulations as well as interpretive-modernist ones. From this perspective, the existence of a real world external to human subjects is assumed, but faith in the timeless, universal nature of the world-knowledge relation and thus the possibility of generating representations that map that world in absolute or foundational terms is rejected.

This shift from "brute facts" to semiotically mediated facts is far from trivial. Among other things, it marks the need to replace a correspondence theory of truth with a consensus theory of truth, which implies a human discourse community as the arbiter of knowledge and truth claims. Gadamer's (1972) work is instructive here. Gadamer argued that truth does not emerge through the application of technical tools or methods but within and through embodied engagement within a "horizon" of experience within a human community. He went even further to claim that truth will always elude capture by technical methods because knowledge is always semiotically and dialogically constructed. Truth is never an act of reproduction but always an act of production within the limited horizon of a community's texts and meanings. Because knowledge (and thus truth) always emerges out of the embodied, rich, and messy process of being-in-the-world, it is always perspectival and conditional.

Within the chronotope of reading and interpretation, the subject-object dualism of the Enlightenment project is also assumed, but subject and object are placed in dialogic tension. This tension is a hallmark of philosophical hermeneutics, which is the foundation (i.e., antifoundation) on which the chronotope of reading and interpretation was built. The term "hermeneutics" derives from the Greek word *hermeneuein* with its obvious linkages to Hermes, the fleet-footed messenger of the gods. This derivation would suggest, then, that the origins of the chronotope of reading and interpretation lie in early Greek thought. Most philosophers of science and social theorists, however, usually place the beginnings of the chronotope reading and interpretation in nineteenth-century German philosophy, especially the work of Schleiermacher and Dilthey.

Although the term *verstehen* is often used as a generic term for interpretive social science, Dilthey (1976/1900) has been credited with developing a specific *verstehen* approach to understanding. This approach basically refers to the process of understanding from another subject's point of view. The *verstehen* approach, according to Dilthey, is achieved through the psychological reenactment or imaginative reconstruction of the experiences of others. In other words, it is intersubjectivity achieved basically through empathy. The extreme psychologism of Dilthey's position has been challenged and tempered by other philosophers including Husserl, Heidegger, and Gadamer.

Most contemporary uses of the term "hermeneutics" refer to the general process of coming to understand a phenomenon of interest (e.g., text, experience, social activity) or constructing an interpretation of such a phenomenon without placing such a heavy burden on intersubjectivity through empathy. Instead, hermeneutic or interpretive inquires are predicated on understanding meanings and practices in relation to the situations in which they occur. Such modes of inquiry draw on the notion of the "hermeneutic circle" as a unique and powerful strategy for understanding and knowledge building. Using this strategy, understanding the "part" (a text, an act, a person) always involves also understanding the whole (the context, the activity setting, the life history) and vice versa.

Heavily influenced by this notion of the hermeneutic circle, qualitative inquiry conducted within the chronotope of reading and interpretation does not aim to generate foundational knowledge claims. Instead, it aims to refine and deepen our sense of what it means to understand other people and their social practices (including language and literacy practices) within relevant contexts of interaction and communication. Put in philosophical terms, these forms of inquiry link the Enlightenment or modernist project of discovering knowledge with a genuine interest in understanding and enriching the "life worlds" (Habermas, 1987) or "lived experience" of others (i.e., our research participants). Researchers operating within a chronotope of reading and interpretation espouse a linguistically mediated view of existence and knowledge wherein both are constituted (and not just represented) in and through human language practices. They study language practices such as conversation, storytelling, disciplinary writing, and the like in order to reveal and understand the contexts and ontologies that they index.

Although the historical roots of the chronotope of reading and interpretation may be traced to nineteenth-century German philosophy, it has grown exponentially during the past two decades. Interestingly, and a bit ironically, this trend was not particularly visible in the major language and literacy journals until just a few years ago, even though it has been quite visible in journals from allied disciplines (e.g., *Anthropology and Education Quarterly*, *International Journal of Qualitative Studies in Education*). It has also been quite visible for some time within dissertations, presentations at professional literacy conferences, and books. The fact that research conducted within the chronotope of reading and interpretation was resisted in our mainstream journals and had to be smuggled into our field through less mainstream venues is testimony to the powerful, pervasive, and long-lasting grip that the chronotope of objectivism and representation has had and still has on qualitative inquiry in our field. Nevertheless, the chronotope of reading and interpretation has managed finally to become a force to be reckoned with in research on language and literacy.

Among the earliest and most durable instances of literacy research representing this force grew out of the ethnography of communication (EOC) tradition, with its focus on the relations among language, community, and identity. Shirley Brice Heath's (1983) now classic *Ways with Words* is one of the best exemplars of this tradition.

In outlining the research strategies she used to conduct the research for her book, Heath (1982) virtually recreated earlier descriptions of the hermeneutic circle, arguing that her research involved "the collection of artifacts of literacy, descriptions of contexts of uses, and their spatial and temporal distribution within the life of members of the community" (p. 47). She went on to claim that she studied how people used literacy artifacts, the activities and events within which the artifacts were used, whether links were made between symbolic representations and their real-world equivalents, how artifacts were presented to children, and what children then did with them (p. 47). Clearly, she came to understand parts in relation to wholes and vice versa.

A central question that motivated Heath's research was "what were the effects of preschool, home and community environments on the learning of those language structures which were needed in classrooms and job settings?" (1982, p. 2). Heath explored and documented language and literacy practices common in the homes of families in three different communities in the Piedmont Carolinas: a working-class black community (Trackton), a working-class white community (Roadville), and an integrated middle-class community (Maintown). Based on findings from ten years of research, Heath argued convincingly for how the knowledges and "ways with words" of people living in these different communities were historically and socially constructed in very different ways. In Heath's words, "the place of language in the cultural life of each social group is interdependent with the habits and values of behaving shared among members of that group" (p. 11). For example, the kinds of interactions that parents and children from the three communities engaged in while reading storybooks were linked to different ways of living, eating, sleeping, worshipping, using space, and spending time. These interactions were also linked to different notions of play, parenting, truth, and morality.

More generally, Heath explained that "for the children of Trackton and Roadville ... and for the majority of the mill workers and students in the Piedmont schools the ways [of the people of Maintown] are far from natural and they seem strange indeed" (1982, p. 262). Importantly, these differences resulted in different consequences for children's success in school. Finally, Heath traced constitutive relations between the identities of people in these communities and their language and literacy practices. In this regard, Heath worked with teachers in the local schools—all of whom were from Maintown—to understand the "ways with words" of the children they taught and to adapt their classroom practices to be more culturally relevant. This process induced changes in the identities, knowledges, and language practices of teachers and students alike.

Central to the work of Heath and other researchers working from within the chronotope of reading and interpretation is the fundamental notion that language practices constitute both individual and community identities. All of these studies presuppose the central assumption that it is not biology or geography or universal structure that constitutes identity and community but the discursive construction of shared meanings and practices. In Heath's work, for example, the predispositions toward books and reading held by the children and parents of Roadville or Trackton have no a priori existence but are continually produced and reproduced through the specific language and literacy practices common to the respective communities. As important as these practices are, however, Heath (and others located within the chronotope of reading and interpretation) never addresses questions about the larger social, political, and economic forces that make specific language and literacy practices visible and available in the first place. These questions are more central to the chronotopes we discuss later in the chapter.

The chronotope of reading and interpretation is embedded within a social constructionist epistemology and deploys hermeneutics as its most common theory-approach complex. From within this chronotope, language is theorized not as a vehicle for representing an already existent world but as the most powerful means available to human beings for constructing what is "really real" (Geertz, 1973) and fundamentally meaningful about that world. This chronotope holds onto the modernist notion of the individual rational subject but views this individual as fundamentally grounded in and constructed within the language and literacy practices of the speech and discourse communities in which he or she participates.

From within the chronotope of reading and interpretation, scholars also reject the idea that science is fundamentally about prediction and control, technical-instrumental rationality, and the gradual accumulation of all knowledge. Instead, researchers operating within this chronotope are committed to reflexively participating in the "language games" (Wittgenstein, 1958) of hermeneutics and the communities that they study with a desire and a willingness to enter into the conversations they find there. From this perspective, ongoing dialogue between researchers and research participants is a primary requirement of knowledge production and understanding.

Chronotope III:
Skepticism, Conscientization, and Praxis

Although the chronotope of reading and interpretation constituted the very foundation of early qualitative research, it came under attack for failing to deal adequately with the power-laden political contexts in which presumably "open dialogue" occurs and "genuine understanding" is constructed. In other words, classical interpretivism rooted in hermeneutics did not address the ways in which dialogue can readily become complicit with the hegemonic structures of power in which it is always embedded. Historically, for example, many ethnographers have also been missionaries or military personnel whose "dialogue" with natives was motivated largely by religious and colonial interests masquerading as paternalistic (or maternalistic) benevolence. This social fact is true even into the middle of the twentieth century, when ethnographers shifted their gaze from "exotic" natives in distant places to equally "exotic" natives in American inner cities (e.g., Blacks, Asians, Jews, etc.). Accusations about the absence of attention paid to ideology and domination within the chronotope of reading and interpretation promoted the development of more critical forms of interpretivism within the Enlightenment or modernist project. We refer to these forms under the rubric of a chronotope of skepticism, conscientization, and praxis.

The roots of a chronotope of skepticism, conscientization, and praxis can be traced to linkages between the hermeneutic tradition and various strands of critical social theory within the tradition of neo-Marxism during the middle of the twentieth century. The name for the chronotope itself is a play on the term "hermeneutics of suspicion," which was introduced by Paul Ricoeur (1970) to refer to modes of interpretation that are radically skeptical about whatever is presumed to be the truth. Building on Ricoeur's basic insights, John B. Thompson (1990) constructed a systematic theory-method complex, which he called depth hermeneutics. Echoing the classic line attributed to Karl Marx, Ricoeur and Thompson argued that ideologies often "operate behind people's backs," which makes it impossible to escape completely the bonds of "false consciousness." Gadamer (1972) had something similar in mind when he claimed that, more than our judgments, our interests or our prejudices constitute who we are. Built largely on the neo-Marxist concerns with ideology and ideology critique, the goal of a critical or depth hermeneutics is to deconstruct or unmask the "reality" or "truth" of prejudicial understanding and to reveal the contingency, relativity, and historicity of consciousness, other people, and the world. Finally, we included Freire's (1970) term "conscientization" in the name of this chronotope to underscore its *praxis* orientation. For Freire, conscientization refers to critical reflection and its articulation with social action to enact individual and collective emancipation.

Like the chronotope of reading and interpretation, the chronotope of skepticism, conscientization, and praxis is grounded in social constructionist epistemologies. Unlike the chronotope of reading and interpretation, the chronotope of skepticism, conscientization, and praxis embraces the challenge of interrogating how ideology functions to "naturalize" and privilege some forms of knowledge and being-in-the-world over others. It also embodies an imperative for democratic social change. Operating within this chronotope, researchers assume that surface-level meanings and actions hide deep structural conflicts, contradictions, and falsities that function to maintain the status quo.

The neo-Marxist foundations of Chronotope III.

To better understand the chronotope of skepticism, conscientization, and praxis warrants a detour into neo-Marxism. Certain neo-Marxists including Antonio Gramsci (1971), George Lukács (1971), and Louis Althusser (1971) challenged the economic determinism of traditional Marxism, arguing that power derives not so much from base economic conditions but from cultural ideologies, which are only informed by economic/political configurations (e.g., feudalism, capitalism, socialism).

Another group of neo-Marxist thinkers known as the Frankfurt School theorists concerned themselves with understanding what they believed to be a set of constitutive relations among capitalism, epistemology, and politics. Although steeped in modernism, many Frankfurt School theorists were downright suspicious about the Enlightenment vision of an increasingly free and more democratic society through technical-instrumental rationality (i.e., science). In the words of Horkheimer and Adorno (1988), "in the most general sense of progressive thought, the Enlightenment has always aimed at liberating men from fear and establishing their authority. Yet the fully enlightened earth radiates disastrous triumph" (p. 3). The radical skepticism of the Frankfurt School did not so much mark a break with the Enlightenment or modernism project as an extension of it, which included a radical critique of the technical-instrumental rationality that had become so central to the project. Frankfurt School theorists were fundamentally concerned with interrogating why the presumed social progress of the project had resulted in "the fallen nature of modern man" (Horkheimer & Adorno, 1988, p. xiv), and the goal of their work was to rescue and reanimate "the hopes of the past" (p. xv).

Frankfurt School theorists did not attempt to disrupt the subject-object dichotomy central to Enlightenment and modernist work, however. Indeed, they struggled to preserve the idea that individuals are both rational and free but wanted to demonstrate how these inalienable characteristics had become distorted and corrupted by what Adorno (1973, p. 5) called "identity logic." Identity logic, according to Adorno, is radically subjectivistic and embodies the desperate human need to eliminate the distance between subject and object. It is rooted in the hubristic desire to know "things-in-themselves," to experience first hand what is indexed by the notion of a "correspondence theory of truth." The propensity for mastery and control, which is implicit in Adorno's identity logic and which was central to the Enlightenment project's notion of human freedom (and freedom from suffering), was viewed by Adorno and other neo-Marxists as the primary cause of the Enlightenment's demise and the disintegration of a logic of verification within the logical positivist tradition. Although Adorno often "affirm[ed] the wildest utopian dreams of the Enlightenment project" (Bernstein, 1992, p. 43), he thought that equating human reason and technical-instrumental rationality would negate the possibility of a critique of ideology and critical self-reflexivity. In this regard, he saw lived experience and material reality as far richer and more complex than could ever be captured by human thought and language. To imagine otherwise, he believed, was wrongheaded and arrogant. Worse than this, he argued that such arrogance eclipsed people's capacity for reflexivity and self-reflexivity in human thought and action.

The work of Frankfurt School scholar, Jürgen Habermas, perhaps went the furthest in laminating an emancipatory logic onto the basic modernist project. In his theory of communicative action, Habermas (1984, 1987) offered a critique of modernism, which shifted the locus of human agency from the Cartesian ego to the possibilities of dialogue inherent in language itself. Importantly, this shift entailed a concomitant shift in the locus of agency from the individual to the social. Finally, he rejected the technical-instrumental rationality of the Enlightenment without rejecting rationality itself, an issue we take up below.

Habermas's (1984, 1987) theory of communicative action is both a theory of rationality and a theory of society. In this regard, he viewed rationality as a social, dialogic process with both political and ethical valences. According to this view, rationality is not a property of the transcendental ego or individual subject. Instead, it is produced within "ideal speech situations" wherein people engage in communicative acts that are free, unconstrained, dialogic, and therefore undistorted. Ideal speech situations are defined or constituted by four "validity claims." Whatever speakers say must be (a) meaningful, (b) true, (c) justified, and (d) sincere. Truth is the goal or promise of this model, and it is defined in terms of agreement or consensus achieved through critical dialogue and debate. Rational consensus is determined on the basis of who offers the better argument with the most adequate evidence and warrants. Reasoned argumentation is thus the ultimate court of appeal.

Habermas's insistence on the importance of the ideal speech situation was rooted in his ethical and political commitments. Because he believed that the colonizing forces of capitalism were rooted in technical-instrumental rationality, he rejected this form of rationality and posited two alternatives: (a) practical rationality and (b) emancipatory rationality. Practical rationality (or Habermas's version of praxis) is the means by which people reach mutual understandings through unfettered dialogue. Emancipatory rationality is a mode of thinking/being that allows people to escape the lures of hegemony and oppression through self-reflection. By acknowledging the workings of these three forms of rationality in social life, Habermas was able to account for how language is a constitutive force *both* in generating shared understandings (and thus truth) *and* in the exercise of power and domination. Social movements such as second-wave feminism, the civil rights movement, and the ecology movement are good examples of how Habermas's rational, emancipatory, de/recolonization project have been concretely realized in history. In our own field, one might argue that "whole language" pedagogies, Gravesian versions of the "writing process" pedagogies, and many incarnations of the "critical literacy" pedagogies are all grounded in Habermas's practical and emancipatory forms of rationality, as well as how these pedagogies have been assaulted by hegemonic regimes rooted in and legitimated by technical-instrumental rationality.

The praxis turn.

The general interest in practical reason or praxis has a long history in philosophy. Aristotle (e.g., Nichomachean Ethics, Book VI) contrasted poesis with praxis, arguing that poesis involves instrumental action that results in *making* or *producing* things whereas praxis involves action that results in acting or doing things with and for others that promote moral goodness and "the good life." Thus, praxis always has to do with what people *do* in relation to each other to enhance their respective lives. Aristotle also believed that, through these acts, people also promote the democratic goals of the state.

More generally, the term "praxis" has often been used to refer to the general process of linking theory and practice, knowledge and action to enhance the possibilities of *communitas* and to make the world a better place to live in for all people. For the most part, knowledge has remained the privileged term in this binary but practical knowledge and not knowledge for its own sake has been emphasized. Since the so-called crisis of representation in anthropology (e.g., Marcus & Fisher, 1986), praxis has often been used to refer to the practical and dialogic/reciprocal relationships that researchers may forge with research participants. Within these relationships, researchers have often imposed mandates on themselves to work with research participants to help them improve the conditions of their lives (e.g., Lather, 1991, 1997). Less common, but at least as important, is a political sense of praxis such as that developed by Gramsci (1971). This sense of praxis unites theory and practice in such a way that neither is subservient to the other. Researchers and research participants enter into reciprocal relationships wherein the common work experience has to be as much a venue for both intellectuals and workers to advance their points of view and interests. Reciprocal relationships must lead to the development of common goals, and these goals must in some ways express the transformative possibilities of a dialogic community.

Chronotope IV:
Power/Knowledge and Defamiliarization

When most people think about "critical" qualitative research, they presume that it is always framed within postmodern and/or poststructural epistemologies and theories. Although we argued against this generalization in the previous section, critical qualitative research has been increasingly grounded in postmodern and poststructural perspectives. Because power/knowledge and defamiliarization are constructs that are central to these perspectives, we have used them to characterize the next chronotope we discuss. Partly because of its almost exclusive alignment with postmodernism and poststructuralism rather than modernism and structuralism, this chronotope is partially discontinuous with the chronotope of skepticism, conscientization, and praxis.

Power/knowledge and games of truth.

Perhaps the hallmark of postmodern and poststructural critical theorists is the extent to which they debunked modernist notions of knowledge, arguing that knowledge is always related to power. For example, they rejected Habermas's (1984, 1987) dialogic/consensus model of knowledge made possible by the inherent potential of language to afford an "ideal speech situation." Contra Habermas, Baudrillard (1983), Foucault (1977), Lyotard (1984), and others warned that consensus is a hopeless vestige of modernism that actually elicits complicity with totalizing regimes of knowledge and truth, and they set out to demonstrate the ways in which knowledge and power are co-constitutive. Foucault's (1975, 1977, 1990) genealogies of madness/the asylum, criminality/the prison, and the discourses of sexuality, for example, showed how what is considered true or false is dependent on specific "games of truth" or "regimes of power" upon which the possibilities of making any and all knowledge claims depend. Different games of truth afford and allow different knowledge claims. For example, Foucault (1990) raised several doubts about the presumed "repressive hypothesis" of modern society beginning with the Victorian age:

> First doubt: Is sexual repression truly an established historical fact? ... Second doubt: Do the workings of power, and in particular those mechanisms that are brought into play in societies such as ours, really belong primarily to the category of repression? ... Third and final doubt: Did the critical discourse that addresses itself to repression come to act as a roadblock to a power mechanism that had operated unchallenged up to that point, or is it not in fact part of the same historical network as the thing it denounces (and doubtless misrepresents) in calling it "repression"? [p. 10]

Foucault went on to claim that these doubts about the repressive hypothesis "are aimed less at showing it to be mistaken than at putting it back within a general economy of discourses on sex in modern societies since the seventeenth century" (1990, p. 10). And he argued that this relocation ushers in new (and more important) questions about sexuality such as "Why has sexuality been so widely discussed, and what has been said about it? What were the effects of power generated by what was said? What are the links between these discourses, these effects of power, and the pleasures that were invested by them? What knowledge (*savoir*) was formed as a result of this linkage?" (p. 10).

The human subject.

Besides reconceptualizing knowledge in relation to power, post-modern/poststructural critical theorists went much further than modernist critical theorists in decentering Enlightenment notions about the human subject and displacing the locus of rationality from the mind of this subject. For example, although Habermas (1984, 1987) rejected the idea of the Cartesian subject and argued for viewing rationality not as a possession of the individual subject but as a dialogic social process rooted in the potential for an "ideal speech situation" inherent in language, he still viewed subjectivity as coherent and progressive.

For postmodern/poststructural critical theorists, the subject is neither autonomous nor coherent nor teleological in nature. Instead, the subject is constructed within various "discursive systems" or "discourses" that normalize what it means to be a subject in the first place (Foucault, 1977, 1990). These discourses are not linguistic and textual alone but involve habituated and largely unconscious ways of thinking, talking, feeling, acting, and being. Discourses are practical "grids of specification" (Foucault, 1972, 1977, 1996) for classifying, categorizing, and diagramming the human subject in relation to the social. Discourses are forms of power that both literally and metaphorically inscribe/produce the individual and the collective social body. Indeed, the residue of such production processes litters our vocabulary: "the culturally literate citizen," "the naturally literate child," "the educated gentleman," "the child author," "the reader of romance," "the functional illiterate," and "the academically prepared student." These classifications are almost always also classed, raced, and gendered.

Language.

Although we have already touched on the views of language and discourse central to the chronotope of power/knowledge and defamiliarization, we want to return to this topic and to address it more explicitly. The roots of understanding language and discourse within this framework seem to lie in postmodern notions of deconstruction. Importantly, however, like Habermas's communicative ethics, deconstruction never entirely escaped from the inherent dualism of transcendental philosophy or the foundational status of subjective experience. Again, Foucault offered some insights that allow us to address/redress these problems. So, we will outline the contours of deconstruction and then show how Foucault identified and responded to some of their inherent weaknesses.

Deconstruction decentered traditional notions of the relationsbetween signs and their referents (e.g., Saussure's signifiers and signifieds). Derrida (1976), for example, made the provocative claim that there is nothing outside of language (or semiotics more broadly conceived). Extending the "negative dialectics" of Adorno, he argued that we can never make the relation between the sign and its referent identical. In uncompromising terms, this claim brought into high relief the possibility that that the referents of all signs and symbols, including those of natural language, are not objects in the world but other signs and symbols. Unmediated knowledge of the referents in themselves is a radical impossibility.

No particular signifier (sign) can ever be regarded as referring to any particular signified (referent). Baudrillard (1983) extended this idea further with his construct of the "simulacrum." According to this construct, the sign is actually more real that the reality it represents. The real forever recapitulates the imagined. Postmodernity, Baudrillard argued, is "hyperreal." We do not live in reality but "hyperreality" where everything is simulation and objects seduce subjects rather than subjects rationally choosing objects. What he meant here is that the boundary between the real and the imaginary has been dissolved. Reality is no longer a court of appeal for experience and knowledge. The "more real than real" has become existence itself. In an age of "hyperreality," signs exert more power and influence over people than material reality, and reality itself is experienced as mysterious and illusionary to a large extent.

Defamiliarization.

The construct of defamiliarization becomes important for exploring the tactics at the heart of conjunctural analysis, and for understanding the ways in which Chronotope IV reflects a sharp break from the other chronotopes, especially with regard to the nature and process of research, and the stances of researchers toward the "objects" of their research. In his efforts to imagine an ethnography for the late twentieth and early twenty-first centuries, Clifford (1988) talked about a "hermeneutics of vulnerability," which foregrounds the ruptures of fieldwork, the multiple and contradictory positionings of researchers and research participants, the imperfect control of the ethnographer, and the utility of self-reflexivity.

In one sense, self-reflexivity involves making transparent the rhetorical and poetic work of the ethnographer in representing the object of her or his study. In another perhaps more important sense, self-reflexivity refers to the efforts of researchers and research participants to engage in acts of defamiliarization in relation to each other. In this regard, Probyn (1993) discussed how fieldwork always seems to result in being "uneasy in one's skin" and how this experience often engenders a virtual transformation of the identities of both researchers and research participants even as they are paradoxically engaged in the practice of consolidating them. This is important theoretically, because it allows for the possibility of constructing a mutual ground between researchers and research participants even while recognizing that the ground is unstable and fragile. Self-reflexivity as defamiliarization is also important because it encourages reflection on ethnography as the practice of both knowledge gathering and self-transformation through self-reflection and mutual reflection with the other. Importantly, these acts of defamiliarization can help people recognize the fragmentary, historically situated, partial, and unfinished nature of their "selves" and promote processes of self-construction/reconstruction in relation to new discourses and others.

Summary and Conclusions

The taxonomy we have used to organize our argument is not meant to be read as a taxonomy in the classic Aristotelean sense. Instead, it should be used as a heuristic device that helps move us down the road in our thinking about the complex and nuanced ways in which particular epistemes, epistemologies, theories, and methods have coalesced in emergent ways to become "regimes of truth" that inform inquiry practices in powerful and pervasive ways. Importantly, we did not find these regimes of truth lying around in the basement of a philosophy department; we produced them. They are neither "real" in any universal sense nor are they mutually exclusive. Together, however, they constitute a useful continuum for thinking about how different articulations or assemblages of subjectivity, rationality, language, knowledge, and truth emerged historically, became durable chronotopes, and continue to affect in very powerful ways how qualitative inquiry is imagined and practiced within literacy studies, education, and the social sciences. Imagined as points positioned on a continuum, the chronotope of objectivism and representation embodies many traditional Enlightenment logics such as Descartes's rational subject and a correspondence theory of truth, whereas the chronotope of power/knowledge and defamiliarization probably goes the furthest in disrupting these particular logics and replacing them with alternatives.

Translating these ideas to research practice, perhaps what is most important is to generate as good a fit as possible between research questions or objects of interest and where to locate oneself on this continuum of chronotopes. This requires deep reflection on the relations among various epistemologies, theories, approaches, and strategies. In some ways, each chronotope is uniquely valuable for pursuing some research projects more than others. But this is a bit of an overstatement. Seldom is a researcher ever really located within a single chronotope. Additionally, depending on their values and goals, two different researchers might choose to locate ostensibly the same research project within different chronotopes. For example, although Heath's famous *Ways with Words* (1983)—the classic ethnography of reading across three communities in the Piedmont Carolinas—located itself quite firmly in

Chronotope II, one could imagine locating similar work within Chronotopes III or IV. Indeed, certain critiques of Heath's work have suggested that this might have been a good idea—that it should be less descriptive and more critical. Similarly, Luke's (1992) poststructual work on discipline and reading in Australian elementary schools could readily have been conducted within Chronotope II. Indeed, many more "neutral" interpretive accounts of read-alouds and story discussions have been written.

So where does this all leave us and our fellow qualitative researchers today? How might our philosophical and historical reflections inform the ways in which we imagine and enact research practices as we move through the twenty-first century? Many metaphors have recently been proposed to describe the possible futures of qualitative inquiry. Each is predicated on particular ontological and epistemological assumptions, and each calls attention to the complexities and difficulties of conducting research a globalized, fast-capitalist, media-saturated world. We conclude with brief descriptions of a subset of these metaphors.

Locating themselves primarily within Chronotope IV, Denzin and Lincoln (1994) famously call for qualitative researchers to be "bricoleurs," mixing and matching the multiple logics and tools of qualitative inquiry in pragmatic and strategic ways to "get the job done," whatever one imagines that job to be. The goal of research, according to this metaphor, is to produce "a complex, dense, reflexive collage-like creation that represents the researcher's images, understandings, and interpretations of the world or phenomenon under analysis" (p. 3).

Located more in Chronotopes I and II, Hammersly (1999) responded to this metaphorically informed call with another one rooted in more cautionary, pragmatic, neomodernist impulses. Briefly, he argues that qualitative researchers should imagine themselves not as bricoleurs but as "boatbuilders." This metaphor derives from what is known as Neurath's boat, named after the German sociologist Otto Neurath, who compared the work of scientists with the work of sailors who must often rebuild their ships at sea, never able to start from scratch and always aware that their reconstructions must result in a coherent whole that floats. Hammersly goes on to argue that producing collage and pentimento can never be a basis for good boat building and that the impulse toward "bricolage" threatens to "sink" the qualitative inquiry ship. "A central message that ought to be taken from Neurath's metaphor," Hammersly claims, "is that because we are always faced with the task of rebuilding our craft at sea, everything cannot be questioned at once" (p. 581). He argues further that "those who want to be poets or political activists, or both, should not pretend that they can simultaneously be social researchers" (p. 583). Unabashedly modernist, Hammersly urges that we "develop a coherent sense of where we are going and of how we need to rebuild our vessel to sail in the right direction" (p. 579), which, among other things, will require thoroughgoing knowledge of where we have been.

A third metaphor, and the one that motivated many of our arguments in this chapter, is the "genealogist." Thinking genealogically forces us to see disciplines as the ongoing work of invested actors, not as paradigms we must uncritically occupy. Traditionally, researchers have been encouraged to see research traditions and methods as immutable, with parameters that are defined a priori. Genealogists have no given lineages, but different histories at their disposal.

Using these histories, they attempt to understand how any "subject" (e.g., a person, a social formation, a social movement, an institution) has been constituted out of particular intersections of forces and systems of forces by mapping the complex, contingent, and often contradictory ways in which these forces and systems of force came together to produce the formation in the precise way that that it did and not some other way. From the perspective of genealogy,

> [h]istory becomes "effective" to the degree that it introduces discontinuity into our very being—as it divides our emotions, dramatizes our instincts, multiplies our body and sets it against itself. "Effective" history deprives the self of the reassuring stability of life and nature, and it will not permit itself to be transported by a voiceless obstinacy toward a millennial ending. It will uproot its traditional foundations and relentlessly disrupt its pretended continuity. This is because knowledge is not made for understanding; it is made for cutting. [Foucault, 1981, p. 88]

Guided by this sense that knowledge is "for cutting," we choose methodological directions strategically but with full knowledge that there no "safe spaces," no alibis for our decisions. Although genealogists call into question naive realism and the authority of experience, they also try to deploy such constructs in thoughtful and partial ways. Deleuze and Guattari (1987), for example, do not claim to rid the world of binaries but to create new ones that are more productive for achieving democratic ideals. Genealogists realize that they need to appropriate extant epistemologies theories, approaches, and strategies to do their work, but they are aware that there are no "pure" choices, no guarantees about what these appropriations will produce or how they will produce it. To understand such outcomes requires intense retrospective analysis, constantly looking back and trying to understand how our accounts were constructed in the ways they were and not in other ways.

In closing, we want to underscore that we have presented these three metaphors because we believe that all of them (as well as others we might have discussed) are powerful and productive for thinking about the central topic of this book—the logics of qualitative inquiry—past, present, and future. These metaphors index tensions that have always existed in the field of qualitative inquiry and will probably always exist. Together, they map the many imperatives and impulses that we, as qualitative researchers, must struggle with in our daily work, especially with respect to locating ourselves strategically within and across chronotopes and creating epistemology-theory-approach-strategy assemblages that are both principled and pragmatic.

References

Adorno, T. (1973). *Negative dialectics* (E. B. Ashton, Trans.). New York: Continuum.

Althusser, L. (1971). *Lenin and philosophy*. New York: Monthly Review Press.

Bakhtin, M. M. (1981). *The dialogic imagination* (C. Emerson & M. Holquist, Trans.). Austin: University of Texas Press.

Baudrillard, J. (1983). *Simulations.* New York: Semiotext(e).

Bernstein, R. (1992). *The new constellation: The ethical/political horizons of modernity/postmodernity.* Cambridge, MA: MIT Press.

Birdwhistell, R. L. (1970). *Kinesics and context: Essays on body motion communication.* Philadelphia: University of Pennsylvania Press.

Bourdieu, P. (1990). *The logic of practice* (R. Nice, Trans.). Stanford, CA: Stanford University Press.

Clifford, J. (1988). *The predicament of culture: Twentieth-century ethnography, literature, and art.* Cambridge, MA: Harvard University Press.

Clifford, J., & Marcus, G. (Eds.). (1986). *Writing culture: The poetics and politics of ethnography.* Berkeley: University of California Press.

Deleuze, G., & Guattari, F. (1987). *A thousand plateaus: Capitalism and schizophrenia* (B. Massumi, Trans.). Minneapolis: University of Minnesota Press.

Denzin, N. K., & Lincoln, Y. S. (Eds.). (1994). *Handbook of qualitative research.* Thousand Oaks, CA: Sage.

Derrida, J. (1976). *Of grammatology* (G. Spivak, Trans.). Baltimore: Johns Hopkins University Press.

Dilthey, W. L. (1976/1900). *Selected writings.* Cambridge, UK: Cambridge University Press.

Flower, L., & Hayes, J. (1981). A cognitive process theory of writing. *College Communication and Composition, 32,* 365–387.

Foucault, M. (1972). *The archaeology of knowledge* (A. M. Sheridan Smith, Trans). New York: Pantheon Books.

Foucault, M. (1975). *The birth of the clinic. An archaeology of medical perception* (A. Sheridan, Trans.). New York: Vintage.

Foucault, M. (1977). *Discipline and punish: The birth of the prison* (A. Sheridan, Trans.). New York: Vintage Books.

Foucault, M. (1990). *The history of sexuality: An introduction* (Vol. 1) (R. Hurley, Trans.). New York: Vintage. (Original work published in 1978).

Foucault, M. (1996). History, discourse and discontinuity. In S. Lotringer (Ed.), *Foucault live (Interviews, 1961–1984)* (pp. 33–50). New York: Semiotext(e). (Original essay published in 1972).

Freire, P. (1970). *Pedagogy of the oppressed.* New York: Continuum.

Gadamer, H. G. (1972). *Knowledge and human interests* (J. J. Shapiro, Trans.). Boston: Beacon.

Geertz, C. (1973). *The interpretation of cultures: Selected essays.* New York: Basic Books.

Giddens, A. (1979). *Central problems in social theory.* Berkeley: University of California Press.

Gramsci, A. (1971). *Selections from the prison notebooks of Antonio Gramsci* (Q. Hoare & G. N. Smith, Eds. and Trans.). New York: International Publishers.

Grossberg, L. (1992). *We gotta get out of this place: Popular conservatism and postmodern culture.* New York: Routledge.

Habermas, J. (1984). *The theory of communicative action: Reason and the rationalization of society* (Vol. 1) (T. McCarthey, Trans.). Boston: Beacon.

Habermas, J. (1987). The *theory of communicative action: Lifeworld and system* (Vol. 2) (T. McCarthy, Trans.). Boston: Beacon.

Hall, S. (1992). Cultural studies and its theoretical legacies. In L. Grossberg, C. Nelson, & P. Treichler (Eds.), *Cultural studies* (pp. 277–294). New York: Routledge.

Hammersly, M. (1999). Not bricolage but boatbuilding. *Journal of Contemporary ethnography, 28*(5), 574–585.

Heath, S. B. (1982). Ethnography in education: Defining the essentials. In P. Gilmore & A. A. Glatthorn (Eds.), *Children in and out of school: Ethnography and education* (pp. 33–55). Washington, DC: Center for Applied Linguistics.

Heath, S. B. (1983). *Ways with words: Language, life, and work in communities and classrooms.* Cambridge, UK: Cambridge University Press.

Hebdige, R. (1979). *Subculture: The meaning of style.* London: Routledge.

Heidegger, M. (1962). *Being and time* (R. MacQuarrie, Trans.). New York: Harper & Rowe.

Hirsch, E. D. (1987). *Cultural literacy.* Boston: Houghton Mifflin.

Holland, D., Lachiotte, W., Skinner, D., & Cain, C. (1998). *Identity and agency in cultural worlds.* Cambridge, MA: Harvard University Press.

Horkheimer, M., & Adorno, T. (1988). *The dialectic of enlightenment* (J. Cummings, Trans.). New York: Continuum.

Lather, P. (1991). *Getting smart: Feminist research and pedagogy with/in the postmodern.* New York: Routledge.

Lather, P. (1997). Drawing the lines at angels: Working the ruins of feminist ethnography. *Qualitative Studies in Education, 10*(3), 285–304.

Lukács, G. (1971). *History of class consciousness: Studies in Marxist dialectics* (R. Livingstone, Trans.). Cambridge, MA: MIT Press.

Luke, A. (1992). The body literate: Discourse and inscription in early literacy training. *Linguistics and Education, 4*(1), 107–129.

Lyotard, F. (1984). *The postmodern condition: A report on knowledge* (G. Bennington & B. Massumi, Trans.). Minneapolis: University of Minnesota Press.

Marcus, G., & Fischer, M. (1986). *Anthropology as cultural critique: An experimental moment in the human sciences.* Chicago: University of Chicago Press.

Morson, G., & Emerson, C. (1990). *Mikhail Bakhtin: Creation of a prosaics.* Stanford, CA: Stanford University Press.

Pinar, W. (2004). *What is curriculum theory?* Hillsdale, NJ: Lawrence Erlbaum.

Probyn, E. (1993). *Sexing the self: Gendered positions in cultural studies.* London and New York: Routledge.

Ricoeur, P. (1970). *Freud and philosophy: An essay on interpretation.* New Haven, CT: Yale University Press.

Rorty, R. (1979). *Philosophy and the mirror of nature.* Princeton, NJ: Princeton University Press.

Strike, K. (1974). On the expressive potential of behaviorist language. *American Educational Research Journal, 11*(2), 103–120.

Thompson, J. B. (1990). The methodology of interpretation. In J. B. Thompson (Ed.), *Ideology and modern culture* (pp. 272–327). Stanford, CA: Stanford University Press.

Turner, J. C. (1995). The influence of classroom contexts on young children's motivation for literacy. *Reading Research Quarterly, 30*, 410–441.

Willis, P. (1977). *Learning to labor: How working class kids get working class jobs.* New York: Columbia University Press.

Wittgenstein, L. (1958). *Philosophical investigations* (G.E.M. Anscombe, Trans.). Oxford, UK: Basil Blackwell.

Chapter 2 | This *IS* Your Father's Pardigm

Government Intrusion and the Case of Qualitative Research in Education

Patti Lather
The Ohio State University

Could quantification settle important issues of public policy? Experience was often disappointing, but hope sprang eternal.
—Porter, 1995, p. 152

Science, as I have known it and practiced it over the years, has had little to do with Washington, DC. I learned early in my academic career that the Reagan administration was not interested in funding my feminist critical qualitative research. I have stayed away from grants and grant culture ever since, doing what might be termed "little science" with little money and getting by just fine. But during the past year or so, I have found myself sucked into an alphabet soup of OERI, NRC, DOE, NSF, Senate subcommittees on this or that, even something dubbed "web scrubbing," where the U.S. Department of Education is deleting research, including ERIC digests, that it deems unsupportive of Bush administrative agendas.[1]

This chapter is an effort to make sense of the federal government's incursion into legislating scientific method in the realm of educational research via the "evidence-based" movement of the past few years. Although I will attend some to the consequent effort to address congressional disdain regarding educational research via the National Research Council's (NRC) (2002) report *Scientific Research in Education*,[2] my primary interest is in the structure of the situation. Hence, in what follows, I address the many factors at play including the "science wars" and the needs of neoliberal states in a time of proliferating insurgent special interests, including that of conservative restoration. Also at play are academic capitalism, entrepreneurship, and ambition, and, with a nod to Adorno and for me, always, Walter Benjamin, the traditions of critical theory in terms of the critique of instrumental reason.

In taking on these latest twists and turns in governmental efforts to effect educational research, the reductionisms of positivism, empiricism, and objectivism are assumed. I do not want to rehearse the various critiques of scientism that have arisen in the thirty-plus years since Thomas B. Kuhn's (1970) *The Structure of Scientific Revolutions*. Instead, I ask three questions about what I find to be a profoundly troubling situation.

First, what is happening to make me willing to return to the scene of my doctoral training in evaluation methods some twenty years ago, to immerse myself in the language of "treatment homogeneity," "setting invariance," the "promiscuous" use of quasi experiments (Cook & Payne, 2002, p. 173), and my favorite, "inadvertent treatment crossovers," in this case, of a principal in the treatment condition married to someone in the control school (Cook & Payne, 2002, p. 163)?

Second, what are the implications for qualitative research of the NRC report, a report that intended a "catholic view toward research methods" in delineating "high quality science" (Shavelson, Phillips, Towne, & Feuer, 2003, p. 25)?

And third, how might the federal effort to legislate scientific method be read as a backlash against the proliferation of research approaches of the past twenty years out of cultural studies, feminist methodology, radical environmentalists, ethnic studies, and social studies of science, a backlash where in the guise of objectivity and good science, "colonial, Western, masculine, white and other biases" are smuggled in (Canclini, 2001, p. 12)?

In surveying a variety of ways this topic could be approached, I will call particularly on discourse practices of Foucauldian policy analysis, feminism via Luce Irigaray, and postcolonialism via Stuart Hall.

Legislating Method:
Science for Policy or Policy for Science?

Education research is broken in our country ... and Congress must work to make it more useful.... . Research needs to be conducted on a more scientific basis. Educators and policy makers need objective, reliable research.

—Michael Castle, U.S. representative,
quoted in NRC, 2002, p. 28

It is, of course, an old argument that the social sciences are not to be subsumed under a natural science model. In my first encounter with this argument as a doctoral student, Marcia Westkott (1979) argued against what she termed "the first positivist assumption": that the methods appropriate for studying the natural world are equally appropriate for the study of human experience. What is new in what I have to say here is that in this moment of what Foucault (1981/1991) termed "our contemporaneity" (p. 40), this old argument against a unified idea of science (Galison & Stump, 1996) is being disavowed via nakedly political and self-aggrandizing moves.

John Willinsky's (2001) call to broaden and deepen federal major policy statements regarding the translation of educational research into practice provided a wake-up call for me regarding movements at the federal level to legislate method. Rather ingeniously, Willinsky attached a critical agenda to one that is decidedly instrumentalist and even shocking in its lack of attention to the past twenty years of "utilization" research on why "'top-down linear' R&D models of the 1950s and 1960s" did not work (p. 7). Arguing for democratic forms of collaboration and exchange rather than "heavy-handed intentions of driving educational practice" (p. 7), Willinsky foregrounded the "productive tensions and radical challenges that mark this play of interpretations within social science research" (p. 7).

Worried about "research-wielding technocrats" (Willinsky, 2001, p. 9), his article scared me so much that at the American Educational Research Association's (AERA) 2002 conference, I broke my usual rule of no 8:00 a.m. sessions to attend Ellen Lagemann's talk about her 2000 book on the history of educational research, *An Elusive Science: The Troubling History of Educational Research*. Although her talk was lovely, the discussion afterward was not. It turned to the attempts of the NRC (2002) report to negotiate between the federal government and the educational research community what it means to do scientific educational research.[3]

In spite of the efforts of the NRC report toward a "big tent" of legitimate methods in educational research (Feuer, Towne, & Shavelson, 2002), Lagemann seemed adrift in addressing how calls for generalizability, objectivity, replicability, and a unified theory of science reinscribe a science under duress for some thirty years. Made aware of an afternoon session where what I call "the suits" would be on the podium in force, I went to that session and became even more aghast at the framing statement from a representative from the Office of Educational Research and Improvement about the need for policy research that supported the present administration's initiatives.[4] This sort of nakedness was either strategic or naive, and these folks did not look naive. I began to think that maybe I was the naive one, that I would think the past thirty years of the social critique of science might actually shape contemporary thought about policy-driven research. And I began to plot this article, as I asked what is happening when at the very time there is a philosophical trend against certainty in the social sciences, "this continual and noisy legislative activity" (Elden, 2002, p. 146), with all of its normalizing authority, is working at the federal level to discipline educational research to a narrowly defined sense of science-based evidence.[5]

When Andy Porter, past AERA president, visited Ohio State University after the 2002 AERA conference, I asked him how scared I should be. "Do I look scared?" he asked back. "No," I replied. "Do I look young?" he asked. "No," I replied, as he stated his view that trends come and go in Washington while the rest of the country gets on with its business. I do not share Dr. Porter's sanguine outlook on this matter. Irrespective of whether the fifteen-year timeline of the Strategic Education Research Program of the NRC will change the face of educational research, this seems about much more than the latest trend in Washington, DC. Elizabeth Atkinson (2004), for example, asks who loses when "a nation of researchers is locked into a government policy agenda" (p. 117) and urges a sort of heresy against "serving policy" to the point where we collude in our own oppression. How can we take Atkinson's charge to heart of "thinking outside the box" at a time when educational research is being told what science is by bureaucrats and Congress, at the very same time that an expansive definition of science is being urged in the more high-status areas of science (e.g., Goenka, 2002)?[6]

As the latest wave of the conservative attack on education, this kind of "activist interventionism and expansion of the scope of government" (Shaker, 2002) gives the lie to the rhetoric of decreased federalism in the conservative restoration. Paul Shaker (2002) wrote of the "reading wars": "This is not a fair fight, it is not what it seems on the surface, and the stakes are high" (p. 11). Learning lessons from its effort to gain control of reading research, the government has targeted math, science, professional development, and comprehensive school reform as its next objects of "high scientific standards." With random field trials (RFTs) now specified by Congress ever more frequently in effectiveness studies of federally funded programs, the design and application of educational research has become a partisan tool, much like standardized tests have functioned for almost two decades now.

What work does the NRC (2002) report do in challenging governmental manipulation of science? The NRC, serving as scientific advisor to the government since 1863, has issued five reports on educational research since 1958. This latest one is trying to speak against the narrow scientism of the Elementary and Secondary Education Act (No Child Left Behind Act of 2001) that was signed into legislation in January 2002. According to Marilyn Cochran-Smith (2002), in an editorial in the *Journal of Teacher Education*, this act "virtually mandates" that to be funded, educational research must be evaluated "'using experimental or quasi-experimental designs ... with a preference for random-assignment experiments'" (p. 188). By 2004, 75% of funded research is targeted to be RFTs. Rather than a focus on randomized experimental trials as the gold standard, the NRC report attempts inclusivity regarding a range of approaches to educational research, both quantitative and qualitative.

In delineating the scientificity of science, although the NRC (2002) report tries to walk a fine line, it is, ultimately, what Foucault (1981/1991) termed "a kind of tribunal of reason" (p. 60). Given the report's often-repeated intentions of balance across multiple methods, it took an article by several committee members on the scientificity of design studies in a later issue of *Educational Researcher* (Shavelson et al., 2003) for it to become clear how objectivity is enshrined and prediction, explanation, and verification override description, interpretation, and discovery.

Although the contested nature of science is much evoked in the report, an epistemological sovereignty is assumed in delineating and applying principles in the doing of "high-quality science." The exclusionary force of its "guiding principles" is striking in its disavowal of different views of evidence, analysis, and purpose. Rationality's domesticating power is particularly fascinating in that the chapter on the specificities of educational research lists all that gets in the way of an engineering approach to science. Values and politics, human volition and program variability, cultural diversity, multiple disciplinary perspectives, the import of partnerships with practitioners, even the ethical considerations of random designs—all are swept away in a unified theory of scientific advancement with its mantra of "science is science is science" across the physical, life, and social sciences. One expects to sort through several voices in a committee-prepared document, but, in the end, its efforts to provide guidelines for rigor and enhance a "vibrant federal presence" (NRC, 2002, p. 129) are complicit with the federal government's move to evidence-based knowledge as being much more about policy for science than science for policy.

Evidence-Based Practice and Science, Money, and Politics

With the NRC (2002) report under my belt and with little time for Derrida and Deleuze, I buried myself in the updates on "Bush science" from *Education Week*, tried to keep up with policy analyses of these twists and turns, and even developed some web access skills. I learned three things from all of this.

The British Scene

The first thing I learned is that Britain has been going through this extremely interventionist regulatory climate policed by statutory bodies for more than a decade [see also Torrance, this volume]. In a "taking stock" edited book published in 2000, *Evidence-Based Practice: A Critical Appraisal*, the focus is largely on health care policy (Trinder & Reynolds, 2000). Appraising strengths and weaknesses across both "champions and critics" (Trinder, 2000a, p. 3), its appeal and, hence, rapid influence is theorized as rooted in the needs of posttraditional societies for ways of managing risk in the face of a paradoxical dependence on and suspicion of experts and expert knowledge. Combined with the push to value for money, the rise of managerialism, consumerism, and political discourses of accountability and performance, neoliberal ideologies of the neutrality via proceduralism of such practices prevail in an "explosion of auditable management control systems" (Trinder, 2000a, p. 9). Here, at last, is a way to manage quality issues by displacing professional judgment with promised effectiveness via the procedural production of evidence. Although "a product of its time" (p. 5), the problem is that there is little evidence that evidence-based practice actually works (p. 2).[7]

In terms of education, Hammersley's (2000) chapter on the British scene notes that in medicine, the focus was on quality of practice whereas in education, the focus has been on the quality of research (p. 163).[8] Hammersley also notes the focus on teaching as opposed to administration and management and how, in spite of the claims of evidence-based practice of being a "radically new venture" (p. 164), research-based teaching has a long history, including a long critique. The shift to qualitative methods in the 1970s was related to the difficulties of measuring what is educationally significant and the limits of causal models given the preponderance of interaction effects. As a result, according to Hammersley, educational research became "embroiled in philosophical and methodological disputes" (p. 167) that cannot be simply overcome. Replicability, for example, is no answer given the "complex web of relationships" (p. 168).

The degree to which the kinds of problems that teachers face are open to solution by research is precisely the question. The importance of contextual judgment mandates a great caution in adapting the medical model. Formulas for transparent accountability are more about politics than about quality of service. Teachers are not as powerful as doctors, so it is worrisome that educational managers can more likely force narrow definitions of effective practice (Trinder, 2000b, p. 238).[9]

For the purposes of this chapter, it is the mutations of the classic approach in the British scene that are particularly instructive. The introduction of qualitative research, the interruption of the top-down approach, and the pluralistic interpretations of what is evidence: this is a sort of translation in diffusion. Calls for effectiveness studies of evidence-based practice displace the hegemony of meta-analysis and randomized clinical trials by capitalizing on the move in focus from advocacy to implementation. Here, qualitative or mixed methods are de rigueur. In nursing research, for example, given displacement of the empiricism of the natural sciences by phenomenology and its rejection of objectivism, the uneasy fit of qualitative, its lack of a sense of certainty, and its eclecticism require considerable adaptation and, hence, might work as a counterforce to prevailing narrow ideas of what constitutes evidence.[10]

From Back in the Day

The second thing I learned is that a handful of advocates are well positioned to push for this. Out of a 1999 conference named, ironically, for Donald Campbell who, of course, championed the case study in later life,[11] emerged a 2002 publication by the Brookings Institution. This book, *Evidence Matters: Randomized Trials in Education Research*, is coedited by Frederick Mosteller, professor emeritus of mathematics at Harvard and early 1970s architect of randomized clinical trials as the gold standard in medical research, and Robert Boruch of the Campbell Collaboration (see note 15). In their introduction, the coeditors laud the government's serious interest in the quality of education research. Permeating the text are terms such as "standards of evidence" and "scientific rigor," with a nod toward "other kinds of research" as "augmentation" to controlled studies, provided "scientific standards" can be delineated.

Driven by "worry about ideology parading as intellectual inquiry" (Boruch & Mosteller, 2002, p. 2), the coeditors' task was to persuade sponsoring agencies "that there is no easier way to get the answers to the right question" than RFTs (p. 3). Shocked by the paucity of "good studies" (p. 4), they called for political and administrative support for rigorous research to address the bad reputation of educational research. Although claiming "refreshed ways of thinking" (p. 4), most of the essays are a response to critics during the past twenty years.[12]

At root is what to do about federal needs for evaluation data on educational initiatives in a time of belt-tightening economies. The good old days of the 1960s are evoked, when the federal trough was rich with program evaluation monies as the research budget soared from US$3 million in 1960 to US$100 million in 1967 (Vivovskis, 2002, p. 123). Foregrounding an expansive federal role in financial, political, and regulatory environments, they long for something like the Food and Drug Administration to "require good evidence" regarding which educational interventions are safe or effective. It is high time then, for "rigorous evaluation" on the part of "randomizers" to assume important positions at the federal level. "Generating better evidence for better education" (Boruch & Mosteller, 2002, p. 14) is the watchword.[13]

Since the Reagan years, the growing perception has been of more money chasing after bad research and evaluation. Federal agencies were increasingly under the gun of a Republican House of Representatives that wanted to win elections on pro–school reform platforms while spending the least dollars. The watchwords of "scientifically sound" and "politically objective" captured the widespread "discontent with the state of current knowledge of what works in education" (Cook & Payne, 2002, p. 150). Cook and Payne saw the rejection of experimental design as "probably a major cause of the impoverished current state of knowledge" (p. 151), blaming Eisner, Guba, Lincoln, Patton, Stake, and Stufflebeam by name.[14]

It is of particular interest how conservative think tanks have ratcheted up their focus on education issues since the late 1980s and how entrepreneurial interests are at work.[15] In *Science, Money and Politics*, Daniel Greenberg (2001) probed the demands for utilitarian science versus scientific autonomy within the National Science Foundation, which he situated as a "little dog" compared to defense, space, and medical research. Greenberg noted that the "politics of the academic pork barrel" (p. 184) work toward a sort of "scientific welfare" (p. 39) within the Enterprise University (p. 356) with its grant economy, where the social sciences are insulted by being largely left out. If real science, as Greenberg suggested, is about skepticism, curiosity, and passion (p. 24), where transparency of process is the only agreed-on fundamental, "could science serve us better" (p. 10) if it moved beyond its "capacity for believing it is the victim of neglect and hostility" (p. 60) and its grant chasing?[16]

It appears that science, money, and politics have combined with prepositioned capability and sweetheart contracts on the part of self-described "ambitious researchers" (Burtless, 2002, p. 193) to court the increased federal role in the adoption of experimental methods. As argued by Baez and Boyles (2002) in their lovely analysis of the discourse of grants, it is not that "academic capitalism" has not become our way of life. The deal has already been struck. The question is the extent to which we can promote critical work within such a milieu, "work which challenges the categories that organize [our] existence" (Baez & Boyles, 2002, p. 45), given the "Faustian bargain" of the federal and corporate embrace.

Toward a Policy Relevant Counterscience: Fieldwork in Philosophy

The third thing I have learned is that we need to put our critical theory to work in this moment of our now. In his discussion of how conservative modernization has radically reshaped the common sense of society regarding education, Michael Apple (2001) asked, "If the right can do this, why can't we?" (p. 194). In addressing such a question, I suggest that the left needs a policy turn (Bennett, 1992; Ferguson & Golding, 1997; McGuigan, 2001; McRobbie, 1997), with a focus on program evaluation as a particularly cogent site where a policy-relevant counterscience might be worked out.

Suggestive here is *Making Social Science Matter* by Bent Flyv-bjerg (2001), a Danish urban developer who argued for a move from a narrowly defined epistemic science to one that articulates a social science that integrates context dependency with practical deliberation. Here considerations of power are brought to bear in delineating a knowledge adequate to our time. Rather than the self-defeating "physics envy"[17] that underlies the objectivist strands of the social sciences, this is a social science that can hold its own in the science wars by contributing to society's practical rationality in clarifying where we are and where we want to be.

Flyvbjerg's (2001) argument for a practical philosophy of ethics that takes power into account "as a point of departure for praxis" (p. 70) focuses on the context of practice as a disciplining of inter-pretation. Mandating on the ground empirical work, theories are constantly confronted with praxis toward public deliberation. Here social science becomes a sort of laboratory toward public philoso-phy, what Bourdieu termed "'fieldwork in philosophy'" (quoted in Flyvbjerg, 2001, p. 167). Case studies assume prime importance as critical cases, strategically chosen, provide "far better access for policy intervention than the present social science of variables" (p. 86). In such a laboratory, against a narrow scientism in policy analysis and program evaluation, the urgent questions become: Where are we going with democracy in this project? Who gains and who loses and by which mechanisms of power? Given this analysis, what should be done?

"Simultaneously sociological, political and philosophical" (Flyv-bjerg, 2001, p. 64), this is a science that does not divest experience of its rich ambiguity because it stays close to the complexities and contradictions of existence. Focusing on practices as event, detect-ing forces that make life work, sociality and history are seen as the only foundations we have. Instead of emulating the natural or, in Foucauldian terms, "exact" sciences, the goal is getting people to no longer know what to do so that things might be done differ-ently. This is the yes of the setting-to-work mode of postfoun-dational theory that faces unanswerable questions, the necessary experience of the impossible, in an effort to foster understanding, reflection, and action instead of a narrow translation of research into practice.

Interrupting a Discourse One Finds So Profoundly Troubling

In my final section, I put into play three discourse practices quite scandalous to that of the NRC (2002) report to explore what it might mean to dissolve the continuities of dominant narratives. In short, the uncompromising discourses of Foucauldian policy analysis and feminist and postcolonial science are called on to evoke the science that might be possible after the critique of science.

A Foucauldian Reading

In Foucauldian terms, policy is one of the three technologies of governmentality, the others being diplomatic/military and economic.[18] Policy is to regulate behavior and render populations productive via a "biopolitics" that entails state intervention in and regulation of the everyday lives of citizens in a "liberal" enough manner to minimize resistance and maximize wealth stimulation. Naming, classifying, and analyzing: all work toward disciplining through normalizing. Such governmentality is "as much about what we do to ourselves as what is done to us" (Danaher, Schirato, & Webb, 2000, p. 83). It is, contrary to those who see Foucault as a pessimist and determinist, much about how understanding such processes might raise possibilities for doing otherwise.

In *The Order of Things*, Foucault (1970) turned to the matter of the status of the human sciences. Here Foucault argued that to look at such sciences as "pre-paradigmatic" is to buy into some "maturation" narrative that belies how the human sciences are about "constantly demystifying themselves" rather than making themselves more precise (pp. 356, 364). Locating the human sciences in the interstices of the mathematizable and the philosophical, "this cloudy distribution" (p. 347) is both their privilege and their precariousness. Language, meaning, the limits of consciousness, the role of representations, this is the stuff of humans seeking to know. Rather than lacking in exactitude and rigor, the human sciences are more a "'meta-epistemological' position" in being about "finitude, relativity, and perspective" (p. 355). Here, their very "haziness, inexactitude and imprecision" (p. 355) is the form of positivity proper to the human sciences: "blurred, intermediary and composite disciplines multiply[ing] endlessly" (p. 358).

Whether this is "truly scientific" or not is a "wearisome" discussion (Foucault, 1970, p. 365). The human sciences do not answer to criteria of objectivity and systematicity, the formal criteria of a scientific form of knowledge, but they are within the positive domain of knowledge as much as any other part of the modern episteme. There is no internal deficiency here; they are not "stranded across the threshold of scientific forms" (p. 366). They are not "false" sciences; "they are not sciences at all" (p. 366). They assume the title to "receive the transference of models borrowed from the sciences" (p. 366). Enacting "a perpetual principle of dissatisfaction, of calling into question, of criticism and contestation" (p. 373), such knowledges are tied to a praxis of unmasking the representations we give to ourselves of ourselves. Here is where we learn to think again, opening ourselves to a future thought of the knowledge of things and their order.

In terms of the recent governing mentality of educational research, the "privilege accorded to ... 'the sciences of man'" is based on the "'political arithmetic'" (Foucault, 1998, p. 323) that makes particular kinds of discourse both possible and necessary. This is not so much about concepts on their way to formation or even the price paid for scientific pretensions, but rather of understanding claims to scientificity as discursive events. Here the "inexact knowledges" become "*a field of strategic possibilities*" (p. 320), a "counterscience" of "indisciplined" policy analysis that troubles what we take for granted as the good in fostering understanding, reflection, and action.

A Feminist Reading

This militantly empiricist and quantitative movement, this desire for hardness with its claims to produce findings that are verifiable, definitive, and cumulative, is set against a softness where interpretation is central and findings are always subject to debate and reinterpretation (Gherardi & Turner, 1987).

French feminist theory is premised on the idea that the classic structure is splitting and opening to becoming and that this becoming will be initiated primarily by women because men have more to lose and psychic structures are more called to the scene of castration (Conley, 2000, p. 25). Irigaray's argument that there are "systems of thought dominated by the logic and linguistics of male sexual organs" is, of course, based on psychoanalytic theory (Olkowski, 2000, p. 91). Her concern is that we have so naturalized such language and logic that we do not see the practical aspects of such domination. Regimes of power and systems of philosophy are designed to "penetrate," interventions are "engineered," "we encourage one another to be 'hard' on the issues" (p. 92).

In contrast is the sort of "embarrassing emotion-fest" of women's work that can be interpreted only as "excess ... wild or crazy, bizarre, remote, or meaningless" to the task of social policy (p. 93). Intelligibility demands that language conform to hegemonic and rigid hierarchies, systems of formulation, standards of truth within a logic of solid mechanics. What Irigaray called "placental economies" of fluid negotiation "make us shudder" within the "order of good sense" (Olkowski, 2000, pp. 96, 99).

The structure of oppositions thus set up reads such claims to truth as "false claimants, 'corrupted by dissemblance' ... made from below, by means of an aggression, an insinuation, a subversion, 'against the father' and without passing through the Idea" (Olkowski, 2000, p. 99). "Disconcerting the erection of the male subject," women's bad copies or fake science are "an abyss in which the Father could no longer recognize himself" (p. 101). Proceeding by alliances, symbiosis, contagion, and what Irigaray called "mucosity," this is a kind of refusal of recognition and of the proper rather than a scene of good daughters making bad copies via replication studies.

Charges of essentialism are, of course, rife here. Arguing what Deleuze called "becoming-woman" as having a "special introductory power," key to all other becomings (Olkowski, 2000, p. 103), women's insight into multiplicity and difference is held to come from the "assemblages that produce minoritarian groups ... those outside the rules" (p. 106) and from an embodiment that is not organized by castration or its threat (p. 107). Depathologizing that which is associated with women, "the uteral, the vulvar, the clitoral, the vaginal, the placental" (p. 107): this would transform the social contract and give purchase to seeing science as a site of contestation, an always already gendered practice.

A Postcolonial Reading

In rereading Stuart Hall (1996) on Gramsci for the introduction to a cultural studies class I recently taught, I was struck with how the right models Gramsci's tactics of a "war of position." Condensing a variety of different relations and practices into a definite system of rules through a series of necessary displacements, the state "'plans, urges, incites, solicits, punishes'" (Gramsci, quoted in Hall, 1996, p. 429).

As a sort of "regressive modernism," this disciplining and normalizing effort to standardize educational research in the name of quality and effectiveness is an attempt to hegemonize and appropriate to a reactionary political agenda deeper tendencies in cultural shifts. These might be termed a "new cultural politics of difference" (Hall, 1996, p. 464) and include the displacement of European high culture, the Americanization of world culture, and the decolonization of the Third World, including the decolonization of First World minorities. Such a politics is marked by unevenness, contradictory outcomes, disjunctures, delays, contingencies, and uncompleted projects.

The danger of the reduction of spaces for the doing of other sorts of research on the part of a cultural dominant is that the decentering of old hierarchies and grand narratives of the past twenty or so years has created new subjects on the political and cultural stage. To try to reinscribe a medical model of the 1970s is to set oneself up to be read as an "aggressive resistance to difference" (Hall, 1996, p. 468; West, 1990). This backlash attempt to transfer a canonical model to educational research is an "assault, direct and indirect, on multiculturalism" (Hall, 1996, p. 468). As Hall noted, "there is no going back" (p. 469).

Overtaken by the carnivalesque, a sort of "low science" has emerged out of this proliferation of difference that challenges the fundamental basis of the mechanisms of ordering and of sense making of European culture. A rich production of counternarratives is alive and kicking, from subaltern studies to indigenous research methodologies, from native as anthropologist to Al-Jazeera, the Arabic TV channel. This is the end of the innocent notion of knowledge production as value neutral. Efforts by the "top" to reject and eliminate the "bottom" for reasons of prestige and status bite back from a place where white masculinities are no longer at the center of the frame.

Hall's (1996) narrative of the coming of feminism to cultural studies is instructive here. Hall told of being targeted as the enemy, "as the senior patriarchal figure": "I was checkmated by feminists; I couldn't come to terms with it" (p. 500). By this, he meant not personally (he noted he was married to a feminist) but in terms of figuring out how to do useful work. "It was time to go," he said.

Conclusion: Indisciplined Knowing

> *Will [man] ever be ready to receive ... a thought that, freeing him from fascination with unity, for the first time risks summoning him to take the measure of an exteriority that is not divine, of a space entirely in question, and even excluding the possibility of an answer, since every response would necessarily fall anew under the jurisdiction of the figure of figures? This amounts perhaps to asking ourselves: is man capable of radical interrogation?*
> —Blanchot, quoted in Plotnitsky, 2002, p. 239

To conclude, I have argued that this move at the federal level is the science wars (Plotnitsky, 2002; Ross, 1996) brought to the realm of educational research in a way much marked by the anxieties, rhetorics, and practices of a decentered masculinist and an imperialist regime of truth. In this, I realize that I am an enemy amid talk of détente and the end of the "paradigm wars" and the call for mixed methods (Tashakkori & Teddlie, 2002). Rather than détente, however, all of this reinforces my interest in what Foucault termed "indiscipline" as a move toward a Nietzschean sort of "unnatural science" that leads to greater health by fostering ways of knowing that escape normativity (Nietzsche, 1974, p. 301). By indiscipline, Foucault (1994) described a mechanism by which a marginalized population/practice is created to exert pressure that cannot be tolerated by the very process of exclusions and sanctions designed to guard against irregularities and infractions (p. 36).

As an irregular trooper in the science wars, I see this latest round of reinscribing the idealized natural science model as an effect of power of a sort of historical amnesia that disavows decades of critique and (re)formulations toward a science after the critique of science. To think about the relation of policy and research in such a place of Foucauldian indiscipline, what I have offered might be viewed, in a Lacanian register, as "the hysteric's discourse" (Fink, 1995). Here "a truly scientific spirit" is commanded by "that which does not work, by that which does not fit. It does not set out to carefully cover over paradoxes and contradictions" like that of the master's discourse with its imperative to be obeyed within its guise of reason (pp. 134–135). The hysteric sees the heart of science as "taking such paradoxes and contradictions as far as they can go" (p. 135) rather than endorsing a monolithic science "based on a set of axiomatic mathematizable propositions, measurable empirical entities, and pure concepts" (p. 138).

In short, the science wars continue; the line between a narrowly defined scientism and a more capacious scientificity of disciplined inquiry remains very much at issue. In terms of the desirability of degrees of formalization—mathematized and not, generic procedures, and rigorous differentiations—there is virtually no agreement among scientists, philosophers, and historians as to what constitutes science except, increasingly, the view that science is, like all human endeavor, a cultural practice and practice of culture. To operate from a premise of the impossibility of satisfactory solutions means to not assume to resolve but instead, to be prepared to meet the obduracy of the problems and obstacles as the very way toward producing different knowledge and producing knowledge differently. Foucault (1981/1991) termed this "the absolute optimism" of "a thousand things to do" (p. 174), where our constant task is to struggle against the very rules of reason and practice inscribed in the effects of power of the social sciences.

Notes

1. *Education Week* on the web (Davis, 2002) reported that the U.S. Department of Education plans to overhaul its website and, in the process, delete thousands of files (including ERIC digests) of non–Bush era educational research as well as that which does not support the current administration's views. Government-document librarians and education librarians all over the country are quite concerned about the archival implications of this plan, political considerations notwithstanding (see also http://www.lib.msu.edu/corby/ebss/accesseric.htm).

It is important to note that such efforts are going on across other areas, including health websites where fourteen House Democrats have charged that the "web scrubbing" of the Centers for Disease Control site in regard to abortion and breast cancer "distorts and suppresses scientific information for ideological purposes" (Clymer, 2002). In addition, the Pentagon is pressuring CIA analysts to tailor their assessments of the Iraqi threat to build a case against Saddam Hussein in a "politicization of intelligence" (Miller & Droglin, 2002). One journalist surmised that this "illustrates how, far below the political radar screen, the Bush administration can satisfy conservative constituents with relatively little exposure to the kind of attack that a legislative proposal or a White House statement would invite" (Clymer, 2002, p. A3).

2. This disdain is quite evident in a 1998 report, *Education at a Crossroads: What Works and What's Wasted in Education Today* (1998), that delineates efforts since the Reagan administration to codify proper scientific method in assessing the outcomes of educational programs.

3. According to Greenberg (2001), the National Academy lives off of the production of "generally dour studies" (p. 297), most of which are ignored. Such studies, Greenberg observed, are produced largely by staff members who know well "the report industry ... [where] much is written but little is read in Washington" (p. 299) while fronted by "overscheduled, part-time committee members" (p. 393). The NRC (2002) report was produced in a particularly quick schedule of six months to inform Office of Educational Research and Improvement reauthorization.

4. Davies (2003), writing from Australia, which is further down the road of accountability culture, pointed out that it is typical of new managerialism that "the objectives will come first and that the 'experimental research evidence' will be generated to justify them" (p. 100).

5. See Friedman, Dunwoody, and Rogers (1999) for a discussion of scientific representations of uncertainty and media and public responses

6. See Katz and Mishler (2003) for the growing interest in qualitative research in medical science. The authors caution that such work not be assigned a supplemental role of secondary and limited value but rather, both quantitative and qualitative need to serve as "a critical vantage point for assessing the other so as to provide a fuller and dynamic understanding of the problem" (p. 49).

7. The British experience becomes most interesting where "a number of cracks are beginning to show" (Trinder, 2000b, p. 236). There is a notable paucity of high-quality evidence evenly distributed; there is little focus on application; the cost of assembling an evidence base may outweigh benefits; and doubts abound about the exclusion of bias, the ethics of randomized clinical trials, and how scientism constrains the answers it can supply. In the British scene of health-care policy, given the well-known trade-off between internal and external validity in randomized clinical trials, clinical judgment remained important as did continual evaluation via effectiveness studies in real-world settings versus the efficacy studies of randomized clinical trials (Reynolds, 2000, p. 30). The problems of transfer to noncontrolled clinical settings were not minor. Given worries about the way such efforts might be used to ration health care, limit professional autonomy, and endorse a distorted view of science, impact has been "remarkable" at the policy level but "patchy" in terms of practice (p. 33).

8. Such talk in education usually disallows the controversy within the medical field regarding the quality of medical research and the uses to which doctors put it in the face of experience-based knowledge (Hammersley, 2000; Trinder & Reynolds, 2000).

9. Rising out of medicine with its strong scientific research tradition, the authors posit that the less scientifically driven areas of social policy will be less effected, given the clash of their long-developed qualitative and nonexperimental quantitative research traditions with the ontological, epistemological, and methodological tents of evidence-based practice. Such prognosis did not take into account Bush science.

10. One note of hope is from the nursing field, where the journal *Evidence-Based Nursing*, founded in 1998, publishes structured summaries of both quantitative and qualitative research. Although "soft" forms of research remain marginal (Blomfield & Hardy, 2000, pp. 121, 123), it is the only British journal of the movement to include qualitative research due to the significant interpretative component of nursing-led research (p. 131). If the evidence-based practice movement is to be embraced by nurses, "it must embrace a broader definition of evidence than is currently allowed" (p. 130).

As an example of this, the Cochrane Collaboration, set up by the British National Health Service in 1992, prepares and disseminates systematic reviews of health-care research (Reynolds, 2000, p. 21), with centers in the United Kingdom, Europe, North and South America, Africa, Asia, and Australasia (Trinder, 2000a, p. 1). Trinder (2000b) noted that a Cochrane qualitative methods group is forming, although she cautioned that such moves must be accepted and valued on their own terms (p. 237) (see http://www.salford.ac.uk/ihr.cochrane/homepage.htm).

11. Flyvbjerg (2001) quoted Campbell: "Qualitative common-sense knowing is not replaced by quantitative knowing.... This is not to say that such common-sense naturalistic observation is objective, dependable, or unbiased. But it is all that we have. It is the only route to knowledge—noisy, fallible, and biased

though it may be" (p. 73). See Hamilton (2002) for a discussion of the (mis)uses of Campbell to warrant the "restorationist attempts to re-instate experimental design at the heart of social research" (p. 8). Hamilton's point, of course, is that Campbell, in his own words, "'recanted'" (Campbell, quoted in Hamilton, 2002, p. 6) his negative view of the single case study.

12. It is no new news that practitioners rarely alter their practice on the basis of research findings (Birnbaum, 2000; Trinder, 2000a, p. 3). It is an attractive picture to think of basing practice on the most up-to-date, valid, and reliable research findings. But how feasible are randomized field trials in an environment where, in the Columbus Public Schools in 1999, 45% of students, 53% of teachers, and 75% of principals change schools each year (Bush, 2003)? Claims for objectivity are overstated and mask hidden assumptions and values. Rather than reifying evidence, especially knowledge accumulation, how might social science serve us better than the parade of behaviorism, cognitivism, structuralism, and neopositivism that have all failed to successfully study human activity in a way modeled after the assumedly cumulative, predictive, and stable natural sciences?

13. Chapters cover pointers on how to "market the experiment" and tales are told of "horrific epithets" lobbied at "randomizers" as comparisons are made to the Tuskegee syphilis study (Mosteller & Boruch, 2002, p. 22). The best persuasion is "obviously" to tie funding to willingness to participate in randomized field trials (p. 33), especially given how participants "will eventually figure out how much is involved" (p. 35). Finally, remember "you are not a 'Nazi'" (p. 38) as you develop a thick skin in the face of press and community group resistance. Admittedly, however, "politics usually trumps research" (p. 43) when the stakes are high and ethical standards "circumscribe the import of RFTs [randomized field trials]" (p. 52).

14. In this return to the center of educational research, what evaluation theorists were "willing to let die" (Cook & Payne, 2002, p. 168), listen to the rhetoric of justification: "policy makers can easily grasp the findings and significance of a simple experiment" that is accepted at "face value" (Burtless, 2002, pp. 183, 184) by news media as well, whereas nonexperimental methodology yields a confusion of differing results. "Many target populations are politically weak. Even if many people in these populations object to random assignment, they may lack the political power to stop randomized trials" (p. 188). Ethical issues are "the biggest practical obstacle," and "if opponents to experimentation are politically influential, their influence can doom the effort to use random assignment" (p. 194). Unfortunately, "American educators are well organized and politically influential" (p. 196), and this has hampered the movement.

15. These include efforts such as that of Robert Slavin of Johns Hopkins University, codeveloper of the Success for All improvement program used in more than 1,800 elementary schools, and Robert Boruch of the University of Pennsylvania–based Campbell Collaboration, designed to do for the social sciences what the British-based Cochrane Collaboration does for health

care. Formed in 1998 as a nonprofit organization, the international Campbell Collaboration, along with the American Institutes for Research, a Washington, DC, think tank, was awarded a five-year US$18.5 million contract in 2002 to develop the What Works Clearinghouse (w-w-c.org) to summarize effectiveness data from randomized field trials of social and educational policies and practices for policy makers and practitioners (see www.campbellcollaboration.org). See Laitsch, Heilman, and Shaker (2002) for a discussion of the role of think tanks in consolidating conservative modernization. One notable exception to the conservative bent of such centers is the Education Policy Studies Laboratory at Arizona State University, where Alex Molnar and David Berliner, among others, are doing research on the issues concerning high-stakes testing (Viadero, 2002).

16. See Baez and Boyles (2002) for a critical review of how "grant culture" characterizes much of what happens in the name of research at universities. They cited an article by Loren R. Graham (1978), "Concerns about Science and Attempts to Regulate Inquiry," that makes clear the issues of this article are not new.

17. This phrase, credited to Freud, was used in the New York Review of Books (Flyvbjerg, 2001, pp. 26–27). It is, interestingly, used in the NRC (2002, p. 13) report, without attribution.

18. This section is from Patti Lather (2004).

References

Apple, M. (2001). *Educating the "right" way: Markets, standards, God, and inequality.* New York: Routledge Kegan Paul.

Atkinson, E. (2004). Thinking outside the box: An exercise in heresy. *Qualitative Inquiry, 10*(1), 111–129.

Baez, B., & Boyles, D. R. (2002). Are we selling out? Grants, entrepreneurship, and the future of the profession. Paper presented at the annual meeting of the American Educational Studies Association, Pittsburgh, Pennsylvania, October.

Bennett, T. (1992). Putting policy into cultural studies. In L. Grossberg, C. Nelson, & P. Treichler (Eds.), *Cultural studies* (pp. 23–37). London: Routledge.

Birnbaum, R. (2000). Policy scholars are from Venus; policy makers are from Mars. *The Review of Higher Education, 23*(2), 119–132.

Blomfield, R., & Hardy, S. (2000). Evidence-based nursing practice. In L. Trinder & S. Reynolds (Eds.), *Evidence-based practice: A critical appraisal* (pp. 111–137). London: Sage.

Boruch, R., & Mosteller, F. (2002). Overview and new directions. In F. Mosteller & R. Boruch (Eds.), *Evidence matters: Randomized trials in education research* (pp. 1–14). Washington, DC: Brookings Institution.

Burtless, G. (2002). Randomized field trials for policy evaluation: Why not in education? In F. Mosteller & R. Boruch (Eds.), *Evidence matters: Randomized trials in education research* (pp. 179–197). Washington, DC: Brookings Institution.

Bush, B. (2003). Columbus schools dumping four-way reading program. *Columbus Dispatch*, February 6, C1.

Canclini, N. G. (2001). The North-South dialogue on cultural studies. In N. G. Canclini (Ed.), *Consumers and citizens: Globalization and multicultural conflicts* (pp. 3–13). Minneapolis: University of Minnesota Press.

Clymer, A. (2002). Changes in health web sites draw flak. *Columbus Dispatch*, December 27, A3.

Cochran-Smith, M. (2002). What a difference a definition makes: Highly qualified teachers, scientific researchers, and teacher education. *Journal of Teacher Education, 53*(3), 187–189.

Conley, V. (2000). Become-woman now. In I. Buchanan & C. Colebrook (Eds.), *Deleuze and feminist theory* (pp. 18–37). Edinburgh: Edinburgh University Press.

Cook, T. D., & Payne, M. R. (2002). Objecting to the objections to using random assignment in educational research. In F. Mosteller & R. Boruch (Eds.), *Evidence matters* (pp. 150–178). Washington, DC: Brookings Institution.

Danaher, G., Schirato, T., & Webb, J. (2000). *Understanding Foucault.* London: Sage.

Davies, B. (2003). Death to critique and dissent? The policies and practices of new managerialism and of "evidence-based practice." *Gender and Education, 15*(1), 91–103.

Davis, M. R. (2002). No URL left behind? Web scrubbing raises concerns. *EducationWeek.* Retrieved September 23, 2002, from http://www.edweek.org/ew/ewstory.cfm?slug=03web.h22

Education at a crossroads: What works and what's wasted in education today: Hearings before the Subcommittee on Oversight and Investigations, of the Committee on Education and the Workforce, 105th Cong. (July 17, 1998).

Elden, S. (2002). The war of races and the constitution of the state: Foucault's *Il faut défendre la société* and the politics of calculation. *boundary 2, 29*(1), 125–151.

Ferguson, M., & Golding, P. (1997). Cultural studies and changing times: An introduction. In M. Ferguson & P. Golding (Eds.), *Cultural studies in question* (pp. xiii–xxvii). London: Sage.

Feuer, M. J., Towne, L., & Shavelson, R. J. (2002). Scientific culture and educational research. *Educational Researcher, 31*(8), 4–14.

Fink, B. (1995). *The Lacanian subject: Between language and jouissance.* Princeton, NJ: Princeton University Press.

Flyvbjerg, B. (2001). *Making social science matter: Why social inquiry fails and how it can succeed again.* Cambridge, UK: Cambridge University Press.

Foucault, M. (1970). *The order of things: An archaeology of the human sciences.* New York: Vintage.

Foucault, M. (1981/1991). *Remarks on Marx: Conversations with Duccio Trombadori.* New York: Semiotext(e).

Foucault, M. (1994). The punitive society. In P. Rabinow (Ed.), *Michel Foucault: Ethics, subjectivity and truth* (Vol. 1, pp. 23–38). New York: Free Press.

Foucault, M. (1998). On the archaeology of the sciences: Response to the epistemology circle. In J. Faubion (Ed.), *Michel Foucault: Aesthetics, method, and epistemology* (Vol. 2, pp. 297–333). New York: Free Press.

Friedman, S., Dunwoody, S., & Rogers, C. (Eds.). (1999). *Communicating uncertainty: Media coverage of new and controversial science.* Mahwah, NJ: Lawrence Erlbaum.

Galison, P., & Stump, D. (Eds.). (1996). *The disunity of science: Boundaries, contexts, and power.* Stanford, CA: Stanford University Press.

Gherardi, S., & Turner, B. A. (1987). Real men don't collect soft data. *Quarderno, 13*, Dipartimento di Politica Sociale, Università di Trento, Italy.

Goenka, S. (2002). A day in the field that changed my methodology. *British Medical Journal, 324*, 493.

Graham, L. (1978). Concerns about science and attempts to regulate inquiry. *Daedalus, 107*(2), 1–21.

Greenberg, D. (2001). *Science, money and politics: Political triumph and ethical erosion.* Chicago: University of Chicago Press.

Hall, S. (1996). *Stuart Hall: Critical dialogues in cultural studies.* London: Routledge Kegan Paul.

Hamilton, D. (2002). "Noisy, fallible and biased though it be" (on the vagaries of educational research). *British Journal of Educational Studies, 50*(1), 144–164.

Hammersley, M. (2000). Evidence-based practice in education and the contribution of educational research. In L. Trinder & S. Reynolds (Eds.), *Evidence-based practice: A critical appraisal* (pp. 163–183). London: Sage.

Katz, A., & Mishler, E. G. (2003). Close encounters: Exemplars of process-oriented qualitative research in health care. *Qualitative Research, 3*(1), 35–56.

Kuhn, T. B. (1970). *The structure of scientific revolutions* (2nd ed.). Chicago: University of Chicago Press.

Lagemann, E. (2000). *An elusive science: The troubling history of educational research.* Cambridge, MA: Harvard University Press.

Laitsch, D., Heilman, E., & Shaker, P. (2002). Teacher education, pro-market policy and advocacy research. *Teaching Education, 13*(3), 251–272.

Lather, P. (2004). Foucauldian "indiscipline" as a sort of policy application. In B. Baker& K. Hayning (Eds.), *Dangerous coagulations? The uses of Foucault in the study of education* (pp. 279–304). New York: Peter Lang.

McGuigan, J. (2001). Problems of cultural analysis and policy in the information age. *Cultural Studies/Critical Methodologies, 1*(2), 190–219.

McRobbie, A. (1997). The E's and the anti-E's: New questions for feminism and cultural studies. In M. Ferguson & P. Golding (Eds.), *Cultural studies in question* (pp. 170–186). London: Sage.

Miller, G., & Droglin, B. (2002). Hawks pressuring CIA, sources say. *Columbus Dispatch,* October 11, A2.

Mosteller, F., & Boruch, R. (Eds.). (2002). *Evidence matters: Randomized trials in education research.* Washington, DC: Brookings Institution.

National Research Council (NRC). (2002). *Scientific research in education* (Committee on Scientific Principles for Education Research; R. J. Shavelson & L. Towne, Eds.). Washington, DC: National Academy Press.

Nietzsche, F. (1974). *The gay science* (W. Kaufmann, Trans.). New York: Vintage.

Olkowski, D. (2000). Body, knowledge and becoming-woman: Morpho-logic in Deleuze and Irigaray. In I. Buchanan & C. Colebrook (Eds.), *Deleuze and feminist theory* (pp. 86–109). Edinburgh: Edinburgh University Press.

Plotnitsky, A. (2002). *The knowable and the unknowable: Modern science, non-classical thought, and the "two cultures."* Ann Arbor: University of Michigan Press.

Porter, T. M. (1995). *Trust in numbers: The pursuit of objectivity in science and public life.* Princeton, NJ: Princeton University Press.

Reynolds, S. (2000). The anatomy of evidence-based practice: Principles and methods. In L. Trinder & S. Reynolds (Eds.), *Evidence-based practice: A critical appraisal* (pp. 17–34). London: Sage.

Ross, A. (Ed.). (1996). *Science wars.* Durham, NC: Duke University Press.

Shaker, P. (2002). Is Washington serious about scientifically based research? Paper presented at the Curriculum and Pedagogy Conference, Decatur, Georgia, October.

Shavelson, R., Phillips, D. C., Towne, L., & Feuer, M. (2003). On the science of education design studies. *Educational Researcher, 32*(1), 25–28.

Tashakkori, A., & Teddlie, C. (Eds.). (2002). *Handbook of mixed methods in social and behavioral research.* Thousand Oaks, CA: Sage.

Trinder, L. (2000a). Introduction: The context of evidence-based practice. In L.Trinder & S. Reynolds (Eds.), *Evidence-based practice: A critical appraisal* (pp. 1–15). London: Sage.

Trinder, L. (2000b). A critical appraisal of evidence-based practice. In L. Trinder & S. Reynolds (Eds.), *Evidence-based practice: A critical appraisal* (pp. 212–241). London: Sage.

Trinder, L., & Reynolds, S. (Eds.). (2000). *Evidence-based practice: A critical appraisal.* London: Sage.

Viadero, D. (2002). Research: Researching the researchers. *EducationWeek,* February 20.

Retrieved October 9, 2002, from http://www.edweek.org/ew/newstory.cfm?slub=23advocacy.h21

Vivovskis, M. (2002). Missing in practice? Development and evaluation at the U.S. Department of Education. In F. Mosteller & R. Boruch (Eds.), *Evidence matters: Randomized trials in education research* (pp. 120–149). Washington, DC: Brookings Institution.

West, C. (1990). The new cultural politics of difference. In R. Ferguson, R. Ferguson, M. Gever, T. T. Minh-ha, & C. West (Eds.), *Out there: Marginalization and contemporary cultures* (pp. 19–36). Cambridge, MA: MIT Press.

Westcott, M. (1979). Feminist criticism of the social sciences. *Harvard Educational Review, 49*(4), 422–430.

Willinsky, J. (2001). The strategic education research program and the public value of research. *Educational Researcher, 30*(1), 5–14.

Chapter 3 | Guarding the Castle and Opening the Gates

Katherine E. Ryan and
Lisa K. Hood
University of Illinois

Like many educational communities, the College of Education at the University of Illinois, Urbana-Champaign, held a seminar and panel devoted to "scientifically based research" (SBR) and the National Research Council (NRC) (2002) report. Liora Bresler, Nick Burbules, Ken Howe, and Tom Schwandt presented brief papers addressing various philosophical and epistemological issues surrounding this topic. Many faculty members made supporting remarks in response to their wide and deep critique of these initiatives. However, one member suggested that the papers essentially guarded the "castle." He confronted the panel by asking if anyone was going to look inside their "castle" or were they just going to "throw stones" at the challenges from SBR and the NRC report. He asked who would engage in conversation with these challengers.

In this chapter, we propose we need to do both: guard the castle and open the gates to engage in dialogue with the proponents of the SBR and NRC perspectives. We say guard the castle because in the short time SBR and the NRC have been part of the discourse on educational research we have identified two or three immediate issues that have serious implications for educational evaluation and educational research. These issues include, for instance, changes in what kind of evidence matters for determining educational program effectiveness.

Educational evaluation involves making a judgment about program merit or worth. Educational evaluation methodology, which involves both judgment and inquiry methods, is particularly critical for studying education reform and for determining effective educational programs. Studying educational reform and determining effective educational programs play key roles in all aspects of educational policy and practice, the centerpiece of the SBR and NRC report agendas.

In contrast to previous critical analyses of SBR and the NRC report, we illustrate some of our concerns with actual field examples from our own work as educational evaluators. Through a critical analysis of our stories from the field and other literature, we identify the move toward educational research standards as a fundamental problem. We close with a brief discussion about how to move beyond just good science by opening the gates to engage the practitioners and the public in deliberations about how to improve education.

Guarding the Castle

Inspecting the Castle Boundaries

In reviewing the literature on SBR and evidence-based policy, it appears that there are clear, conceptual links between these two terms. Basically, in the No Child Left Behind Act of 2001 (NCLB), SBR is defined as "apply[ing] rigorous, systematic, and objective methodology to obtain reliable and valid knowledge appropriate to the research being conducted, employing systematic, empirical methods that draw on observation or experiment" (NCLB, 2002, p. 116). The Coalition for Evidence-Based Policy (2002) defined evidence-based policy as that based on research that has been proven effective by randomized controlled experiments replicated on a large scale.

In response to the U.S. Department of Education's (DoE) strong focus on method as a basis for SBR, the NRC convened the Committee on Scientific Principles for Educational Research to study this issue. This committee developed six guiding principles of scientific research in education that they presented in their report (NRC, 2002). These guidelines include: (a) ask significant questions that can be empirically studied; (b) relate research to relevant theory; (c) choose methods that allow direct inquiry into the research question; (d) explain the findings using a logical chain of reasoning; (e) replicate studies and make generalizations; and (f) disseminate research for critique by the professional scientific community. Therefore, using this logic, educational evaluation is "scientific" if it follows these six principles and is sensitive to the study context.

These guidelines are much broader than the DoE's idea of scientific research and evaluation as reflected in NCLB. Nevertheless, the authors of the NRC (2002) report remain committed to their assertion that scientific inquiry, including evaluation, should be objective and that quantitative and qualitative inquiry are epistemologically similar. Feuer, Towne, and Shavelson (2002) clarified their definition of scientific research in education within the context of the six guiding principles. Scientific inquiry in education (SIE) is embedded within a culture of inquiry that is objective and promotes replicability of studies. Studies are exchanged among the scientific community for the "free flow of constructive critique" (Feuer et al., 2002, p. 7). Members of this scientific community are trained in the habits of mind that focus on evidence, eliminate alternative explanations, and reduce or eliminate biases to evaluation. This scientific culture establishes and enforces these norms of SIE fostering the exchange, critique, and revision of assertions based on SIE.

Who is not conducting SIE? Feuer et al. (2002) delineated between scientific educational research and educational scholarship. Educational scholarship is clearly not viewed as scientific, although they do not dismiss the importance of these studies to improve and inform education. These scholarship studies include "humanistic, historic, philosophical, and other nonscientific forms" (p. 5). The committee believes that scholarship studies should be exchanged among peers for critique and revision just like scientific inquiry studies. Doing so will advance educational scholarship and what is known about the field of education.

The same reasoning applies to educational evaluation. Obviously, there are scientific educational evaluation approaches reflecting postpositivist epistemology that use experimental, quasi-experimental, and other designs that are intended to be replicable (Cook, 2002; Mark, Henry, & Julnes, 2000). On the other hand, there are other evaluation approaches like fourth-generation evaluation, responsive evaluation, and democratically oriented approaches that are analogues to "educational scholarship." These approaches are anchored in epistemological foundations such as constructivism, critical theory, or postmodernism that reflect the interpretive turn in the social sciences (Guba & Lincoln, 1989; House & Howe, 1999; Ryan & DeStefano, 2001; Schwandt, 1997; Stake, 1983). For the purposes of this article, we propose the umbrella term educational inquiry, which includes SBR, SIE, educational scholarship, and all forms of educational evaluation.

The SIE principles articulate a clear basis for educational research and evaluation. However, a deeper examination of the SIE principles is revealing (Gee, 2003). A foundational issue underlies these principles: Who gets to decide? There are several relevant questions including, what is a significant question and what is a relevant theory? Further, how can a question be directly investigated and what is a coherent and explicit chain of reasoning? Most important, who is part of the professional community that critiques the assertions made by researchers and evaluators and in general, who is a part of this scientific community charged with answering these questions (Gee, 2003)? We find that who gets to decide is already changing. We illustrate some of these changes in a story about how to determine educational program effectiveness.

The demise of professional judgment.

During the past several years, one of us has been involved in a project that has identified effective postsecondary educational programs. This project received federal funding initially for five years. Using an expert judgment model, these programs were evaluated through a panel review process in which panels consisting of subject matter experts, practitioners, and researchers/evaluators at federal, state, and local levels were convened. Examining program documents mailed to project staff, these panels submitted quantitative scores and qualitative comments based on established criteria and their own professional knowledge. Program outcomes data were heavily valued in the review process, which included certification, degree, or licensure; matriculation to further education; and student and stakeholder satisfaction, among others.

Highest-rated programs moved into the next round of reviews in which project staff followed up with program personnel gathering additional data. From this, project staff convened another panel of reviewers to conduct site visits to those programs who survived the second round of reviews. During these visits, these on-site evaluators interviewed program stakeholders, examined documents, and observed and toured classrooms, labs, and other institutional facilities. After this third round of reviews, programs were identified as "exemplary," "promising," or "neither." Project staff disseminated this information in various project publications and at conferences to share this information with fellow researchers and mostly educational practitioners.

During the three years the expert judgment model was used, project staff continuously refined the review process, becoming more rigorous with each cycle. At the end of three years, seven programs out of more than fifty applications were named "exemplary."

Each year, project directors completed a continuation proposal to receive the next year's federal monies. Before the third year of funding in 2001, the project team began to hear about SBR, and it became increasingly clear that the expert judgment model might not measure up to SBR standards. After submitting the fourth-year continuation proposal in December 2002, the proposal was stalled. It became evident that the model would have to change to be eligible for continued funding. The principal investigator was informed that educational research receiving federal funds should be concerned with "what works." The purpose of this project was always concerned with identifying programs that "worked," but now "what works" meant practices or programs that were identified as such through experimental and quasi-experimental design.

As soon as the What Works Clearinghouse went public on the web (http://www.w-w-c.org), the project team investigated and became aware of the rubric that establishes whether educational research is able to make the claim that an intervention works. The

Coalition for Evidence-Based Policy gave the following recommendations to the DoE about how the federal government could support evidence-based policy. Essentially, this coalition recommended building the knowledge base by promoting educational interventions that have been proven effective using randomized controlled experiments and have been proven over large-scale replications. Further, they suggested providing incentives to adopt these proven interventions by offering federal funds to those who adopt them. Pushing this idea even further, on the DoE's SBR website (http://www.ed.gov/nclb/methods/whatworks/research/index.html), various research designs are ranked. Randomized control group experimental designs have been given the "gold" standard, whereas quasi-experimental designs get the "silver," correlational studies with statistical controls get the "bronze," and so forth. In the eyes of the group that designed this clearinghouse, the expert judgment model did not provide the evidence needed to claim the identified programs "really worked."

Continuing this story, during the next few months, the project director wrote at least three more proposals. In the end, the proposed project evolved from one that relied on the expertise of educational experts and that was based on data that included the voices of program stakeholders and program outcomes data. Instead, the proposed project became one that incorporated a quasi-experimental design involving data from student transcripts and pre- and posttest results analyzed using various statistical techniques. These data would be supported with qualitative descriptive data on interventions, setting, and program participant's experiences. However, most of staff time and resources would be devoted to data collection activities that support the experimental design.

The team is deeply concerned at the undemocratizing effect SBR can have on evaluation and research. In essence, SBR takes the ability to evaluate out of practitioner's and evaluator's hands from all levels, as we included practitioners and evaluators from federal, state, and local agencies. In the redesign process, the DoE required from the project team, project staff watched as this project, one that had been guided and developed by educational researchers and practitioners, changed. The original intent of this project was to identify and share "exemplary and promising" programs, models, and practices so other practitioners may learn from them. In the redesigned project, a high priority was placed on scientific knowledge—a special kind of knowledge, which many do not possess. Qualitative and professional, practical forms of knowledge are not "scientific" so they were not considered important forms of evidence. Therefore, the DoE questioned our claims that the exemplary and promising programs we identified worked. This new experimental design would essentially disregard the expert's and practitioner's knowledge and their view of what makes an effective educational program, and it would avoid what SBR might consider subjective knowledge about whether or not a program works.

The notion that the randomized experiment is the sole methodology for deciding if a program works by establishing causal relations is clearly part of the SBR agenda that is reflected in the DoE's (2002) Strategic Plan. Further, the Strategic Plan calls for making changes in educational policy based on findings from experimental studies of what works. There are two key assumptions reflected in the plan. First, there is a fundamental notion that the initiation and implementation of educational policy is a rational process. That is, results of a randomized educational experiment provide knowledge that is going to be used to make educational policy decisions. Second, qualitative research has no role in the study of causality.

However, we see qualitative methods and other forms of knowledge (e.g., practical) as essential in educational research and evaluation. In particular, qualitative approaches are critical for disentangling causal relations (Erickson & Gutierrez, 2002). Further, we propose that educational policy decisions are influenced by many factors (e.g., economic) other than educational evaluation research results (Weiss, 1983). We illustrate our points with a brief tale about "The Perfect Experiment." One of us has told this story faithfully to an introductory evaluation methods course for the past four years. This experiment is briefly summarized in the NRC report in Box 3-3. This box is located in the section describing "Scientific Principle 3: Use Methods that Permit Direct Investigation of the Question" (NRC, 2002, p. 62).

The perfect experiment.

As evaluators, we agree that randomized field trials, where students, classes, or even organizations are randomly assigned to one or more interventions (Boruch & Mosteller, 2002), are an important methodology. Because groups are statistically equivalent, with no systematic differences present at the initiation of the experiment, they continue to be known as the "gold standard" for determining whether an intervention works or which intervention works better, in spite of problems (Cook, 2002). No doubt educational evaluation and research could benefit from carefully articulated, well-designed randomized field trials.

However, the potential problems with randomized field trials and educational evaluation have a long and storied history (Berliner, 2002; House, In press; House, Glass, McLean, & Walker, 1978). Nevertheless, in more recent history, there is an example, the Tennessee Class Size Experiment or Project STAR (Student-Teacher Achievement Ratio), characterized as "one of the great experiments in education in U.S. history" (Mosteller, Light, & Sachs, 1996, p. 814). The story goes something like this.

Kindergarten students were randomly assigned to participate in small classes (n = 13 to 17), larger classes (n = 22 to 26) and larger classes with an aid. Students' academic achievement was followed for several years. Seventy-nine elementary schools in forty-two Tennessee school districts participated. Study outcomes consisted primarily of performance on standardized tests in Grades 1 through 3. As a follow-up in Grades 4 and 8, information on students' classroom behavior was collected. Performance indicators (e.g., grade retention) were recorded annually. No classroom process data were collected.

Until recently, findings were uniformly positive. Statistically significant findings from the first two years of the experiment showed that small class sizes consistently improved student achievement (Finn & Achilles, 1990). The longer-term findings had educational policy implications: the effects of small classes in K-3 were found to affect students' achievement in later grades (Grade 4 and beyond), and the class size effects were consistent across schools (e.g., low socioeconomic status) (Finn & Achilles, 1999; Nye, Hedges, & Konstantopoulos, 2000). However, the relationship between educational policy and the results of the experiment were never resolutely linked. Interestingly, although other states (e.g., California) implemented some form of class size reduction, Tennessee chose not to implement a statewide reduced class size educational policy because of the costs.

There are other instances of failures to implement educational policy based on solid (and scientific) evidence like the positive impact of quality early childhood education on student achievement (Berliner, 2002). However, to further complicate matters, there are also cases of large-scale educational policy initiatives based on scientific evidence that fail. For example, in contrast to Tennessee, California did implement a US$3 billion class size reduction policy based on the science of the Tennessee Project STAR findings. However, unlike the Tennessee study, the class size reduction initiative in California was not successful. Apparently, this was because, unlike Tennessee, there was a shortage of teachers in California. As a consequence, many class size reduction positions were filled by personnel with temporary certification, suggesting professional teaching credentials, not just a small class size, matters (see Cohen, Raudenbush, & Ball, 2002, on instruction and resources).

Now, there is a turn in this story—which may change the name of the tale to "The Almost Perfect Experiment." Further, the importance of qualitative research in randomized field trials is revealed. A recent examination of differential small class size effects was equivocal (Nye, Hedges, & Konstantopoulos, 2002). Mathematics small class effects are smaller for low-achieving students in comparison to high-achieving students. Although small class size does benefit reading achievement, there are no differences between low- and high-achieving students. This recent investigation cites the lack of information about the particular mechanisms involved in small class size effects. They suggest ethnographic studies of classroom processes would probably provide rich information about how class size influences instruction and student achievement (Nye et al., 2002).

Whether one thinks this a problem concerning local knowledge or the complexity of interactions is perhaps not so important. The results of this experiment, like others, illustrate the power of context and underscore the importance of qualitative methodologies for educational research and evaluation. Randomized field trials are not enough. Qualitative methods were also needed to directly investigate this question.

We have concerns about how both SBR and SIE are incorporating notions about educational contexts in their respective agendas. Within the SBR framework, the notion of context is notably absent. Instead, as reflected in the DoE's (2002) Strategic Plan, education is characterized as susceptible to fads and deeply rooted in ideology. The SBR initiative proposes that educational research and evaluation should be shielded from particular ideologies reflected in politics and values. This plan calls for making educational research an evidence-based field by developing standards for judging the quality and relevance of educational research. The relevance and quality of educational research and evaluation can be improved by developing and enforcing rigorous standards for awarding federal research funds. These rigorous standards will be used in the peer-review process by "qualified scientists who have high levels of methodological and substantive expertise pertinent to projects being reviewed" (DoE, 2002, p. 51).

On the other hand, the NRC report (2002) provides an important contribution by devoting substantial attention to discussing the features of education and educational research. The NRC perspective considers the complexity of education by identifying salient features such as values and politics, human volition, variability in education programs, the educational organization, and diversity that affect educational research. These features form the context of educational research that powerfully shapes educational inquiry.

Aimed primarily at an abstract level, we propose the kinds of issues identified in the NRC report need to be instantiated for clarification. Abstract description of these contextual features simply does not convey the importance of some of the taken-for-granted educational practices and how powerfully these practices shape educational field experiences. These educational practices are at odds with some of the research practices the SBR and SIE initiatives advocate. We offer two concrete instances from our field experiences, one foundational and the other more practical, to demonstrate how the SBR and SIE visions do not completely correspond to everyday educational practices.

Implementing educational interventions and experiments.

In discussing values and politics, the NRC report describes how the multiple stakeholder groups (teachers' unions, interested citizens, business groups) with conflicting agendas influence policy and practice, thereby creating substantial tension. Further, the stakeholder groups "impact research that attempts to model and understand it [policy and practice]" (NRC, 2002, p. 86). We think there is critical framing here that needs to be exposed and discussed. Our questions would be: Do these stakeholder groups affect research that attempts to model and understand educational policy and practice? Or are these stakeholder groups part of policy and practice and so need to be incorporated in educational policy and practice models? We think the latter; as a consequence, any educational policy and practice models that do not include these groups will not contribute to deeper understanding or policy and practice changes.

For example, one of us recently completed an evaluation of the implementation of a federally funded program to improve reading. A critical part of the intervention involved improving reading instruction in low-achieving schools in Grades K-3 through professional development activities. In addition to participation in professional development by outside vendors, literacy coach positions in targeted schools were funded to provide support for classroom teachers. Of course, determining the extent to which reading instruction changed during the course of the intervention was part of the evaluation plan. Consequently, an observation instrument was piloted and developed that the evaluation team used during site visits to document changes in reading classroom instruction over time. In addition to the external evaluation team conducting the classroom observations, the original evaluation plan called for the literacy coaches and teachers to be trained in using the classroom observation instrument to build formative evaluation capacity. However, when the team discussed having observations conducted by the literacy coaches and teachers, in at least two districts the teachers' union's concerns about how the results of these observations might be used were strong enough that attempts to do this were abandoned.

Obviously, in these two districts, the teachers' union is explicitly part of educational policy and practice. To effectively model and understand educational policy and practice involves understanding the kinds of politics and values that are part of educational policy and practice. Effective interventions and educational evaluation research will directly acknowledge this by including politics and values in planning educational interventions and evaluations instead of seeing them as something outside educational research and evaluation.

We provide yet another example from some work one of us is doing in a study of stereotype threat and standardized math test performance. In this instance, it is the study logistics that are a problem. As the NRC report states, education takes place in educational organizations. Not surprisingly, there is an order and structure to educational organizations; the educational day begins at a certain time, is divided into time units, and ends at the same time everyday. Researchers contend with significant obstacles when attempting to implement classroom research that does not fit within these structures. For example, although schools were especially interested in the standardized math test performance project, the project design involved a sixty-minute randomized experiment with participants. The participants were to complete a questionnaire about test taking and a thirty-item math test. About 20% of the students would participate in individual follow-up interviews.

Logistics were a major problem in securing research partnerships with the schools. First, locating two rooms for the experimental and control groups is not easy. Large rooms are needed so all students can participate during one class period to minimize disruption. The cafeteria and the library are usually the best possibilities, but not easy to secure. The library often has to be shared with students and classes who are using the library. Second, needing sixty minutes for questionnaire and test administration was an enormous obstacle because class periods are only forty-five minutes long. Although the research team worked to decrease the number of items in the test and questionnaire, sixty minutes was needed to obtain adequate information. As a result, many school and school administrators were not willing to have another class period disrupted, so they chose not to take part. Many of them said that because the amount of standardized testing now routinely implemented is so time consuming, they are very limited in the number and kind of research projects in which they can participate.

Standing Castle Watch

The professional consensus methodology represented in our first illustration is characterized by SBR as subjective and lacking in the kind of objective information that is needed to make policy decisions about which programs are exemplary and thus worthy of replicability. Our second and third examples illustrate that there are philosophical, political, and even logistical problems with implementing randomized field trials as either sole methodology or even privileging it as such an important approach for establishing causality.

Although what we characterized in our examples have direct implications about how educational research and evaluation are conducted, we are more concerned about this need for educational research standards as a long-range issue. Our examples above suggest this is not always so, but essentially, the SBR initiative locates educational problems in the notion that current educational research and evaluation practices are inadequate. Their position can be summarized as follows. The SBR initiative proposes that the problem in education is the poor quality and irrelevance of educational research and evaluation. Educational research and evaluation will be advanced by improving educational research and evaluation methodologies through the application of rigorous educational research standards in deciding what kinds of research and evaluation will get funded. When educational research and evaluation gets better, the findings from this information can be used to improve education. In contrast, the NRC proposes a scientific culture anchored by a broader set of methodologies, although some forms of educational scholarship (e.g., historical) are marked as "not scientific."

We find this story—that educational evaluators and researchers are not up to the task of determining what constitutes high-quality and relevant research—too much like the story of teachers and educational instruction (House, In press). Although historically, educational problems such as low achievement have been situated in the student, now NCLB shifts the problem to one embedded in teachers and schools. If teachers and schools were different, student achievement would be improved. Consequently, educational standards and large-scale assessments are currently being implemented in every state. This is because teachers are not trusted to do an adequate job of teaching without some kind of standards and tests to make them do a better job.

Now educational researchers and evaluators are being cast as needing the same kind of monitoring. If educational researchers did better research, student achievement would be improved. As a consequence, they need to be directed on what kinds of research methods are best and important. The direction will come from multiple sources through several mechanisms. In addition to the new educational research standards, decision makers (congressional staff, governors' aides, state board superintendents, educational administrators, etc.) will be surveyed to find out which issues they need studied. The online What Works Clearinghouse has been established to make available funded and unfunded research on the topics identified in the survey. The research in this clearinghouse is screened to ensure these rigorous educational research standards are met. Finally, in contrast to capitalizing on practitioner knowledge, guides based on "rigorous" research are being developed for dissemination to educational practitioners so they engage in evidence-based education.

Clearly, this is a shift to a hierarchical, linear approach intended to direct educational research, evaluation, and ultimately educational practice reflecting a climate of control. Due to educational contexts and complexities, attempts to implement this model in the 1950s and 1960s were unsuccessful (House, In press; Lagemann, 2000). Fundamentally, locating educational problems in the students, teachers, schools, and now educational researchers takes the focus away from systemic issues.

Systemic issues include unequal distribution of financial and human resources in schools, effects of institutionalized racism (current and historical), varying levels of parental involvement, and the like. These issues are not amenable to "social" engineering as if a new car design was needed. There is no technical solution to these issues (e.g., unequal distribution of resources) because these are not technical problems. Instead, they are practical problems involving wise and prudent decision making (Ryan, 2002; Schwandt, 1997).

This is a matter of understanding what can be and will be done to improve education in general and low-performing schools in particular.

More important, however, these issues surface in the kinds of educational scholarship that have been cut out of educational research when defined as "not scientific." For instance, educational evaluations and studies about the hidden curriculum show what low-achieving students do learn in school (e.g., Fine, Wise, Weseen, & Wong, 2000; Porro, 1994). This kind of work, however, is characterized as value laden or as advocacy (Howe, 2003). Although "scientific" research may address systemic concerns, it is educational scholarship that has brought attention to these critical systemic issues.

Opening the Gates

A Defense at the Gates

Conducting a critical analysis of the SBR and SIE perspectives is a first step in engaging in a conversation with the SBR and SIE advocates. Although we think more work remains, the educational community is currently engaged in this analysis as reflected in our summary below. Of course, the NRC report is the first official response to SBR that suggests the SBR framework is too narrow for conducting educational studies. A 2002 issue of *Educational Researcher* and many papers from the American Educational Research Association 2003 meeting are devoted to criticisms of SBR as well as SIE, the framework advocated by the authors of the NRC report (Berliner, 2002; Cazden, 2003; Erickson & Gutierrez, 2002; Pellegrino & Goldman, 2002; St. Pierre, 2002; Willinsky, 2003).

These criticisms are broad and diverse. In contrast to the narrower views of SBR and SIE, these criticisms suggest that the educational community needs to focus on avoiding fractionation within their community, acknowledge the importance of educational contexts, understand that a mix of approaches are probably needed to solve educational problems successfully, and be respectful of different epistemological perspectives and educational practitioners' knowledge (Berliner, 2002; Cazden, 2003; Erickson & Gutierrez, 2002; Pellegrino & Goldman, 2002; St. Pierre, 2002; Willinsky, 2003).

We propose that these criticisms lay the foundation for a broadened educational community. This kind of educational community monitors its own research and evaluation processes through rigorous peer review and creates its own agenda in partnership with educational practitioners and other stakeholders by engaging in critical reflection. These goals and commitments include a shared respect and regard across disciplinary, epistemological, and methodological differences. The partnership with educational practitioners and others includes a dialogue about what educational problems need to be studied and the implementation of these studies (Pelligrino & Goldman, 2003).

We acknowledge the substantial obstacles involved in creating and sustaining such a community. Clearly, the change can begin when the current educational community decides to move beyond their respective disciplinary, epistemological, and methodological differences. This commitment sets the stage for graduate training that is substantially broadened (Pelligrino & Goldman, 2002). Some suggest that a methods core include a balance of quantitative and qualitative methods (Pelligrino & Goldman, 2002). Although we are concerned that trading breadth for depth may lead to less methods expertise, the notion that qualitative and quantitative methods are complementary is an important improvement in how the educational community talks about differences. We propose that enabling a mutual respect and regard for different methods is the greatest priority. We suggest this can best be accomplished in coursework devoted to differing epistemologies and philosophies of inquiry.

Forming Castle Alliances

The relationship between educational research and practice is not well articulated. The criticism that educational research has not connected to problems of educational practice is warranted (Pelligrino & Goldman, 2002). Within the SBR framework, this relationship can be characterized as a top-down, receiver-sender, translation model (see DoE, 2002). That is, knowledge from educational studies will be transmitted to practitioners who will improve their instruction by making changes in what they do based on this new knowledge. However, if the educational community is committed to forming a community that includes educational practitioners, the character of this relationship will need to shift substantially.

Practitioner knowledge tends to be normative, personal, particular, and experiential (Larabee, 2003). To date, this kind of knowledge is portrayed as "in contrast to," even "at odds with," scientific and academic knowledge. To see practitioner knowledge as "in addition to" traditional scientific and academic knowledge will require significant changes in doctoral training programs. These changes include, for example, field experiences as a team member in educational inquirer-practitioner collaborative projects or postdoctoral study on educational practice issues (Pelligrino & Goldman, 2002). More important, this collaboration will require an agreement that practitioners can be informed by new knowledge, question this knowledge, and in turn, propose new questions (Willinsky, 2001).

However, these kinds of changes (e.g., including practitioners in the educational inquiry community) need to take place not only in graduate school but also in the larger society by changing the idea that knowledge must be translated for educational practitioners, policy makers, and the public. The translation model assumes that findings from educational studies cannot be understood by educational practitioners or anyone else. As a consequence, this model effectively limits the kinds of critical conversations educational practitioners, policy makers, and the public can have about educational issues (Willinsky, 2001). Although SIE acknowledges that findings about education should be brought to the "professional and public domain" for public engagement, they focus on the peer review among the community of scientists. Public engagement involves finding a place or space for public dialogue and deliberation about educational inquiry in a democratic society.

Public Engagement at the Castle Gates

We are aware that the kind of informed participation we are proposing is easier to talk about than it is to create. We find the notion of a public culture about educational inquiry as part of a critical reflection compelling (Willinsky, 2003). To critically engage with educational practitioners, policy makers, and the public about findings from educational inquiry, this knowledge must be accessible. A public culture is fostered when educational-research knowledge is accessible and widely circulated within the public discourse (Willinsky, 2003).

At present, the public culture reflects a public discourse preoccupied by the problems with educational inquiry. No doubt there are further criticisms that are warranted beyond those identified by SBR and SIE perspectives. Nevertheless, we think it is time to examine what might be the accomplishments in education research and evaluation since the 1960s. Even the authors of the NRC report clearly acknowledged that educational research suffers from a "perception" of low quality because of criticisms from lawmakers, educational researchers themselves, and others (Feuer et al., 2002).

The NRC remedy to the perceptual problem is to propose a set of scientific principles for conducting educational research. However, a concerted effort to improve how the public and others perceive educational research and its impacts is an alternative strategy (Willinsky, 2003). Clearly, the problems with educational research and evaluation are part of the public discourse. It is also possible to make what is right and good part of the public discourse by emphasizing what has been accomplished—correcting current misperceptions.

Clearly, there are challenging educational issues to be addressed that are not amenable to technical solutions. Finding the wisdom and prudent judgment to address these issues is a major challenge. We propose that one place to find such wisdom is in public engagement about education and what is in the best interests for creating and sustaining a democratic society. Creating a public culture about education sets the stage for public engagement with these issues, making educational inquiry more than just good science.

References

Berliner, D. C. (2002). Educational research: The hardest science of all. *Educational Researcher, 31*(8), 18–20.

Boruch, R., & Mosteller, F. (2002). Overview and new directions. In R. Boruch & F. Mosteller (Eds.), *Evidence matters: Randomized trials in educational research* (pp. 1–14). Washington, DC: Brookings Institution.

Cazden, C. (2003). Panorama and close-up views: The complementarity of quantitative and qualitative research. Paper presented at the annual meeting of the American Educational Research Association, Chicago, April 21.

Coalition for Evidence-Based Policy. (2002, November). *Bringing evidence-driven progress to education: A recommended strategy for the U.S. Department of Education.* Retrieved December 1, 2002, from http://www.excelgov. org/usermedia/images/uploads/PDFs/coalitionFinRpt.pdf.

Cohen, D. K., Raudenbush, S. W., & Ball, D. L. (2002). Resources, instruction, and research. In R. Boruch & F. Mosteller (Eds.), *Evidence matters: Randomized trials in educational research* (pp. 1–14). Washington, DC: Brookings Institution.

Cook, T. D. (2002). Randomized experiments in education: Why are they so rare? *Educational Evaluation and Policy Analysis, 24*(3), 175–199.

Erickson, F., & Gutierrez, K. (2002). Culture, rigor, and science in educational research. *Educational Researcher, 31*(8), 21–24.

Feuer, M. J., Towne, L., & Shavelson, R. J. (2002). Scientific culture and educational research. *Educational Researcher, 31*(8), 4–14.

Fine, M., Weis, M., Weseen, D., & Wong, L. (2000). For whom? Qualitative research, representations, and social responsibility. In N. K. Denzin & Y. S. Lincoln (Eds.), *Handbook of qualitative research* (3rd ed., pp. 107–132). Thousand Oaks, CA: Sage.

Finn, J. D., & Achilles, C. M. (1990). Answers and questions about class size: A statewide experiment. *American Educational Research Journal, 2,* 557–577.

Finn, J. D., & Achilles, C. M. (1999).Tennessee's class size study: Findings, implications, misconceptions. *Educational Evaluation and Policy Analysis, 21*(2), 97–110.

Gee, J. P. (2003). It's theories all the way down: A response to scientific research in education. Paper presented at the annual meeting of the American Educational Research Association, Chicago, April 21.

Guba, E., & Lincoln, Y. S. (1989). *Fourth generation evaluation.* Newbury Park, CA: Sage.

House, E. (In press). Qualitative evaluation and changing social policy. In N. K. Denzin & Y. S. Lincoln (Eds.), *Handbook of qualitative research* (4th ed.). Thousand Oaks, CA: Sage.

House, E. R., Glass, G. V, McLean, L. D., & Walker, D. F. (1978). No simple answer: Critique of follow through evaluation. *Harvard Educational Review, 48,* 128–160.

House, E. R., & Howe, K. (1999). *Values in evaluation and social research.* Thousand Oaks, CA: Sage.

Howe, K. (2003). Qualitative knowing scientifically based research. Symposium conducted at the University of Illinois, Bureau of Educational Research, Champaign, May 2.

Lagemann, E. C. (2000). *An elusive science: The troubling history of education research.* Chicago: University of Chicago Press.

Larabee, D. F. (2003). The peculiar problems of preparing educational researchers. *Educational Researcher, 32*(4), 13–22.

Mark, M. M., Henry, G., & Julnes, G. (2000). *Evaluation: An integrated framework for understanding, guiding, and improving policies and programs.* San Francisco: Jossey-Bass.

Mosteller, F., Light, R. J., & Sachs, J. A. (1996). Sustained inquiry in education lessons learned from skill grouping and class size. *Harvard Educational Review, 66,* 797–842.

National Research Council (NRC). (2002). *Scientific research in education* (Committee on Scientific Principles for Educational Research, R. J. Shavelson & L. Towne, Eds., Center for Education, Division of Behavioral and Social Sciences and Education). Washington, DC: National Academy Press.

No Child Left Behind Act of 2001, Pub. L. No. 107-110, 115 Stat. 1425 (2002).

Nye, B., Hedges, L. V., & Konstantopoulos, S. (2000). The effects of small classes on academic achievement: The results of the Tennessee class size experiment. *American Educational Research Journal, 37,* 123–151.

Nye, B., Hedges, L. V., & Konstantopoulos, S. (2002). Do low-achieving students benefit more from small classes? Evidence from the Tennessee class size experiment. *Educational Evaluation and Policy Analysis, 24*(3), 201–218.

Pelligrino, J. W., & Goldman, S. R. (2002). Be careful what you wish for—You may get it: Educational research in the spotlight. *Educational Researcher, 31*(8), 15–17.

Porro, B. (1994). Playing the school system: The low-achiever's game. In E. W. Eisner (Ed.), *The educational imagination: On the design and evaluation of school programs* (3rd ed., pp. 253–272). New York: Macmillan.

Ryan, K. E. (2002). Shaping educational accountability systems. *American Journal of Evaluation, 23*(4), 453–468.

Ryan, K. E., & DeStefano, L. (2001). Dialogue as a democratizing evaluation method. *Evaluation, 7,* 195–210.

Schwandt, T. A. (1997). Evaluation as practical hermeneutics. *Evaluation, 3*(1), 69–83.

Stake, R. (1983). Program evaluation, particularly responsive evaluation. In G. Madaus, M. Scriven, & D. Stufflebeam (Eds.), *Evaluation models* (pp. 291–300). Norwell, MA: Kluwer Academic.

St. Pierre, E. (2002). "Science" rejects postmodernism. *Educational Researcher, 31*(8), 25–27.

U.S. Department of Education (DoE). (2002). *U.S. Department of Education strategic plan 2002–2007.* Retrieved June 2003, from fromhttp://www.ed.gov/about/reports/strat/plan2002-07/index.html

Weiss, C. A. (1983). Ideology, interest, and information: The basis for policy decisions. In D. Callahan & B. Jennings (Eds.), *Ethics, the social sciences, and policy analysis* (pp. 213–245). New York: Plenum.

Willinsky, J. (2001). The strategic education research program and the value of research. *Educational Researcher, 30*(1), 5–14.

Willinsky, J. (2003). The democratic responsibilities of scientific inquiry in education. Paper presented at the annual meeting of the American Educational Research Association, Chicago, April 21.

Chapter 4 | The Politics of Evidence

Janice M. Morse
University of Alberta

The title that I have used, "The Politics of Evidence," [1] is an oxymoron. *Evidence* is something that is concrete and indisputable, whereas *politics* refers to "activities concerned with the acquisition or exercise of authority" (Abate, 1996, p. 1152) and is necessarily ephemeral and subjective.

Here, I will examine how the politics of evidence, the politics of ignorance, stigma, and conflicting agendas (which extend to academic and governmental levels) are impediments to health research—and perhaps also educational research—and constrict qualitative inquiry. This oppressive movement is impeding how, when, and to whom qualitative inquiry is taught, contracted, funded, conducted, published, read, and implemented. I will argue that the long debate over the qualitative/quantitative paradigm issues has now gone beyond preferences for a style of approaching research and has become a more serious concern.

> [This] political economy of evidence … is not a question of evidence *or* no evidence, but who controls the definition of evidence and which kind is acceptable to whom. [Larner, 2004, p. 20, emphasis in original]

This Is the Story

A model to evaluate research rigor was introduced in 1972 by Archie Cochrane (1972/1989). In his book *Effectiveness and Efficiency*, he recommended standards for medical research. This model placed randomized control trials as the gold standard for evidence and mere opinion at the lowest level. The model, intended as criteria for the evaluation of drug trials to determine treatment efficacy, has been embraced in medicine as a new standard. The *standards for quality of evidence* were classified by Sackett (1993) as:

> Grade A. Randomized trials with low false positive (alpha) and/or low false negative (beta) errors supported by at least one (preferably more) Level 1 randomized trial.

> Grade B. Supported by at least one (preferably more) small randomized trials with high false positive (alpha) and/or high false negative (beta) errors. These are usually inadequate for implementation, but meta-analytic techniques used to analyze the results of 2 or more trials may obtain statistically significant results to move these into Level 1.

> Grade C. These consist of Level 3, nonrandomized two-group concurrent cohort comparison (historical control or another site as comparison); Level 4, with no comparison group; and Level 5, opinions of expert committees. Grade C is not recommended to inform practice. Qualitative inquiry is classified as Grade C.

Evidence and *evidence-based practice* have become the new mantras for medical care; they have spawned meta-analyses and the Cochrane Library: a depository of these reviews assessing evidence by evaluating series of trials or replications. This new agenda has resulted in conferences, societies, journals, and databases, and in new approaches to care—evidence-based practice—in which modifications of therapy are made based on its recommendations.

Despite its main criticisms—basically, that the trial conditions are not replicable in day-to-day clinical care and the trial's mean score does little to inform the individual case (Kravitz, Duan, & Braslow, 2004)—evidence-based practice is a trend that is here to stay.

Where Does This Leave Qualitative Inquiry?

Obviously, qualitative inquiry is a poor fit, for it has never purported to be a method that can be used to evaluate the efficacy of drugs or other treatments. But rather than excluding qualitative inquiry from the Cochrane criteria because of the nature of qualitative data, (textual, interviews, conversation, observations), qualitative research was immediately classified as "mere opinion," as Grade C, the lowest level of evidence, not recommended for implementation.[2] Thus, perceived as clinically useless for their agenda of treatment efficacy, it was not taken seriously nor given any credence, until recently.

But my major concern is that disciplines that were the primary users of qualitative inquiry with a mandate for health were virtually excluded from the resources provided for medical research. That is, research from disciplines such as nursing, rehabilitation, occupational therapy, counseling, social work, and the humanistic specialties in medicine, such as family practice and psychiatry, became less credible. Specialties that were not primarily concerned with drug therapy, or that extended beyond this—specialties that valued the *art* of care as well as the science of care, disciplines that were primarily concerned with relationships, interactions, and the context of care—these all slipped from the priority list of medical funding agencies.

The immediate *political* response of many medical granting agencies was to adopt the Cochrane criteria as the standards for evaluating *all* research proposals and, hence, for allocating research funding. In foundations and granting agencies that applied the Cochrane criteria carte blanche, this meant that qualitative research was not considered fundable.

In the United States, nurses had their own funding source in the NIH (National Institutes of Health), NCNR (National Center for Nursing Research) now NINR (The National Institute for Nursing Research), and NIDA (National Institute on Drug Abuse) and they were less affected by this trend. But in Canada, Australia, and New Zealand (and probably the United Kingdom), where the control of health care funding was in the hands of medical researchers, this trend was crippling.

Federal organizations and private foundations that fund research are excellent mirrors of the state of the science. Their health-care priorities and the grants that they fund reveal what research is perceived to be necessary and of outstanding design. Requests for data to both NIH and to CIHR for the percentage of qualitative grants received and funded have bought the response that they do not keep such statistics.[3] Yet, in the United States, since the 1980s, groups of nurses have lobbied consistently to increase the number of qualitative members on the research committees or to establish special committees with the expertise to review qualitative applications.

The agencies' response that other methods do not have special review groups is not exactly correct. Presently, the review groups are predominantly quantitative by default. For instance, the review groups in nutrition understand and respect the methods used by nutritionists, or in engineering, methods used by engineers. There are two problems with the committee structure in NIH for qualitative researchers to get funding. The first problem is the preference that most committee members should have NIH funding, although this is not a requirement. Such a practice perpetuates the status quo and makes it difficult for enough qualitative researchers to establish the track records necessary to "break in." Thus, the second problem is that the membership of these committees is heavily weighted toward quantitative research. In all fairness, if the committee does not have the qualitative expertise needed within the committee membership, another reviewer may be brought in, in person or by phone. But the *dis*advantage of this system is clear. How can one unknown outsider sway a committee (in which friendships and power relations are already established) and, if on the phone, without even the advantages of a personal presence? And it is worse in Canada (from my experience as a reviewer in New Zealand, Australia, Great Britain, and South Africa), where only the external reviewer's written report is considered by the committee, and the "expert" does not have the privilege of listening to and participating in the committee's discussion and debate, nor of voting. These problems continue to this day.

The first response of the qualitative researchers to this inequity in funding in the 1980s and 1990s was an immediate appeal, but their voices were soft. Criticisms were often published in sources that were not on the reading lists of the policy makers. Furthermore, because research is squeezed into most medical curricula—and qualitative inquiry is not usually included in the syllabus—these appeals came from nursing, occupational therapy, speech therapy, and counseling, these being disciplines that were tangential to the mission of the medical foundations, disciplines that were focused on the *person* rather than the therapy and that were not funded as mainstream priorities by the medical review boards. The objections came from stakeholders who were perceived to be outside the core mission of the review boards, so that these complaints were of little concern to the councils approving the funding decisions. And the appeals came over the heads of quantitative health researchers (mainly experimental psychologists and epidemiologists), who were better established, and better funded, and who probably agreed with the medical scientists and decision makers.

The second response of qualitative researchers ("If you can't beat 'em join 'em") was to become a part of the Cochrane movement. A large group of qualitative researchers formed a group that met regularly, with the agenda of including "contextual evidence" in the reviews. Their initial task was methodological—that is, to determine how one should incorporate qualitative findings into the quantitative reviews. Previously, I wrote,

> I am now suggesting that it is time to be honest with ourselves. The assumptions underlying evidence-based medicine are a poor fit with the assumptions of qualitative inquiry. Furthermore, we have contrary research agendas: Whereas the epidemiological and experimental designs for clinical drug trials seek to decontextualize, qualitative research asks them to consider the context. We have different definitions and agendas for "providing care": their focus is on the pill and if it works; our focus is different—why patients might decide whether to swallow the pill or to accept, reject, or modify the prescribed treatment, or how it affects patients' lives. Both perspectives are equally important for "efficacy" but produce complementary information rather than information that may be incorporated into the same reviews. [Morse, 2005, p. 3]

Despite these words, I now believe that this group has made headway in raising the consciousness and status of qualitative inquiry. They are making a difference in the way qualitative inquiry is perceived. Some medical journals, such as the British Medical Journal, now routinely have a qualitative section, perhaps due, in part, to this lobby. But this is a "side effect" of their work.

The final response was methodological—to develop methods for conducting qualitative meta-analyses. This task itself was onerous, because, of course, textual data are not additive; qualitative studies do not intentionally replicate, and so forth. Following meta-ethnography (Noblit, 1984), the effort was spearheaded by

Margarete Sandelowski and her colleagues and is recently completed.. The primary approach followed quantitative meta-analyses: select pertinent studies, critique these studies according to identified standards (Sandelowski & Barroso, 2002), and then use some technique to develop a model according to the major theoretical commonalities (Thorne et al., 2004).

So that is the story to date. But from my perspective, now, in 2005, this *emphasis on evidence* is not going to go away. Indeed, for those of you who are heaving a sigh of relief that you do not do health research or are thanking your lucky stars that you are not entrenched in a health-care discipline, my prediction is that, as it has spread from Britain, to Canada and Australia, and then to the United States, so it will spread laterally, invading other applied disciplines, in particular, education. Politically, qualitative researchers are in for a long and rough ride.

I believe the second problem that we face is not with qualitative inquiry itself but with mainstream medicine's entrapment in clinical drug trials, experimental design, and quantitative analysis—in other words, their perception of their discipline as a biological/physiological rather than a humanistic discipline. I maintain that despite the recent rise of humanistic medicine, their unwavering adherence to randomized drug trials, epidemiological designs, and insistence on the criteria outlined by Cochrane (1972/1989) as The Standard, and fueled by the pharmaceutical industry, is actually occurring in health care at the expense of more significance advances—advances that may make even greater contributions in reducing morbidity and mortality. I maintain that medical granting agencies' limited support for qualitative inquiry, and their limitations in acknowledging, respecting, and funding qualitative modes of inquiry and accepting alternate evidences, will impede advances in health care (Morse, 2006a).

Two factors are driving the health care/medical agenda, and these factors cannot be ignored. The first is that the public lobby for cure is stronger and louder than the public lobby for care. Medical research is expected to reduce morbidity and mortality. The second factor is the political and public lobby of reduced costs, that is, efficiency in care. Medical care is becoming too expensive. These questions are interrelated. Let us ask instead …

Does Qualitative Research Save Lives?

When I look at the outcomes of most publications in *Qualitative Health Research*, authors claim that their research creates models for practice that "provide insight and understanding" into the experience of patients, families, and caregivers. It is important to be understanding, but in the hardball of everyday life, our "soft" research, with such nebulous outcomes, is not useful to policy planners and those responsible for the health of the nation. From this perspective, our research is not directly relevant to our health care agenda, which is intent on reducing mortality, lowering morbidity, and reducing costs.

Ironically, medical knowledge is dependent on qualitative inquiry. The compendium of signs and symptoms, albeit developed somewhat haphazardly in the eighteenth and nineteenth centuries, was dependent on observations and description. This continues, particularly in the identification of new diseases, for example in the identification of AIDS during the early 1980s. New medical procedures are documented using case study design (consider the evolution of heart transplants). Qualitative research is also being used to explicate symptoms (e.g., the early signs of heart attacks in females; Brink, Karlson, & Hallberg, 2002). But pointing out such obvious inconsistencies is not enough. This basic research (and I use that term deliberately) is not adequate for our critics—they need to see the numbers!

Can We Develop "Proper" Evidence?

Theoretically, we could use a mixed-methods design and calculate any impact on mortality resulting from our research, but in reality our research—when it *has* an intervention—uses designs that are not relevant to Cochrane (1972/1989) standards. Excellent clinicians (and excellent teachers) do not use behavioral interventions that consist of rigid protocols but, rather, use a blend of science and clinical wisdom. Interventions based on modifying behaviors and working through relationships lack the scientific rigor required by evidence based protocols. Our problems include (a) the impracticality of using double-blind treatment and control groups with replication in at least two independent sites with behavioral interventions (e.g., consider family therapies); (b) the reduction of such interventions to rote and precise rules counters the flexibility in approaches when underlying philosophies and treatment realities require uniqueness when caring for individuals; and (c) an extraordinarily large contextual variation within the presentation of illnesses and needs, and in the contexts, cultures, and expectations of patients. Clearly, another form of evidence must be developed to justify qualitative inquiry as legitimate, appropriate, and desirable.

Alternate Forms of Evidence

What are these "alternative evidences" for demonstrating efficacy? I am thinking of problems that are too chaotic to be explored using experimental design—for example, qualitative problems. I am thinking of demonstrating and extending our findings using *logic* and *common sense*, and, if necessary, our repertoire of *qualitative designs* that have previously not been part of mainstream qualitative health research.

Expanding Qualitative Methods to Expand Types of Evidence

What are these designs?

I am thinking of designs used in the fields of engineering, such as nonhuman models in trials using simulation; also of methods used in biomechanics. I am also thinking of putting interventions in place following a single "near miss," rather than waiting for statistically significant disasters, and the deliberate trialing using *n of 1* research. And I am thinking of legitimizing ethological qualitative microanalysis, used in anthropology, as evidence in its own right.

These research designs are well funded outside of health care but, strangely, are not considered rigorous within health care. How serious is the problem? My own trauma room research has identified "talking through" to help terrified patients with overwhelming pain, when analgesics are ineffective or withheld, to maintain control and not to fight caregivers (Proctor, Morse, & Khonsari, 1996). The efficacy of such human interventions cannot be readily demonstrated in a two-group design, but it could be demonstrated using logic and modeling (*How does resisting/fighting care increase the severity of a head injury?*). Although the intervention is expensive (another nurse is needed), the cost savings in reducing trauma and the severity of head injuries would be remarkable. I could also argue for other advantages—"talking through" synchronizes the trauma team, so that care is actually administered faster. If care is administered with in the first "golden hour" after the accident, mortality is reduced.

Beyond Social Science: Additional Modes of Qualitative Inquiry/Established Types of Evidence

What are these methods?

The first group I have classified as *Qualitative microanalysis*. These are characterized often by a single case, by abduction, and by attention to detail.

1. Forensic designs.

This research is conducted "detective-style" on a single case or incidence, usually following a serious incident or major disaster, including loss of life. The goal of these methods is to identify causation and, hence, prevent recurrence, rather than—as in police work—to convict or—as in journalism—to expose. At the Qualitative Health Research Conference in 2004, Linda Connell (2004), NASA scientist, described the Aviation Safety Reporting System (ASRS), which collects reports on aviation safety events and incidents, and the role of qualitative inquiry in identifying cause: "Black box cockpit recordings are qualitative data." From such research, there are invariably changes of policy and procedure, changes of design of the aircraft, or further investigation into human limitations that may have contributed to the incident. This is a qualitative design that indisputably saves lives.

Forensic designs are used by many disciplines—obviously by police at crime scenes, in cases of sexual assault, domestic violence, missing persons, fraud investigations, and audit procedures. There are also fields of forensic engineering in anthropology and archeology. Of course, when a building has collapsed or a mummy has been discovered, qualitative methods are the only sensible way to proceed, and these techniques are accepted as standard practice.

Nevertheless, according to Connell (2004), the methods used by NASA to "diagnose" aviation errors are now being used in hospitals in the United States to investigate medical errors (Barach & Small, 2000). This is perhaps the most basic of applied research, for it is from examination of these single cases that pattern recognition and principles emerge. This new focus on patient safety will make this one of the most expanding areas of qualitative inquiry, and we should officially embrace these techniques and add them to our repertoire.

Closely associated with the previous aviation model is a new ASRA, NASA Ames Research Center project, in collaboration with the U.S. Department of Veterans Affairs, that evaluates reports describing "near misses." In this case, the "incident" has not actually occurred, but from a single report of "almost," the circumstances are investigated, warning bulletins released, and policy changed. In other words, an intervention is in place before the "problem" becomes an actual event. How to demonstrate efficacy? Just as avoiding a pedestrian at the last minute does not create a statistic, or dodging another vehicle and avoiding a fender bender does not result in actual cost savings, except at the population level and over time, such proven efficacy remains hypothetical.

Because the researchers are not waiting until there is loss of life—they are responding to a hypothetical case—that is the converse of statistical significance: it is hard to claim credit, to demonstrate a drop in mortality. These researchers are working from a theory of causality that states if something *almost* happened once, it could *actually* occur; they are using logic and experience, not experimental design. Their data rely on anonymity in reporting and a guarantee of "no reprisal" to those who report the incidents; hence, they leave no audit trails and cannot demonstrate the validity of their data. But these conditions ensure both that the researchers receive necessary data and that data are as comprehensive as possible; such conditions enhance validity. These are conditions of evidence, of hypothetical outcomes, and are devoid of the quantitative criteria of replication—*the ultimate ethic.*

What do I mean by the ultimate ethic? Simply put, it is to learn from near misses and to modify practices and develop policy from them. Connell's (2004) example of the disregard for this model was a B757 wake turbulence accident at John Wayne Airport in Orange County, California, in December 1993.

The pilot did not know that the air traffic controller had descended a B757 (which has extreme wake [vortex] frequencies [from its wings]) through his intended flight path. The captain was aware of the danger of wake vortices (although he was not told that the preceding aircraft was a B757) and "was acting appropriately, according to what we've all been taught. The Westwind crashed in uncontrolled flight three miles short of the runway" (Pendleton, 2003, para. 10).

At the congressional hearing, the congressman for Orange County, responding to the comment that one near miss was not statistically significant, asked with sarcastic sadness, "And how many bodies on the runway is statistically significant?" (Connell, 2004).

2. Deliberate trial or testing of interventions with n − 1 *research.*

An example of this type of research is the first heart transplant, and may or may not be happening today with human cloning. The design is usually experimental and outcomes unknown or uncertain, and the nature of the trial demands qualitative microanalysis, perhaps combined with some repeated quantitative measures design. Case study design is an inadequate description of this type of research.

This method has tremendous potential in health care for the examination of rare events, such as heart transplantation or the separation of conjoined twins. Are the findings of such research important? I believe Piaget (1954/1999) used this design when he observed and took careful notes observing his infants, and we know the impact his research has had on our understanding of infant behavior.

3. Observation and precise, microanalytic observational description.

This is classic qualitative inquiry, which is not used enough, and it is the method most in need of development in qualitative inquiry. The use of video recordings enables microanalysis of movement, touch, and talk, and examination of the pacing of the care, so that behaviors, interactions, and responses can be examined.

Is this research of any *assistance* to our agenda of saving lives?

This method is used in biomechanics and can be used, for example, in observing patient mobility when studying patient falls. This will enable bioengineering solutions, in the form of a safer bed or walking aids, to be developed and trialed.

Video is often used for conducting research with nonverbal patients, such as those with advanced Alzheimer's, or in exploring infants' response to pain, or the study of the breastfeeding dyad, and so forth. Thus, qualitative analysis using videotapes is powerful. It enables us to document, to illustrate our practice, and to communicate our findings, and certainly should be used more often.

4. Simulation.

This is the "crash test dummy" type of research. To reduce risk, simulation replaces people in certain high-risk situations. Despite the use of models used in teaching, I do not know of a single case of this type of research being used in qualitative research. This does not mean, however, that we should forget this option exists.

Developing Qualitative Evidence

As researchers, we are tired of conducting underfunded research that seemingly goes nowhere. Yet, forcing ourselves into a quantitative system does not appear to be the answer. Although we know that our research is significant and addresses problems that may otherwise be declared not researchable, our seemingly insurmountable problem is to convince those who control research funding, curricula, and the publication of texts and mainstream journals that our work is significant. We need to convince them that logic and common sense can produce powerful forms of evidence, and that sometimes we cannot afford, both in terms of morbidity and mortality and of dollars, the cost of quantitative inquiry.

Qualitative researchers sit on the fringes of research, but remember that it is on the fringes where the greatest advances are often made. We are addressing the confusing and chaotic problems that are too difficult to tackle quantitatively. But they are important problems.

Let us look internally, to ourselves, and bring together all our resources, all we know methodologically, and all that we know as professionals. Then, with a united voice, a rising chorus, demand the resources and attention that our research deserves.

Notes

1. This was the opening plenary address presented at the First International Congress of Qualitative Inquiry, May 5–7, 2005, University of Illinois, Urbana-Champaign. Reprinted with permission from *Qualitative Health Research*, 16 (Morse, 2006b). I am grateful to Linda Connell, M.A., director of ASRS, NASA Ames Research Center, Moffett Field, California, for her comments on an earlier draft.

2. Elsewhere, I suggest that Cochrane (1972/1989) intended to target clinical opinion or clinical judgment regarding treatments in this level, and not qualitative inquiry and the type of problems it addresses, in this categorization. In fact, Cochrane probably did not know anything about qualitative inquiry as it is practiced today (Morse, 2006a). Thus, it is an error—and invalid—to categorize qualitative inquiry into the Cochrane review criteria.

3. NIH-funded applications (with rare exceptions) are in the public domain, but this information could not feasibly be obtained one application at a time.

References

Abate, F. (Ed.). (1996). *The Oxford dictionary and thesaurus: American edition.* New York: Oxford University Press.

Barach, P., & Small, S. D. (2000). Reporting and preventing medical mishaps: Lessons from non-medical near miss reporting systems. *British Medical Journal, 320,* 759–763.

Brink, E., Karlson, B. W., & Hallberg, L. (2002). To be stricken with acute myocardial infarction: A grounded theory study of symptom perception and care-seeking behavior. *Qualitative Health Research, 7,* 533-543.

Cochrane, A. L. (1972/1989). *Effectiveness and efficiency: Random reflections on health services*. London: British Medical Journal.

Connell, L. (2004). Qualitative analysis: Utilization of voluntary supplied confidential safety data in aviation and health care. Presentation to the Qualitative Health Research Conference, Banff, Canada, April/May.

Kravitz, R. L., Duan, N., & Braslow, J. (2004). Evidence-based medicine, heterogeneity of treatment effects, and the trouble with averages. *Milbank Quarterly, 82*(4), 661–687.

Larner, G. (2004). Family therapy and the politics of evidence. *Journal of Family Therapy, 26,* 17–39.

Morse, J. M. (2005). Beyond the clinical trial: Expanding criteria for evidence [Editorial]. *Qualitative Health Research, 15,* 3–4.

Morse, J. M. (2006a). It is time to revise the Cochrane criteria [Editorial]. *Qualitative Health Research, 16*(3).

Morse, J. M. (2006b). The politics of evidence. *Qualitative Health Research, 15*(3), 395–404.

Noblit, G. (1984). *Meta-ethnography: Synthesizing qualitative studies.* Newbury Park, CA: Sage.

Pendleton, L. (2003). *Wake turbulence—An invisible enemy.* Retrieved November 26, 2005, from http://www.avweb.com/news/airman/183095-1.html

Piaget, J. (1954/1999). *The construction of reality in the child*. London: Routledge.

Proctor, A., Morse, J. M., & Khonsari, E. S. (1996). Sounds of comfort in the trauma center: How nurses talk to patients in pain. *Social Sciences & Medicine, 42,* 1669–1680.

Sackett, D. L. (1993). Rules of evidence and clinical recommendations. *Canadian Journal of Cardiology, 9*(6), 487–489.

Sandelowski, M., & Barroso, J. (2002). Reading qualitative studies. *International Journal of Qualitative Methods, 1*(1), Article 5. Retrieved March 10, 2005, from http://www.ualberta.ca/~ijqm/

Thorne, S., Jensen, L., Kearney, M., Noblit, G., & Sandelowski, M. (2004). Qualitative metasynthesis: Reflections on methodological orientation and ideological agenda. *Qualitative Health Research, 14*(10), 1342–1365.

Chapter 5 | Methodological Fundamentalism and the Quest for Control(s)

Ernest R. House
University of Colorado

When the evaluation of educational and social programs began as a large-scale endeavor in the late 1960s, only quantitative research methods were accepted by many scholars as being sufficiently rigorous for evaluating government programs. After several disappointing high-profile evaluations, and a lengthy debate within the evaluation community, qualitative methods gradually became acceptable. Evaluation became multimethod.

However, during the administration of George W. Bush, the U.S. Department of Education mandated that evaluations should use randomized experimental designs as the strongly preferred method. Other research methods were insufficiently scientific. The ideological basis for this shift lay in the neofundamentalist policies of the Bush administration, in which the quest for control and authority rested on fundamentalist beliefs. In the field of evaluation, this attitude was expressed in the policy that only randomized experiments could produce true findings, a belief in a single method as the sole source of truth—methodological fundamentalism—analogous to the belief that the Bible is the sole source of religious truth. From a broad perspective, all fundamentalisms are attempts to maintain or restore traditional authority relationships.

Early Evaluation Policies

In 1965, the U.S. Congress passed the Elementary and Secondary Education Act. At the insistence of Senator Robert Kennedy, this bill included an evaluation rider that became the stimulus for large-scale program evaluation. That same year, President Lyndon Johnson introduced the Program Planning and Budgeting System (PPBS) to the U.S. Department of Health, Education, and Welfare. The goal was to develop government programs that could be stated, measured, and evaluated in cost-benefit terms. Economists William Gorham and Alice Rivlin headed the evaluation office (McLaughlin, 1975).

Federal policy stipulated that key decisions regarding educational and social services would be made at the higher levels of the federal government. The only true knowledge about such services was a production function specifying stable relationships between inputs and outputs, and the only way of obtaining such knowledge was through experimental and statistical methods. "Information necessary to improve the effectiveness of social services is impossible to obtain any other way" (Rivlin, 1971, p. 108). To that end, several large-scale experiments were funded.

Campbell and Stanley's (1963) classic work became the methodological guide, and experimental studies became the research standard, with Campbell and Stanley describing experiments

> as the only means of settling disputes regarding educational practice, as the only way of verifying educational improvements, and as the only way of establishing a cumulative tradition in which improvements can be introduced without the danger of a faddish discard of old wisdom in favor of inferior novelties. [p. 2]

During the early days of professional evaluation, many policymakers and evaluators put their faith in large-scale studies, such as Follow Through, Head Start, and the Income Maintenance experiment. They thought these national studies would yield definitive findings that would demonstrate which programs worked best. The findings could serve as the basis for mandates by the central government to reform inefficient social services. In time, these studies proved disappointing. One problem was their scale. The Follow Through experiment cost $500 million, and during one data collection, the evaluators collected twelve tons of data. The evaluators were overwhelmed to the point where they could not produce timely reports. Eventually, the government reduced the study by limiting the number of sites and variables.

Another serious problem was that the findings were equivocal.

The studies did not produce clear-cut results that could be generalized easily. For example, when the Follow Through data were analyzed, the variance in test scores across the dozen educational programs was nearly as great as the variance within the programs. In other words, if an early childhood program had been implemented at six sites, two sites might have good results, two might have mediocre results, and two might have poor results. This was not a definitive finding on which the government could base strong national recommendations. After years of frustration and hundreds of millions of dollars, officials and evaluators became disenchanted with large-scale experiments.

Alternative Methods

Meanwhile, evaluators were developing alternative approaches, including qualitative studies, meta-analysis, and program theory. Small qualitative studies were practical. For example, if a school district wanted an evaluation of its early childhood education program, interviewing administrators, teachers, and students was simple and cheap and the findings were easy to understand. Furthermore, generalizability was not the problem that it was for national studies. The demand on the local study was that the results be true for this place at this time, not for sites all over the country.

However, some evaluators still did not consider qualitative studies to be scientific, particularly those who had championed experimental designs. Evaluators engaged in intense debates about the scientific legitimacy of qualitative methods. This dispute occupied the profession for twenty years, even as qualitative studies became popular. After considerable discussion, the field accepted the idea that evaluation studies could be conducted in different ways (Reichardt & Rallis, 1994). Evaluation became methodologically ecumenical, though personal animosities lingered. By 2000, the quantitative-qualitative dispute seemed to be history.

A second alternative to large-scale quantitative studies was meta-analysis (Glass, 1976). Meta-analysis was more acceptable to quantitative methodologists because it was based on experimental data. In some ways, meta-analysis is the natural successor to large-scale quantitative studies. Meta-analysis assembles the results of many experimental studies—studies that have control groups—and combines the findings quantitatively by focusing on differences between performances of the experimental and control groups. This technique is more radical than it sounds because researchers might combine outcomes that are different in kind into the summary results. Meta-analysis became very popular in social and medical research.

A third alternative to experimental studies was program theory (Chen & Rossi, 1987). Program theory consists of constructing a model of the program as part of the evaluation. Previously, some had advocated basing evaluations on grand social theories, but those attempts failed. There were two reasons why. First, there were few social theories that had much explanatory power. Second, if such theories existed, there was a question of whether they could be used to evaluate social programs. For example, given the task of evaluating automobiles, could evaluators use theories of physics to do the job? It seems unlikely.

Evaluators reduced the concept to theories about individual programs. This worked better. The program formulation was concrete enough to guide evaluations and communicate directly with program participants. Program theory delineated points where evaluators might confirm whether the program was working and enabled evaluators to eliminate rival hypotheses and make causal attributions more easily (Lipsey, 1993). Qualitative studies, meta-analysis, and program theory all worked better because each approach took account of a more complex social reality by framing studies more precisely, albeit in different ways. Qualitative studies showed the interaction of people with other causal factors in context, thereby limiting causal possibilities (Maxwell, 1996). Meta-analysis used individual studies that occurred in circumstances of rich variation, making generalization better (Cook, 1993). Program theory specified the program more exactly, allowing the posing of more precise questions (Lipsey, 1993).

Neofundamentalist Policies

Although many evaluators moved away from quantitative methods and value-free studies toward multiple methodologies and studies more open to stakeholders, these trends were not universally accepted. Not only did many conservatives and neoconservatives view such studies as too permissive—and, indeed, many studies were not very good—some did not like the direction in which the entire society and the evaluation field were headed. Pointing to what they saw as excesses, especially in studies labeled postmodern, they railed against such trends, mostly to little avail. Various methods flourished side by side.

However, the events of September 11, 2001 changed this permissive pluralist atmosphere. Before the terrorist attacks, President George W. Bush struggled to find traction. As he assumed office, he emerged from a contested presidential election with his legitimacy in question, his personal ability the butt of jokes, and his popularity in decline. After the terrorist attacks, Bush assumed the mantle of wartime president. The moral fervor with which he embraced this role expressed his personal, born-again, religious fundamentalism. During his younger days, he had been a heavy drinker and drug user who converted to religion, saving himself from personal ruin, in his own view. He embraced the new mission that had been thrust on him with religious intensity, and he projected moral certainty onto his administration and the country, a traumatized country seeking strong leadership. The simple world-view of good and evil suited him. Condoleezza Rice, his national security advisor and later secretary of state, reflected that the worst possible thing she could say to him was that an issue was complex.

Fundamentalism has several characteristics.

First, there is one source of truth, be it the Bible, the Koran, the Talmud, or whatever.

Second, this source of authority is located in the past, often in a Golden Age, and is associated with particular individuals. Believers often hark back to that time.

Third, true believers have access to this fundamental truth, but others do not, and applying the truth leads to a radical transformation of the world for the better. Fundamentalists have a prophetic vision of the future, that is, revelatory insight.

Fourth, having access to this source of truth means that believers are certain they are correct. They have moral certitude, a defining attribute.

Fifth, fundamentalists are not open to counterargument.

Indeed, they are not open to other ideas generally. They do not assimilate evidence that contradicts their views. They dismiss contrary information or ignore it.

Sixth, they are persuaded by arguments consistent with their beliefs even when outsiders find these arguments incomplete, illogical, or even bizarre.

Seventh, people who do not agree with them do not have this insight, and fundamentalists do not need to listen to them. In fact, sometimes it is all right to muscle nonbelievers aside because they do not understand.

Eighth, believers associate with other true believers and avoid nonbelievers, closing the circle of belief and increasing inner certainty.

Ninth, they promulgate their beliefs by means other than rational persuasion—by decree, policy, or laws—through forcing others to conform rather than persuading them—in short, through pressure or coercion.

Tenth, and last, fundamentalists try to curtail the propagation of other viewpoints by restricting the flow of contrary ideas and those who espouse them.

The Bush administration exercised this new fundamentalism in foreign and domestic policies. In foreign policy, the new fundamentalism was evident in the invasion of Iraq. The Golden Age for neoconservatives was the Reagan administration, and Reagan was the sacred figure. Conservatives and neoconservatives hoped to restore the age during which the United States brought down the Soviet Union and won the cold war. Bush's speeches took on a quasi-religious, moralistic tone, including references like "axis of evil." Bush believed that he was a great leader like Reagan, Churchill, or Lincoln. By his own admission, he talked to God every night. He surrounded himself with fellow evangelicals who saw him as "chosen." No matter what evidence was presented against his position on Iraq, it had no effect. If the Iraqis had no weapons of mass destruction, they were hiding them. If the Iraqis admitted to having weapons, they had violated the UN mandate. If war might destabilize the region, if most nations were opposed, no matter. Others did not understand. They were "old Europe," unwilling to take risks.

The Bush team was closed to counterevidence. Administration members presented arguments seen by others as inconclusive, at times strange, and sometimes false. They concocted a revelatory vision of democratic transformation for Iraq that foreign policy experts viewed as incredible. The more criticism they encountered, the more they banded together. Coercion was the tool of choice for securing compliance with their policies, used against enemies and allies alike. They had little sense of how others might react to their actions or didn't care. They did not understand that people they bullied might react negatively, even contrarily to the direction in which they were pushed.

All in all, George W. Bush's leadership exemplified a disdain for deliberation and an embrace of decisiveness and action, a "bullying" impatience with doubters and critical questions. He kept a tight inner circle of advisors so that alternative ways of framing problems did not arise. He believed, and his staff believed, that will, determination, and power would carry the day. One White House official told a reporter, "We are an empire now, and we create our own reality" (Suskind, 2004). Character, certainty, fortitude, and godliness were primary virtues. Bush felt that his reelection was a manifestation of divine purpose and that "God put me here" to deal with the war on terror (Hersh, 2005, p. 43). The fundamentalism of the Muslim terrorists was countered with the fundamentalism of the American president.

Methodological Fundamentalism

This fundamentalist attitude permeated other government policies as well. In evaluation, the policy took the form of "methodological fundamentalism." The U.S. Department of Education aggressively promoted "evidence-based" programs. The core of the evidence-based doctrine was that research and evaluation must be "scientific." In this interpretation, scientific meant that evaluation findings must be based on experiments, with randomized experiments given strong preference. Other ways of producing evidence were not scientific and not acceptable. There was one method for discovering the truth and one method only—the randomized experiment—a fundamentalist position.

The doctrine was embedded in Bush's education legislation, No Child Left Behind. The Department of Education established a What Works Clearinghouse to screen evidence-based projects and encouraged the construction of lists of researchers who complied with the methodological strictures—a white list as opposed to a black list. The rationale for evidence-based evaluation was outlined in a report prepared for the U.S. Department of Education by the Council for Evidence-Based Policies (2002), a group of Washington insiders, bureaucrats, and think tank fellows, plus some social researchers. The basic argument of the council was that education is a field of fads in which there has been no progress, as measured by national tests. By contrast, there has been great progress in medicine:

> Our extraordinary inability to raise educational achievement stands in stark contrast to our remarkable progress in improving human health over the same period—progress which . . . is largely the result of evidence-based government policies. [p. I]

And progress in medicine resulted primarily from randomized field trials.

Hence, the Department of Education should build a "knowledge base" of educational interventions proved effective by randomized trials and provide strong incentives for the use of such interventions. "This strategy holds a key to reversing decades of stagnation in American education and sparking rapid, evidence-driven progress" (Council for Evidence-Based Policies, 2002, p. i). Such was the revelatory vision for the transformation of American education. The council recommended that all discretionary funds for research and evaluation be focused on randomized trials. In accepting the report, Secretary of Education Rod Paige remarked that Bush's education policy was based on four concepts: accountability through testing, options for parents, local control, and evidence-based instruction. Accountability and options had been long features of neoconservative educational policy. As for evidence-based studies, "for the first time we are applying the same rigorous standards to education research as are applied to medical research" (Paige, 2002).

In addition to a revelatory vision that promised radical transformation, methodological fundamentalism exhibited other features of neofundamentalism. It had a simple credo: only randomized experiments produce the truth. There was one source of truth—the randomized experiment, and if we but follow, it will lead us to a Golden Age. Methodological fundamentalism had a storied past, the key figure being Don Campbell, who championed the concept of experiments as the only way to evaluate social programs. Campbell himself later conceded there were other ways of acquiring valid knowledge about social programs, but some followers did not. The methodological fundamentalists found new opportunities in the Bush administration, as neoconservatives found opportunities for their long-held preemptive war policies.

A Department of Education mandate for randomized trials was enacted without extensive discussion with professional communities. Avoiding contrary ideas is part of the orientation. As required by law, the proposed regulations were posted in the Federal Register to solicit public comments. The department noted: "In response to our invitation in the notice of the proposed priority, almost 300 parties submitted comments on the proposed priority. Although we received substantive comments, we determined that the comments did not warrant changes" (Federal Register, 2005, p. 3586). No significant changes were made. There is no reason to make changes if you already know the truth and others do not, even in the face of 300 comments. What can you learn? And the prescription was enforced by government decree. So, after forty years, evaluation policy came full circle back to experiments, this time with the force of religious authority.

Fundamentalism as a Movement

Since its founding, the United States has been swept repeatedly by strong evangelical movements that claim to possess absolute truth and attempt to restrict the flow of other ideas. During the twentieth century, these movements often took the form of anticommunist crusades and they had a strong effect on American social science. Indeed, one reason American social research is so methodologically oriented has been the attempt by social scientists to avoid political controversy (Ross, 1991).

Historically, fundamentalism is the term applied to a religious movement that began in the United States in the early twentieth century. At that time, Darwinism and German biblical criticism were eroding belief in the literal truth of the Bible. The threat to traditional religious authority engendered strong reactions among those who saw themselves as the guardians of true religion. Between 1910 and 1920, traditionalists published a series of booklets called The Fundamentals: A Testimony to the Truth. Fundamental beliefs included biblical inerrancy, the divinity of Jesus, the Virgin birth, the Atonement, and the Resurrection (Brash, 2001). The fundamentalists rejected core tenets of the Enlightenment—the divorce between revelation and reason, the separation of church and state, and faith in science and technology to solve all human problems. They opposed pluralist beliefs and Christians who acted on behalf of the poor and oppressed. Social concerns were diversions from God's message, they thought; God's law should override human rights.

In the 1970s, a new wave of fundamentalists arose against the excesses of modernism and the mass media, which were undermining religious authority. In the United States, this resurgence was led by television evangelists Jerry Falwell and Pat Robertson, who allied themselves with conservative Republicans and used their television followings to influence politics. Religious nationalism was a central theme. At the same time, religious nationalism also fueled Islamic fundamentalism, the most dramatic event being the overthrow of the U.S.-supported Iranian government and establishment of a theocratic Islamic state. Islamic fundamentalists rejected Christian domination and dedicated themselves to driving infidels from the Muslim holy land. They opposed pluralism, civil rights, and female rights. Like Christian fundamentalists, they supported male authority (Furnish, 2001).

Contemporary fundamentalist movements seem to be stimulated by globalism's corrosive effects on traditional society, gender roles, beliefs, and authority structures. Socially, the fundamentalists tended to be secondary male elites led by charismatic male leaders (e.g., the Promise Keepers led by former Colorado football coach Bill McCartney). These groups strongly supported male and patriarchal authority and opposed female rights, civil rights, gay rights, abortion, and divorce. They supported group authority over individuals and were confrontational in style. In their view, they were a religious remnant of true believers battling against worldliness. In general, fundamentalist movements are attempts to maintain or restore control and authority. They seek authority and certainty via holy script that supports traditional authority relationships, and the text interpreters are almost always male (Wellman, 2001).

I believe methodological fundamentalists are motivated by similar concerns as the religious fundamentalists. They have witnessed an erosion of social science, in their view, and are reacting to what they see as serious breaches of research authority. Since the broad acceptance of qualitative studies, experimental studies have lost ground. Such studies do not carry the respect and authority they once did, nor do their advocates and practitioners. With the advent of postmodern studies questioning the concept of truth itself, the situation has become acute. Experimental advocates regard such studies as blasphemous and lament the disrespect to scientific truth. In their view, they are reestablishing the authority of social science, particularly the authority of the methodology they learned as graduate students and nurtured as professors.

This reaction leads some to disdain methodological pluralism. And individual personal histories may account for the moralistic fervor with which some embrace randomized experiments. Certainly, not all who support randomized studies are methodological fundamentalists, any more than all Christians or Muslims are fundamentalists. One can believe randomized experiments are the best designs possible without being fundamentalist in attitude. The defining fundamentalist traits are whether one believes randomized experiments are the only ultimate source of truth, the moral fervor with which this conviction is held, and the degree to which one is willing to force others to accept such a view. Fundamentalism carries heavy authoritarian overtones.

A Few Words on Randomized Designs

What about randomized experiments in their own right? None of my analysis weighs against such studies. I am strongly in favor of randomized experiments, though not of mandating one method, whatever it is. In my view, there is no single avenue to discovering truth or determining causal relationships. Randomized designs are extremely valuable, and we should use more of them, but they are not appropriate in every circumstance, and they do not provide the best answer in every situation. The critical question is when to employ them. Although discussion of randomized designs requires a separate paper, I will make a few observations.

First, I agree with Council for Evidence-Based Policies that education is riddled with fads that have no research backing. Indeed, neoconservatives have promoted many such reforms—vouchers, charter schools, retention of students, and accountability via test scores—that have no strong research backing. I also agree that the schools have not improved much and that medicine has shown substantial progress. However, medical progress has not been due to randomized field trials. Medicine is the beneficiary of decades of breakthrough research in biophysics, biochemistry, and molecular biology. These basic sciences have resulted in detailed theories about disease. As far as I know, no scientist has received a Nobel Prize in medicine for promoting randomized studies. Experiments test ideas—an extremely valuable service for sure—but they do not produce the ideas.

Unfortunately, education has no corresponding theory on which to base its practices. The social sciences that might have produced the underlying theory, primarily psychology and sociology, have failed to do so, even though psychology relies on randomized trials extensively. Nor has there been significant progress in criminology or mental illness, fields that also employ many randomized trials. Randomization is neither the problem nor the cure. We could use more randomized trials, but they are not a panacea.

From a philosophy of science perspective, extreme faith in randomized designs is based on an inadequate conception of social causation, namely the regularity or Humean theory. Social programs are not closed to outside influences in the same way as experiments in the physical world can be. Hence, once-and-for-all definitive experiments to test theories or programs are not possible, as they sometimes are in the physical world. This is not to say that experiments cannot be extremely useful. They can be if used appropriately and supported by evidence that provides context for interpreting findings. Theory like that in medicine and the physical sciences is not available for interpretation, so social research findings are often interpreted ideologically or politically. Cronbach (1982), among others, raised in-depth criticisms of experimental studies decades ago, and these concerns have never been answered adequately by randomized design advocates.

In my view, the best situation for using randomization is when the objects being evaluated are similar to physical entities. For example, evaluating drugs by way of randomized designs is extremely appropriate because the drugs themselves can be reproduced in identical form. Drug treatments do not vary nearly as much as social programs and they do not interact with the environment to the same degree, though even here people react to the same drugs differently. When the treatments are entities difficult to standardize and reproduce exactly, the findings of experiments become more equivocal. For example, when educational programs are implemented in different settings, there are dozens of influences impossible to control, even by randomization. Findings can vary because of interaction effects even when the program appears to be the same. Most discussions of experimental design do not recognize this difficulty and portray the treatment or program as an "X" that does not vary from setting to setting. Of course, experiments can still be extremely valuable if one is careful in interpreting the findings.

Nor does randomization eliminate all biases, as some advocates mistakenly believe. For example, drug studies are among the most biased studies now being conducted, even though they are randomized experiments. Why? Pharmaceutical companies have gained control over many drug trials, and the companies are adept at biasing studies in favor of their particular drugs. They do this by clever choice of comparison treatment (often a placebo rather than a competitor drug), altering of dosages, selection of samples, selection of outcome variables, ignoring side effects, publishing only positive outcomes, and changing time scales, among various manipulation techniques. None of these biases are controlled by randomization. Whose interests control a study often determines the findings more than technical considerations.

One final concern is that experimental designs usually eliminate stakeholder perspectives, views, and interests. Many other methodologies incorporate the perspectives of stakeholders, increasing the fairness, accuracy, and utility of such studies, in my view. Most experimental studies exclude stakeholder views and interests, though there is nothing inherent that requires exclusion. Randomized studies could include stakeholder interests, but experimenters rarely do; that is not the traditional way of conducting experiments. By not including other interests and perspectives, such studies remain in the hands of the evaluator-researchers and their clients; in other words, the studies maintain traditional authority relationships that promulgate the interests and viewpoints of clients. For example, drug studies often incorporate drug company interests, but not those of patients. This inherent bias passes unnoticed, with some experimenters sincerely, though falsely, believing they are conducting unbiased studies. They believe randomization takes care of all biases. Again, none of this argues against doing randomized experiments. The question is when, how, and under what circumstances.

Summary

In the wake of September 11, 2001, neofundamentalists sought to control the world by imposing their beliefs on others and restricting the flow of ideas that conflict with fundamentalist beliefs. When scientific findings have conflicted with those beliefs, as with evolution, abortion, birth control, and global warming, the Bush administration has changed, distorted, or deleted the findings from government statements (Glanz, 2004). The administration has also sought to promote "scientific" educational research and evaluation by instituting one method as the certain pathway to true findings.

From a broader perspective, this apparent contradiction turns out to be another form of fundamentalism—methodological fundamentalism—that embodies belief in a single source of truth and restricts other ideas. One anticipates that not only will government determine method but also the outcome variables, who can participate in studies, what data they can collect, who can conduct studies, and how studies are reported—in short, the features that determine findings. Drug companies have demonstrated how findings of such studies can be controlled.

Like religious fundamentalism, methodological fundamentalism is an attempt to control ideas and restore, protect, and maintain traditional authority relationships. These traditional relationships include the authoritative role of government, the relationship between government and researchers, the restriction of what information is allowed to influence policy, the central role of certain methods in research, and the status of particular groups within the research community.

References

Brash, B. E. (Ed.) (2001). *Encyclopedia of fundamentalism*. New York: Routledge.

Campbell, D. T., & Stanley, J. C. (1963). *Experimental and quasi-experimental designs for research*. Chicago: Rand McNally.

Chen, H., & Rossi, P. H. (1987). Evaluating with sense: The theory-driven approach to validity. *Evaluation Review, 7,* 283–302.

Cook, T. D. (1993). A quasi-sampling theory of the generalization of causal relationships. In L. B. Sechrest & A. G. Scott (Eds.), *Understanding causes and generalizing about them* (pp. 39–82) (New Directions in Evaluation, No. 57). San Francisco: Jossey–Bass.

Council for Evidence-Based Policies. (2002). *Bringing evidence-driven progress to education: A recommended strategy for the U.S. Department of Education.* New York: William T. Grant Foundation.

Cronbach, L. J. (1982). *Designing evaluations of educational and social programs.* San Francisco: Jossey–Bass.

Federal Register. (2005). *Vol. 70* (15), 3586.

Furnish, T. R. (2001). Islamic fundamentalism. In B. Brash (Ed.), *Encyclopedia of fundamentalism* (pp. 235–240). New York: Routledge.

Glanz, J. (2004). Scientists say administration distorts facts. *New York Times,* February 19, A18.

Glass, G. V. (1976). Primary, secondary, and meta-analysis of research. *Educational Researcher, 5,* 3–8.

Hersh, S. M. (2005). Up in the air: Where is the Iraq war headed next? *The New Yorker,* December 5, pp. 42–54.

Lipsey, M. W. (1993). Theory as method: Small theories of treatments. In L. B. Sechrest & A. G. Scott (Eds.), *Understanding causes and generalizing about them* (pp. 5–38) (New Directions in Evaluation, No. 57). San Francisco: Jossey–Bass.

Maxwell, J. A. (1996). Using qualitative research to develop causal explanations. Working paper, Harvard Project on Schooling and Children, Harvard University, Cambridge, Massachusetts.

McLaughlin, M. W. (1975). *Evaluation and reform.* Cambridge, MA: Ballinger.

Paige, R. (2002). Remarks at Consolidation Conference, Washington, DC, November 18.

Reichardt, C. S., & Rallis, S. F. (Eds.). (1994). *The qualitative–quantitative debate: New perspectives* (New Directions in Program Evaluation, No. 61). San Francisco: Jossey–Bass.

Rivlin, A. (1971). *Systematic thinking for social action.* Washington, DC: Brookings Institution.

Ross, D. (1991). *The origins of American social science.* Cambridge, UK: Cambridge University Press.

Suskind R. (2004). Without a doubt. *New York Times,* Oct 17, Magazine Section, p. 44.

Wellman, J. K. (2001). Secularism. In B. Brash, (Ed.), *Encyclopedia of fundamentalism* (pp. 440–442). New York: Routledge.

Chapter 6 | The Challenge of Tailor-Made Research Quality

The RQF in Australia

Julianne Cheek
University of South Australia

Introduction: What This Chapter Is about

In Australia, as in most Western countries over the past decade, there has been a steady rise of the influence of audit culture and the desire on the part of governments to ensure value for money in terms of research investment. Strathern (1997) notes that "Audit culture is audit enhanced" (p. 309), linked to a more general idea of accountability and one in which "audit rewards the self-examining self" (p. 314). An outworking of such audit culture has been the emergence of schemes designed to measure and reward research performance.

The Research Assessment Exercise (RAE) in the United Kingdom was a forerunner in this regard. The RAE was established in 1992 (Broadhead & Howard, 1998) by the then conservative government, whose rationale was a "wish to see selectivity in the allocation of research resources based on the assessments of the quality of research" (p. 3). In 2005, using similar rhetoric and rationales, the Australian federal government moved rapidly to introduce a Research Quality Framework (RQF) designed to assess the quality and impact of Australian research both within Australia and globally. The RQF will be in operation from 2007 onward. In the discussion that follows, I explore challenges that the imminent imposition of the RQF poses for qualitative researchers in Australia and for qualitative research more generally.

The RQF: Desperately Seeking Research Quality and Standing

Brendan Nelson, the then federal minister with responsibility for the portfolio of Education, Science and Training in Australia, provided the following imprimatur for the imposition of the RQF: "For Australia to be competitive in a knowledge based economy, our research must be of the highest international quality and standing" (Nelson, 2005a, p. 3). Nelson's rhetoric inextricably links research and researchers to a global marketplace and the concept of a knowledge-based economy. Indeed, one possible conclusion from such rhetoric is that the greater the contribution of research to that marketplace, the greater the quality and standing of that research. Thus, in Australia we are seeing research increasingly viewed and framed as an enterprise shaped and colonized by economically driven, market-derived and -sustained understandings and premises.

Such a view and framing of research is in keeping with the contemporary political climate in Australia that, as in most Western nations, can be defined broadly as neoliberal. Neoliberal governments, and the political regimes of truth that emanate from them, promote "notions of open markets, free trade, the reduction of the public sector, the decrease of state intervention in the economy and the deregulation of markets" (Torres, 2002, p. 368). Embedded within notions of the marketplace and using the rhetoric of competition and enterprise, neoliberal thought is productive of a range of apparatuses and technologies designed to "actively create the conditions within which entrepreneurial and competitive conduct is possible" (Barry, Osborne, & Rose, 1996, p. 10, emphasis in the original). In many ways, this is somewhat paradoxical in light of neoliberalism's avowed intent to limit the intrusion of the state into the world of the individual (Barry, Osborne, & Rose, 1996).

At the same time, researchers in Australia find themselves confronted by a resurgence of neopositivist influenced and derived approaches to research. A form of methodological fundamentalism (House, 2005) is emerging, fueled by the evidence-based movement that has become so pervasive in the past decade. Central to this movement is the notion of "scientific" research where:

scientific means that research and evaluation findings must be based on experiments, with randomized experiments being given strong preference. Other ways of producing evidence are not acceptable... . This is a fundamentalist position. [House, 2005, p. 1078]

Although there is no doubt that the RQF poses challenges for all researchers in Australia, it poses particular challenges for qualitative research and researchers. Perhaps the most serious is the potential for the RQF, with its neopositivist influences and concomitant fundamentalist tendencies, to erode many of the gains made by qualitative researchers in terms of gaining recognition for qualitative approaches as legitimate in their own right.

The collision and confluence of neoliberal and neopositivist thought in the contemporary Australian context produces new and refracted understandings of research and research outcomes. The RQF is an outworking of such understandings in that it is both produced by them and in turn productive of them. The RQF operates to construct and create conditions within which research activity can be thought about in certain ways, thus relegating to the margins other ways of thinking about research and research outcomes.

Researchers in Australia are increasingly confronted with pressure to act within the conditions of possibility emerging from the understandings underpinning the RQF. Thus, when operating within the parameters of the RQF, researchers experience a form of delimited autonomy both with respect to the research methods they choose to use and the basis on which they are able to claim impact and quality of their research. In other words, what emerges is a form of autonomy but only within the conditions of possibility enabled by the understandings of research implicit within the RQF. Such conditions of possibility shape the spaces in which qualitative researchers find themselves. In these spaces qualitative researchers twist and turn (Lather, 2004), relentlessly buffeted by competing demands and seemingly incompatible discourses about research and research outcomes.

Of course, it is possible for qualitative researchers to resist occupying these delimited spaces. However, there is a price to be paid. Nelson makes that clear by what he outlines as happening once the framework is in place:

An RQF will provide a consistent and comprehensive approach to assessing publicly funded research. It will drive positive research behaviours, encouraging researchers and research organisations to focus on the quality and impact of their research. [2005a, p. 3]

Further,

once implemented, the RQF will provide the Australian Government with the basis for redistributing research funding to ensure that areas of the highest quality of research are rewarded. [2005b, p. 3]

The framework is not to be just for measuring research in order to reward areas of "high" research performance. Rather, it is to be used to actively drive behavior with respect to what, and, importantly, how research is conducted. The type of research to be encouraged is research that fits predetermined measures of quality and impact. The RQF is thus a technology of power that is designed to actively create the conditions within which particular understandings of research can emerge, assume mainframe, and be rewarded. Resources, such as funding, will follow from how well researchers comply and work within these understandings, or put another way, spaces of delimited autonomy.

Nelson's comments highlight the overt political agenda in play. Here we see the mutation and evolution of the desire to measure research impact and quality, to one in which the overt agenda is to modify researcher behavior and then reward that modified behavior accordingly. The RQF thus becomes a disciplinary technology (Foucault, 1977), not only normalizing understandings of research and research outcomes, but also disciplining both those who do and those who do not comply with such understandings. In turn, it enables a range of self-disciplining behaviors, on the part of researchers, to emerge based on various forms of examination—the self-examining self referred to by Strathern (1997). Increasingly, researchers find themselves examining their research and subjecting their research to examination to determine how well it "fits" or "scores" in such a disciplinary technology. For example, researchers in my institution are already being urged to think about where they publish in terms of the RQF emphasis on journal impact factor in determining quality and impact of research.

To encourage them to do so, they will be rewarded with financial incentives if they publish in high-impact factor journals.

Examination of research and researchers' activities is central to the RQF as a normalizing and disciplining technology. Groups of "experts," such as those individuals appointed to the RQF panels, scrutinize research output and productivity to compare, rank, and identify any deficits. So, too, do universities, departments within universities, and individuals within those departments. Thus, we have the development of cascading levels of scrutiny and examination of the research context and those who work in it. Foucault (1977) points out that the examination is a highly ritualized and structured use of power designed to bring into focus, classify, and categorize individuals in certain ways:

> The examination combines the techniques of an observing hierarchy and those of a normalizing judgement. It is a normalizing gaze, a surveillance that makes it possible to qualify, to classify and to punish. It establishes over individuals a visibility through which one differentiates them and judges them. [p. 184]

The RQF enables the overt surveillance of research and researchers' activities, along with associated disciplinary regimes premised on examination, observation, and above all normalization. The push toward normalization is evident from the comment by the chair of the expert advisory group advising Nelson that it is an "exciting challenge to produce a tailor-made research quality framework that will drive and deliver positive behaviours in Australia's research system" (Roberts, 2005, p. 5). The positive behaviors to be driven and delivered are those in keeping with the understandings of research implicit within the RQF and its associated metrics. An alternate reading of a "tailor-made research quality framework" is as a form of regulation that codifies knowledge production and normalizes understandings of research, reducing them to key performance indicators and metrics such as number of publications, economic benefits, and number of research dollars obtained. Mentoring, thinking time, community service, and unfunded research are some of the potential casualties of such reductionist understandings (Cheek, 2005).

Metrics as Material Apparatus of the RQF: Effects on, and Challenges for, Qualitative Research

Strathern (1997) notes that "audit has its own material apparatus" (p. 317). Part of the material apparatus of the RQF is the metrics used to determine quality, impact, and ultimately research performance. At the time of writing this chapter, the final metrics to be used to determine performance in the RQF were yet to be announced. However, the writing and rhetoric around the development of the RQF have consistently emphasized that the process of assessment must be practical and cost effective. The Australian government commissioned the Allen Consulting Group, a company that provides policy analysis and advice to business and government, to develop a report detailing how benefits from publicly funded research can be realized and identifying practical metrics by which returns on funded research can be assessed (Allen Consulting Group, 2005). The report suggested that efficient and collectable quality indicators related to research impact in the social sciences and humanities (areas where much qualitative research has historically been located) include:

- the number of highly cited papers published,
- the number of papers in high quality journals, and
- the number of citations of papers within papers published in high-quality journals.

Given such a view, emphasizing as it does "the number of," it is not surprising that terms such as "highly cited" and "high quality" have increasingly become synonymous with quantitative bibliometric indicators such as citation analysis figures and the impact factor of journals (Cheek, Garnham, & Quan, 2006). Elsewhere, I have shown that such assumptions are flawed and pose particular challenges for qualitative researchers (see Cheek, Garnham, & Quan, 2006). The main challenges are understanding how these bibliometrics work, what they can demonstrate, and, most importantly, what they can not.

Other challenges are how best to respond to imperatives emanating from such bibliometric techniques and determining what the effects of those responses might be. For example, I have noted a trend among the journals for which I review and/or sit on editorial boards, all of which publish qualitative research, to be increasingly concerned with either gaining an impact factor or improving it. The discussions are invariably framed from a marketing point of view. Gaining an impact factor involves applying to Thomson Scientific and meeting their criteria for inclusion.[1] This requires the journal to conform to the requirements of the database. In so doing, there is the danger that journals themselves will become normalized, forced to conform to particular understandings of what journals are for and should look like. For example, journals written in English dominate these databases. So do journals based in the United States. Seglen (1997, para. 12) notes that one effect of this is that:

> American scientists, who seem particularly prone to citing each other, dominate these databases to such an extent (over half the citations) as to raise both the citation rate and the mean journal impact of American science 30% above the world average.

Further, what of the implicit assumption in all of this that a researcher's most important contributions are in the form of journal articles? Researchers in the social sciences (where most qualitative research is located) publish far fewer journal articles than researchers in the natural and medical sciences (Archambault & Vignola-Gagne, 2004). One reason for this may be that they have used books and book chapters to convey their work. How will the RQF affect this tradition? How will qualitative researchers position themselves in relation to this? Will this see the demise of the extended argument and exegesis that has been such an important part of the development of qualitative research?

Another metric that appears in the initial list proposed by the consulting group is the value of research contracts received from industry and government. The value of research contracts is equated to the number of dollars received—thus, a specific and limited understanding of "value" is in play. The number of dollars received will be used to rank and scrutinize individual researchers, departments, and universities. This is despite the fact that some research projects do not require large amounts of money to conduct. Much qualitative research, for example, does not cost as much to carry out compared to, for example, research in physical or engineering sciences that require expensive pieces of equipment.

Nelson has made it very clear that government research–funding schemes will be reengineered to suit particular types of research and to fit with particular assumptions about research, quality, and impact. Therefore, it follows that government dollars allocated for research will only go to those working within these set understandings of research in the first place. This is of great concern, given another of the metrics proposed in the initial Allen Consulting Group report—namely, success rates in securing competitively allocated research grants, many of which are government funded. The potential exists for unprecedented government and bureaucratic control of research and research agendas. In fact, in Australia we are already seeing the outworking of such control: in the last Australian Research Council round of funding, the minister refused to sign off on seven projects recommended for funding by the peer review process.

> Three of those projects were on a hit list of 27 drawn up by conservative newspaper columnist and Quadrant magazine editor Padraic McGuinness, whom Dr Nelson appointed to the ARC's quality and scrutiny committee. It's understood that five of the seven grants Dr Nelson vetoed were in the humanities and two were in the social sciences. [Illing, 2005, p. 3]

The RQF and the metrics embedded within it have the potential to establish a self-perpetuating and -fulfilling cycle in which only certain types of research and researchers will be considered high quality and as having impact. It is these researchers who will have the right kind of track record to secure competitive research funding. The gaining of such funding will ensure that these researchers score well on RQF metrics, thereby reinforcing prior and extant notions of quality and impact in research. Researchers working outside these definitions, and this will include some (or many) forms of qualitative research deemed unfundable or not fitting with RQF-influenced research agendas and directions, will be marginalized and find resources for their research increasingly difficult to come by. Further, they will increasingly be faced with difficult decisions in a context and world of metrics that constructs and labels researchers as "either competent, scientific, rigorous, and therefore concerned with truth and quality—or soft, non-intellectual, lacking reasoning abilities, and therefore of poor quality and with no or negative impact" (Lincoln & Cannella, 2004, p. 8). Such difficult decisions include whether to persist with forms of qualitative research that may never attract funding.

Emerging Databases: New and Different Challenges for Qualitative Researchers

The metrics that form part of the material apparatus of the RQF compel qualitative researchers to confront the challenge of how best to capture and convey their research output. Increasingly, valuable researcher time is taken up preparing for, and undertaking, the reporting requirements rather than conducting the research. As Traynor and Rafferty noted in 2001:

> there is a tendency for those whose activities and characteristics are being measured to turn considerable attention towards the measure, rather than the quality supposedly being measured, in order to achieve some kind of reward, or, more usually in the public sector, stave off some penalty. [p. 167]

Five years later, nothing has changed in this respect. In fact, if anything, it has intensified. Already the institution in which I work has participated in a trial run of an RQF assessment exercise to review its processes and ensure that it has the correct procedures in place to meet the reporting requirements of the RQF. Thus, the RQF itself becomes the defining frame rather than the research it is designed to measure. As happened with the roll-out of the RAE (Broadhead & Howard, 1998), large amounts of scaffolding now surround the RQF, supporting it, responding to its understandings and imperatives, and, in so doing, providing the infrastructure for even greater layers of measurement and control. One part of this scaffolding is the increasing evolution and prominence of databases that provide and manipulate data to enable the scrutiny, inspection, and measurement of research and researchers.

For example, ResearchMaster, a company that produces software for research administration, advertises that:

When the New Zealand government introduced a derivative of the UK's Research Assessment Exercise (RAE) called Performance Based Research Funding (PBRF), ResearchMaster met the extended collection and reporting need by enhancing ResearchMaster Enterprise (RME) for the New Zealand market…. ResearchMaster is confident that if and when Australia introduces a RAE derivative, RME clients will be ready to meet the challenges of this new system. [2005, p. 5]

Here we have the development of software designed to assist in the collection and presentation of data according to the requirements of particular research assessment exercises. Although this may seem benign and helpful, especially for university administrations that have to navigate much data and conform to onerous reporting requirements, such development marks an interesting shift in the way databases are located in the spaces occupied by qualitative researchers. Researchers are forced to conform to reporting in the way that the database or software requires and this, in turn, influences the way that they think about their research and what they and others consider research outputs. For example, no place exists for recording an avowed humanistic and social justice commitment, which is a fundamental principle of many forms of qualitative research (Denzin & Lincoln, 2005, p. xvi). The ever-present danger is that the development of databases both technically and in the way that they are thought about in terms of their use will contribute to and perpetuate rigidity with respect to the way in which research performance and quality are thought about and measured.

It is even more concerning to note the way in which some of the software programs are being marketed in terms of the array of sorting and ranking purposes to which they can be put. Such marketing reflects the confluence of neoliberal and neopositivist influences. For example, consider Essential Science Indicators (ESI), a software program developed by Thomson Scientific, based on journal article publication counts and citation data from Thomson Scientific databases. ESI is designed to enable "researchers to conduct ongoing, quantitative analyses of research performance and track trends in science" (Thomson Scientific, 2005). It states that its intended users are government policymakers, a variety of corporate research administrators, analysts, researchers or information specialists in government, academia, industry, publishing, financial services, and research foundations.

The proponents of ESI are overt in terms of claiming a market niche for this program directly related to the ranking of research and researchers. They advertise that it offers "data for ranking scientists, institutions, countries and journals" (Thomson Scientific, 2005). The advertisements indicate that ESI can rank "top" countries, journals, scientists, institutions, and companies by field of research, as well as enabling users to evaluate potential employees, collaborators, reviewers, and peers. Thus, an example of the way that ESI can be used, is given by Thomson Scientific on its ESI web page under the heading "Measuring Research Performance":

> **Challenge**: The Rector of a large German university wants to allocate a new source of research funding where it will have the biggest positive impact on the University's scientific standing.

> **Application**: Essential Science Indicators makes it possible for the Rector to compare the research performance of its departments with other universities. Funding is then allocated to the departments that are showing the greatest potential in their field, leading to greater scientific success for the university. [Thomson Scientific, 2005]

Here, the allocation of resources is directly linked to the use of the data in this database to rank research performance. This reinforces the shift in the way that these databases are now being viewed and used. Such ranking is overt, as departments are compared with other departments both within and without the university in order to identify departments showing the greatest potential in their field. Here, "potential in their field" is equated to the way that they score on the measures in the database. If they score well, they are rewarded with more resources; as a result, the cycle is perpetuated and notions of success are solidified and normalized. Scientific standing is assumed to be synonymous with the numerical ranking obtained from such a database. At the heart of all this is normalization—the normalization of the way in which research is scored, the way success in research is thought about and measured, and the way in which researchers can be ranked and compared.

Thus, we see the mutation of databases based on a citation index originally designed to allow researchers to track the use of their and others work (Garfield, 1955), to ones that enable government officials and administrators to use the data to draw up lists of performance and rank individuals, institutions, and even countries. The emphasis is on the production of the relative rankings and indicators of performance; any shortcomings in either the data used to draw up those rankings or the limited scope of that data are relegated to the margins (see Cheek, Garnham, & Quan 2006). What emerges is the normalization of the use of this type of database and the type of data it collects and presents in the research arenas in terms of establishing the relative worth of both research and researchers. Once the norm is established as to how to rank and measure performance, then ways can be developed to locate individuals in relation to that norm and compare them to each other. When this is done, it is possible to make statements about "poor" and "good" research performance and to make judgments about individuals' performance. Put another way, the database enables a form of surveillance of both research and researchers. The surveillance and the relative rank of research become the important foci with the premises that underpin the numbers forgotten or taken for granted in the push for timely responses to imperatives created by apparatuses such as the RQF.

Daring to Hesitate:
The Challenge for Qualitative Researchers

The opening decade of the twenty-first century has seen the emergence and consolidation of a context replete with "tensions, contradictions, and hesitations" (Denzin & Lincoln, 2005, p. xi) for both qualitative research itself and for those who carry out this research. My purpose, and the position that I have adopted in writing this chapter, is to encourage qualitative researchers to embrace an informed and considered activism with respect to how they twist and turn in the spaces that they find themselves in. In so doing, I argue for the need for an increased hesitation on the part of qualitative researchers when interacting with, and locating themselves in, increasingly conservative and potentially hostile contexts. I have used the imminent imposition of a research quality framework in Australia as a vehicle to explore aspects of the conservative challenge that face the community of qualitative researchers and scholars at this time. The RQF epitomizes an outworking of what Lincoln and Cannella (2004, p. 6) term "dangerous discourses," namely, a return to high modernism, a backlash against diverse forms of research, and direct government actions to create a science for the "common good."

The relentless pace of the colonization by these discourses of the spaces that we as qualitative researchers find ourselves in exacerbates the dangers that they pose. In these colonized spaces we find new forms and refracted variants of old issues—including the seemingly relentless quest for how to assess the quality and establish the impact of research; how to determine what is a "good" and "useful" research outcome; and what constitutes "evidence" of impact and quality of research.

As a qualitative researcher in Australia, I find myself incessantly twisting and turning as I struggle to position myself in relation to the demands being placed on me. This applies particularly to the demands that are flowing, and will continue to flow, from the RQF and the disciplinary practices emanating there from. Questions I have found myself asking include the following:

1. How do I, as a qualitative researcher, position myself in relation to all of this?

2. Can I accept and live with the tensions and contradictions confronting me as a funded qualitative researcher in the reality in which I live and work every day?

3. Do I try to fit my research and my belief in, and commitment to, qualitative research as a research approach in its own right into the spaces created for me by the RQF?

4. What should I defend and what might I give up?

5. How do I respond to the enterprise culture of neoliberalism increasingly so pervasive in every aspect of the research process?

6. How do I respond to postdoctoral research fellows and research students when they ask me about how best to forge a funded research career or where they should publish, given

the increasing emphasis on specific metrics for tenure, promotion, and funding?

Questions such as these create hesitation for me when thinking about the RQF, the potential positions that are constructed for me within it, and how I act on, and within, those positions. Such hesitation requires me to think deeply about what I am doing, and why, in order to confer "a new kind of intelligibility upon the strategies that seek to govern [me]" (Barry, Osborne, & Rose, 1996, p. 16) and the research that I do. Importantly, it also requires me to consider the "ways in which [I] have come to understand, embrace or contest such strategies" (p. 16).

In writing this chapter, I have attempted to destabilize aspects of the present I find myself in, to challenge the obvious and seemingly inevitable. In so doing, I am making a plea for hesitation on the part of qualitative researchers; for an untimely response to the rapid and relentless pace of the infiltration of audit culture and its attendant demands on understandings of research. Such an untimely response is one that embraces Strathern's (1977) idea of productive nonproductivity to focus on thinking deeply about what we are doing and why. This may well suspend, or at least slow, the relentless twisting and turning that many of us currently experience while being buffeted by the ever-increasing demands for quality, impact, and improvement as defined in increasingly narrower terms. Otherwise, we risk remaining always on the margins, twisting and turning to someone else's tune and open to the charge of being there because we cannot "cut it" in the normalized and taken-for-granted world of rankings, numerical measures, and narrowly defined evidence-based approaches to research.

One way in which we might be able to resist the push for expediency in terms of fitting qualitative research into the "what is," is to hesitate and focus instead on the "what might be" (Cheek, 2005), with respect to the way qualitative research is thought and spoken about. This highlights the layers of political action that are required to address deep residual practices that can hinder and even subvert the development of qualitative research. Without taking such political action, we run the risk of remaining on the surface and playing the politics of the system rather than changing that politics. As Morse (2003) points out:

This is a task for us all to do collectively and systematically, for it involves changes such as broadening research priorities and perspectives on what is considered researchable and what constitutes research. It involves political problems, such as expanding and sharing research funds to new groups of investigators. In this light, the administrative changes involved, such as developing appropriate review criteria, expanding committee membership, and educating other scientists about the principles of qualitative inquiry ... appear trivial. [p. 849]

To conclude, this chapter is offered in the spirit of critique. French social philosopher Michel Foucault notes that:

critique is not a matter of saying that things are not right as they are. It is a matter of pointing out on what kinds of assumptions, what kinds of familiar, unchallenged, unconsidered modes of thought the practices that we accept rest. [1981, p. 154]

The goal of such critique is "not so much to establish the limits of thought, but to locate the possible places of transgression" (Gordon, 1986, p. 75). The challenge each qualitative researcher faces in relation to the imperatives of the contemporary contexts that they find themselves twisting and turning in is to work out where and what those places of transgression might be.

Note

1. Journal evaluation editors take into account factors such as the journal's basic publishing standards, its editorial content, the international diversity of its authorship, and the citation data associated with it (Thomson Scientific, 2004).

References

Allen Consulting Group. (2005). *Measuring the impact of publicly funded research*. Report to the Australian Government, Department of Education, Science and Training. Available online at http://www.dest.gov.au/sectors/research_sector/publications_resources/profiles/measuring_the_impact_publicly_funded_research.htm

Archambault, É., & Vignola-Gagné, É. (2004). *The use of bibliometrics in the social sciences and humanities* (Report prepared for the Social Sciences and Humanities Research Council of Canada). Montréal, Canada: Science-Metrix.

Barry, A., Osbourne, T., & Rose, N. (Eds.). (1996). *Foucault and political reason: Liberalism, neo-liberalism and rationalities of government*. Chicago: University of Chicago Press.

Broadhead, L., & Howard, S. (1998). "The art of punishing": The Research Assessment Exercise and the ritualisation of power in higher education. *Education Policy Analysis Archives, 6*(8), 1–13. Available online at: http://epaa.asu.edu.epaa/v6n8.html

Cheek, J. (2005). The practice and politics of funded qualitative research. In N. K. Denzin & Y. S. Lincoln (Eds.), *Handbook of qualitative research* (3rd ed., pp. 387–410). Thousand Oaks, CA: Sage.

Cheek, J., Garnham, B., & Quan, J. (2006). What's in a number?: Issues in providing evidence of impact and quality of research(ers). *Qualitative Health Research, 16*(3), 423–435.

Denzin, N. K., & Lincoln, Y. S. (Eds.). (2005). *Handbook of qualitative research* (3rd ed.). Thousand Oaks, CA: Sage.

Foucault, M. (1977). *Discipline and punish: The birth of the prison*. London: Allen Lane.

Foucault, M. (1988). Practicing criticism—Interview with Didier Eribon. In L. Kritzman (Ed.), *Politics, philosophy, culture* (pp. 152–158). London: Routledge.

Garfield, E. (1955). Citation indexes to science: A new dimension in documentation through association of ideas. *Science, 122*, 108–111.

Gordon, C. (1986). Question, ethos, event: Foucault on Kant and enlightenment. *Economy and Society, 15*(1), 71–87.

House, E. F. (2005). Qualitative evaluation and changing social policies. In N. K. Denzin & Y. S. Lincoln (Eds.), *Handbook of qualitative research* (3rd ed., pp. 1069–1082). Thousand Oaks, CA: Sage.

Illing, D. (2005). ARC feeds on Nelson's silence. *The Australian*, November 23, p. 3.

Lather, P. (2004). This *is* your father's paradigm: Government intrusion and the case of qualitative research in education. *Qualitative Inquiry, 10*, 15–34.

Lincoln, Y. S., & Cannella, G. S. (2004). Dangerous discourse: Methodological conservatism and governmental regimes of truth. *Qualitative Inquiry, 10*(1), 5–14.

Morse, J. (2003). A review committees guide for evaluating qualitative proposals. *Qualitative Health Research, 13*(6), 833–851.

Nelson, B. (2005a). Minister's foreword. In *Commonwealth of Australia. Research quality framework: Assessing the quality and impact of research in Australia—Issues paper.* Canberra. Available online at: http://www.dest.gov.au/sectors/research_sector/policies_issues_reviews/key_issues/research_quality_framework/issues_paper.htm

Nelson, B. (2005b). Minister's foreword. In *Commonwealth of Australia. Research quality framework: Assessing the quality and impact of research in Australia—Preferred model.* Canberra. Available online at: http://www.dest.gov.au/sectors/research_sector/policies_issues_reviews/key_issues/research_quality_framework/issues_paper.htm

ResearchMaster. (2005). Advertisement in Australasian Research Management Society Inc. *Up in arms*—Newsletter, April, no. 7, p. 1.

Roberts, G. (2005). Chair's foreword. In *Commonwealth of Australia. Research quality framework: Assessing the quality and impact of research in Australia—Issues paper.* Canberra. Available online at: http://www.dest.gov.au/sectors/research_sector/policies_issues_reviews/key_issues/research_quality_framework/issues_paper.htm

Seglen, P. O. (1997). Why the impact factor of journals should not be used for evaluating research. *British Medical Journal, 314*, 497–502. Retrieved December 13, 2005, from http://bmj.bmjjournals.com

Strathern, M. (1997). "Improving ratings": Audit in the British University System. *European Review, 5*(3), 305–321.

Thomson Scientific. (2004). The ISI database: The journal selection process. Available online at http://scientific.thomson.com/free/essays/selectionofmaterial/journalselection/

Thomson Scientific. (2005). *Essential science indicators.* Available online at http://scientific.thomson.com/products/esi/

Torres, C. A. (2002). The state, privatisation and educational policy: A critique of neo-liberalism in Latin America and some ethical and political implications. *Comparative Education, 38*(4), 365–385.

Traynor, M., & Rafferty, A. M. (2001). Editorial—Bibliometrics and a culture of measurement. *Journal of Advanced Nursing, 36*(2), 162–168.

Chapter 7 | Research Quality and Research Governance in the United Kingdom
From Methodology to Management

Harry Torrance

Education and Social Research Institute
Manchester Metropolitan University, UK[1]

Introduction

Internationally, over several years now, educational researchers have witnessed, and been subject to, sustained attack over the quality and relevance of their work. Americans will be most familiar with the recent debate over the No Child Left Behind legislation (2001) and associated reviews of the quality and utility of educational research (Feuer, Towne, & Shavelson, 2002; NRC, 2002, 2005).

But similar attacks and debates have been taking place in the United Kingdom and over a longer period (Hargreaves, 1996; Hillage et al., 1998; Tooley & Darby, 1998); have been noted and commented on in Australia (Yates 2004); and are beginning to emerge in the European Union (Bridges, 2005; Brown, 2003). As a result, we seem to be faced with the emergence of an almost global "new orthodoxy" in educational research (Hammersley, 2005; Hodkinson, 2004; Lather, 2004; Oancea, 2005). This new orthodoxy seems perversely and wilfully ignorant of many decades of debate over whether, and if so in what ways, we can conduct enquiry and build knowledge in the social sciences, pausing only to castigate educational research for not being more like (supposedly unproblematic) medical research (Hargreaves, 1996; Oakley, 2000, 2003).

The new orthodoxy seeks to discipline both the purpose(s) and methods of educational research: finding "evidence" for "what works" in current, assumed-to-be given, circumstances, as opposed to, for example, problematizing and investigating the social and classroom constructions of what counts as success and failure and how they are realized in action, and privileging large-scale correlational and even experimental approaches, rather than detailed qualitative and/or critical enquiry. There seems to be an assumption that all educational researchers are, or should be, involved in a uniform, homogeneous, almost corporate endeavor to solve short-term problems on behalf of the modern, neoliberal, managerial state.[2] For example, in the United Kingdom, the Hillage Report (Hillage et al., 1998), sponsored by the Department for Education and Skills (DfES), concluded that "there is an overwhelming need for an overall strategy and ... some form of National Educational Research Forum needs to be established" (p. 56). And the most recent report from the National Research Council (NRC) assumed that "federal funding agencies, schools of education ... and professional associations [should] work together" (NRC, 2005, p. 7) and asked whether "existing training and professional activities [are] sufficient ... to respond to the demands of practitioners and policy makers?" (p. 5).

The debate in educational research is only one particular example, albeit a particularly acute one, of a more wide-ranging trend toward the regulation of social research and indeed research activity more generally. Key elements of the new orthodoxy derive not only from methodological advocacy within the research community, but also from policy assumptions within government that more central control, selective funding, and research management will improve the quality and utility of research in general, and social and educational research in particular. It is this latter set of assumptions that I want to address in this chapter, especially with respect to developments in the United Kingdom.

Debates about quality in research, particularly in qualitative research, have traditionally revolved around questions of epistemology and methodology. Quality cannot be reduced to methodological prescriptions, of course, and standards are realized in action through the lived experience of methodological communities of practice (see Hodkinson, 2004). Central control, managerialism, and the audit culture threaten these by both shifting the locus of control outside the communities of practice and embedding definitions of quality in quality assurance procedures that change the social relations of research. The elements of audit culture policy that comprise this drive in the United Kingdom include a general higher education funding policy that concentrates research resources in fewer universities, specific arguments for central orchestration of and integration of the "national research effort" in educational research, and the increasing application of "quality assurance" arguments and procedures to definitions of research quality across the social sciences. I will address each of these elements in turn, the first two fairly briefly, the third at more length.

Concentrating Research Resources— Literally Reinventing "Big Science"

Rhetorically at least, the government in the United Kingdom, along with others, is concerned about maintaining economic competitiveness through knowledge production and the continuous improvement of labor market skills. In a global market, we cannot compete on price, we have to compete on top-end science (bioengineering, pharmaceuticals, etc.), quality of design ideas, and the supply of human and financial services. Widening participation in higher education and developing research capacity is taken to underpin these goals, but resources cannot be spread too thinly. While attempting to encourage more young people to attend university, and move the "age-participation rate" close to 50% of the cohort, the government is simultaneously concentrating research resources. A recent parliamentary "White Paper," laying out the argument for policy stated:

> Research lays the long-term foundation for innovation, which is central to improved growth, productivity and quality of life. This applies not only to scientific and technical knowledge. Research in the social sciences ... can also benefit the economy.... . But competition is fierce ... we need to think carefully about how research is organised and funded. [DfES, 2003, p. 23]

The argument is that research resources must be concentrated to bring most benefit from "economies of scale":

> The challenge now is to make best use of the money by making sure that research funding is allocated, organised and managed effectively ... [ ] ... by focussing resources ... on the best research performers.... We therefore intend to reward research that is more concentrated and better managed. [DfES, 2003, pp. 26–29]

Lone researchers, working to criteria of quality deriving from their disciplines may still attract funding, but "concentration ... and ... collaboration" (p. 28) are assumed to be the way forward.

The mechanism for achieving this in the United Kingdom is the Research Assessment Exercise (RAE), a periodic review of research output for which quality grades are awarded and from which government funding flows. Such exercises have also been introduced in Australia and New Zealand modeled on the UK experience (Middleton, 2005; Yates, 2005) and are being discussed in Europe (Bridges, 2005; Brown, 2003). They seem to be being introduced for similar reasons of research productivity: to compete in a global (knowledge) economy, research resources must be concentrated in larger, better-funded units.

The minutiae of the RAE are now pored over by academics in the United Kingdom in obsessive detail. Success brings significant material and reputational rewards, failure the reverse, and game playing is widespread. The details need not concern us here, but briefly, every several years, all universities that wish to receive research funding from the treasury (via the Higher Education Funding Council) must submit the "research output" (essentially publications) of their "active researchers" for scrutiny via the RAE. Subject panels allocate grades and funding follows grading. Currently, funding is restricted to the top three grades awarded (4, 5, and 5*), with a very steep "selectivity slope" resulting in the top-rated departments (those that have been rated 5* in successive exercises) receiving nine times the funding of those rated 4 (Commission on the Social Sciences, 2003, p. 56).

The White Paper cited above noted that 75% of research funding now goes to the "top" twenty-five universities (out of more than 100 eligible to bid), but proposes still further selectivity for the next exercise in 2008. The emergent details of the next RAE have delineated four grades, three of which are meant to be at increasing levels of international excellence, with only "world-leading" research attracting the highest grades and, in turn, the most funding. Clearly, such concentration and competition drives the system toward larger-scale and very proactively managed activity. In turn, assessment of the "research environment" (i.e., culture, levels of activity and management) has and will continue to form an important element of overall judgments of quality in addition to the assessment of individual outputs (HEFC, 2005, pp. 24–25). Of course, it can be argued that given competing demands on government funding, selectivity and concentration of research resources are both necessary and inevitable to extract the most value from the investment. But the case is not proven and begs many issues with respect to protecting smaller units and promoting diversity and the generation of new ideas rather than the promulgation of orthodoxy.

Coordinating the "National Research Effort" in Education

The attack on the quality of educational research in the United Kingdom is nested within this more general disciplining of the universities and the concentration of research funding in a small number of highly successful units. It also goes hand-in-hand with attacks on the quality, relevance, and utility of teacher education reminiscent of U.S. debates reviewed by Cochran-Smith and Fries (2001). The consequence for educational research is that most university departments of education are now cut off from general research support:

Current (2001–2008) RAE Grades and Funding for the United Kingdom

University Education Departments

RAE grade 5*	good funding	two departments
RAE grade 5	adequate funding	twelve departments
RAE grade 4	limited funding	nineteen departments
RAE grades 1, 2, 3b, & 3a	no funding	fifty departments

Within this general trend toward selectivity and concentration of research, specific attacks on the quality and utility of educational research have also led to calls for more centralized national planning of educational research (see Hillage et al., 1998, cited above). This is somewhat ironic given that the competitive concentration of resources obviously undermines the notion of a nationally coordinated effort, but the argument is that educational research has been too thinly spread, is too fragmented and has produced too many individual small-scale (qualitative) studies that are not linked and have not built a cumulative "knowledge base" for educational policy and practice (Hargreaves, 1996; Oakley, 2003). Here, the arguments are very similar to those being made in the United States (NRC, 2005, p. 36 & ff) and dovetail with and reinforce the new orthodoxy's claims for "scientifically based research ... [and] ... rigorous evidence" (U.S. Department of Education, 2003, p. iii).

Of course, the arguments over quality and utility are disputable, and much of the criticism has been partial and even prejudiced. A great deal of what has now passed into "accepted wisdom" as to the poor quality of educational research in the United Kingdom would not remotely pass muster if subjected to the tests of "scientific evidence" that critics propose for others but not themselves. Thus, Hargreaves's (1996) influential views were presented in a polemical lecture; Tooley and Darby's (1998) review, although based on some evidence, was selective, not comprehensive or "systematic," and sponsored and published by the government's Office for Standards in Education (OfSTED), the chief inspector of which (at the time) had gone on record as referring to educational research as "badly written dross" (Woodhead, 1998, p. 51). MacLure (2003, 2005) and Oancea (2005) subject these and other similar sources to detailed analysis and critique. Nevertheless other evidence-based groups in social policy now routinely cite the poor quality of educational research as a cautionary tale for the rest of the social sciences (e.g., Boaz & Ashby, 2003; Grayson, 2002), and these criticisms have been extremely influential, as they both add to and draw strength from current political agendas promoting selectivity and research management.

One result of these criticisms was a government-sponsored

review of *Research on Schools* (Hillage et al., 1998), which took a broadly positivist and corporatist perspective, concluding that "the research system is too fragmented. It could benefit from some strategic coherence … and greater collaboration" (p. 55) and recommending, as we have seen, that "some form of National Educational Research Forum needs to be established" (p. 56). Just such a forum has been established (NERF 2001), housed in the DfES although notionally independent of it. Its establishment has parallels in congruent fields, including Health and Social Care. Thus, we now have a National Health Service "R&D Forum" (DoH, 2005, p. 45), while the Social Care Institute for Excellence (SCIE), also established and funded by government though claimed to be independent (SCIE, 2004, p. xiii), has recently called for a "national research and development strategy for social care" (p. 54).

In practice, NERF has rather limped along since its inception, as the DfES has equivocated about its role and funding. Indeed, its demise has recently been announced (with effect from April 2006) and what, if anything, will replace it is unclear. In this respect, we should never ignore the "turf wars" that occur within policy circles. NERF clearly required sufficient policy support and resources to orchestrate the "national research effort," but not too much or it could become a rival organization to the DfES, open to lobbying and "capture" by the researchers themselves. Its creation added to a sense of centralization, however (Ball, 2001), and the perceived need for concerned educational researchers to engage with such centralizing "quality control" and "capacity building" measures if they are to argue for a larger share of research resources for educational research per se. Here, then, we can see that although some may simply wish to destroy educational research (see Woodhead, above), others engage with and become subject to the discourse of quality control and improvement to argue the case for more funding (but only, of course, for "better" research). It is here that the tentacles of accountability and performativity are at their most embracing.

Quality Assurance and Management in Social and Educational Research

NERF's establishment is but one example of a more general trend across UK social policy and the social sciences more broadly for government to act as orchestrator and arbitrator of what counts as high-quality research. This trend is part of a continuing post-Thatcherite critique of public services in the United Kingdom. The professional "producers" of the public sector are claimed to act only in their own interests, rather than those of their clients (service users). Government intervention is thus needed to regulate the producers and protect both the subjects and consumers of research activity. This basic critique is now wedded to a "new managerialism" under recent Labour governments, whereby a renewed commitment to providing resources to the public sector is linked to accountability and quality-assurance mechanisms. In turn, accountability is linked to measures of utility usually expressed in terms of auditable outputs (such as research outputs in the RAE). Quality assurance is linked to concentration, critical mass, and effective management of the "business" of producing research.

Thus, to look beyond education for a moment, the Department of Health's "Research Governance Framework for Health and Social Care" sets mandatory legislative standards for all research conducted in health and social care settings. Compliance is monitored by reference to the "Duty of Quality," which all health care organizations have to meet under legislation (DoH, 2005, p. 2). The framework claims that its development and implementation will "assure quality in health and social care research" (p. 5), and it "is offered as a model for the governance of research" in order to bring "general performance up to that of those at the leading edge" (p. 3). A diagram used to illustrate the way in which the framework will operate indicates a top-down model, with the "effective management of research to national standards" at its core (p. 5).

One might well ask why "national" appears to be the key word here—what privileges "the nation" in this discourse rather than health professionals, or local communities, or indeed the international scientific community? Interestingly, the answer seems to concern methodology, since one outcome of the model is claimed to be "dependable local delivery of research" (p. 5) that will "forestall poor performance … research misconduct and fraud" (p. 3). Within such a taken-for-granted discourse of benign management and recalcitrant researchers it is a very small step to the elision of "high quality" with "single method," in exactly the way we have seen with respect to educational research in the United States (U.S. Department of Education, 2003).

Another feature of the DoH framework (2005) is that "quality" in research and in a research culture seems to be taken to be synonymous with the "management" of research. Thus, there are injunctions to develop quality-assurance procedures including "detecting and preventing scientific misconduct" (p. 32), "arrangements to archive the data" (p. 33), and with all data to be "available at the request of the inspection and auditing authorities" (p. 33). Furthermore "careful attention [must be paid] to monitoring compliance" (p. 37), whereas "delivery systems [i.e., research organizations] … should be designed to facilitate … random monitoring and audit" (p. 45). Of course, all of these "quality indicators" derive from the logic of having such a "quality-assurance framework" in the first place—once it is assumed and accepted that a framework is appropriate and necessary, then monitoring compliance with its implementation will become a research management responsibility.

As it happens, medical and health-related research in the United Kingdom have come in for particular criticism of late with respect to some especially high profile cases of malpractice, (all the more ironic, of course, that they are held up as models for educational research). Vulnerable persons (and animals) are very often involved in such research and clearly interventions that carry potential or actual risks to health and well-being need to be fully explained, conducted under an ethical code, and, if necessary, governed by legislation.

The DoH framework is addressed as much to these sorts of high-risk circumstances as to more generally health-related social research. Nevertheless, the framework is intended to be implemented across the full range of health- and care-related research and represents a particularly draconian example of state intervention in and regulation of social research. Similarly, as we have also seen, assumptions about the concentration and management of research resources pervade other elements of government research funding policy such that quality is no longer considered an issue in the design and conduct of individual pieces of research, or even the integrity of individual investigators, but rather is now considered a feature of the management of research across studies. You cannot be doing "quality" research if you are not managing and quality-assuring research.

Equally problematic, however, with respect to the particular framework developed by the DoH, is the fact that its presumptions are all about the control of irresponsible or incompetent researchers. Although the framework insists on a key role in quality assurance for the scientific community with respect to refereeing proposals and peer reviewing publications (DoH, 2005, pp. 13–14), none of the principles or guidelines for the conduct of research are addressed to sponsors (including government departments) that might wish to exert undue pressure on researchers to produce particular results or prevent publication of unwelcome results. The presumption throughout is that the government, sponsors, and research managers are benign and disinterested guarantors of research quality, which, in turn, is enshrined in the processes and procedures of the quality assurance system. Follow the procedures and high-quality research will be produced. Independent thinkers, insightful researchers, and methodological innovators need not apply.

Although the extent of managerial control and legislative regulation is particularly exemplified in the DoH framework, the general trend is apparent across the social sciences, even being ensconsed in (mandatory) guidelines issues by the UK's Economic and Social Research Council (ESRC), a quasi-independent "arm's length" agency that funds individual research student and research grant applications.

The ESRC is the most prestigious body from which social science researchers can secure funds in the United Kingdom and has traditionally been associated with funding "blue skies" research in response to individual proposals. However, it has attracted criticism recently because much of its current funding has been awarded for research projects within predefined themes and programs (Commission on the Social Sciences, 2003, p. 54). Moreover, the ESRC's recently issued "Research Ethics Framework" not only expects individual projects to be conducted according to ethical guidelines (as they should), but also expects grant-holding institutions that employ researchers to have "proper ... oversight ... of ethical research governance ... and [ ] ... arrangements to ensure ... that its research complies with this Framework" (ESRC, 2005a, pp. 1–2).

The guidelines go on to assert that "research governance concerns the development of shared standards and mechanisms that permit proper management and monitoring of research" (ESRC, 2005a, p. 23), and that "researchers and research organisations should ensure that appropriate governance procedures and mechanisms are in place to oversee social science research" (p. 26). If this is not the case, and is not confirmed in writing, no funds will be released irrespective of any individual proposal securing funds and de facto being assessed by ESRC as of the highest social scientific quality.

Similarly, for departments to be "recognized" by the ESRC for receipt of studentship grants, the ESRC Research Training Guidelines require "generic training in research methods" (ESRC, 2005b, p. 7), including "general research skills and transferable employment-related skills" (p. 18) and "research management skills" (p. 21). In general terms, such requirements might be considered to be perfectly reasonable, but again, they assume research concentration, critical mass and the privileging of research management over excellence in a specific theoretical or substantive field. Small units with specific strengths in a particular area will not be recognized for receipt of studentships, unless they develop a generic training program, even though they may be exactly the right place for particular students to be located. There is a recurrent and discursive disciplinary process at work here (Foucault, 1975).

Quality Control in Qualitative Research?

Some argue further, that one particular approach to the design and conduct of research is and should indeed be preeminent— that of randomized control trials (Oakley, 2000, 2003). This is

at the heart of the push for the development of so-called systematic reviews of previous research and the evidence-based practice
movement (Gough and Elbourne, 2002; Oakley, 2003). Such
arguments are not without significant and influential critics (e.g.,
Hammersley, 2001; MacLure, 2005), but in resisting the "one
best method" argument, the debate about quality has started to
invade the research community itself as a fear of marginalization (and the concomitant exclusion from resources as indicated
above) seems to have generated a sense of "better do it to ourselves
before they do it to us." The NRC reports in the United States
(2002, 2005) and indeed the various ESRC guidelines seem to be
examples of this tendency.

With respect to qualitative research, Hammersley (2005)
himself, in a recent article, argues that some discussion of what
should count as appropriate governance of educational research
is required. Meanwhile, the ESRC has also produced a report
on Assessing Quality in Applied and Practice-Based Research"
(Furlong & Oancea, 2005), which will be used by the Education Subject Panel in the next RAE. At the same time, government agencies as diverse as the devolved Welsh Assembly and the
UK Cabinet Office have sponsored reviews of how to evaluate
action research (Welsh Assembly, 2003) and qualitative evaluation (Cabinet Office, 2003a, 2003b).

The Cabinet Office report is particularly interesting and illumi-
nating, given the argument so far. Independent academics based
at the National Centre for Social Research (a not-for-profit organization) were commissioned by the Strategy Unit of the Cabinet
Office to produce a "framework for assessing research evidence"
with respect to qualitative evaluation (Cabinet Office, 2003a).
The rationale seems to have been that government departments
are increasingly commissioning policy evaluations in the context
of the move toward evidence-informed policy and practice and
that guidelines for judging the quality of qualitative approaches
and methods were necessary.

The report is in two parts: a seventeen-page summary, including the quality framework (Cabinet Office, 2003a), and a 167-
page full report (Cabinet Office, 2003b), including discussion of
many of the issues raised by the framework. One presumes it is

the short summary report that is expected to get the most attention—especially from policymakers and civil servants commissioning research on behalf of their departments. The summary report states that the framework has been "designed primarily to assess the outputs of qualitative enquiry ... and.... It is also hoped that the framework will have a wider educational function in the preparation of research protocols, the conduct and management of research and evaluation and the training of social researchers" (Cabinet Office, 2003a, summary report, p. 6, emphasis in original).

So, the framework is a guide for the commissioners of research when drawing up tender documents, managing the research, and reading reports. But it also has ambitions to influence the training of social researchers, a particularly noteworthy ambition given our previous discussion of the centralizing tendencies of government. Also, of course, if it becomes apparent that research commissioners are indeed using the framework to write tenders and evaluate proposals, then the framework will certainly influence the response of social researchers to tenders.

The full report claims that "there are no explicitly agreed standards regarding what constitutes quality in qualitative policy evaluation methods and no agreed criteria for judging the quality of qualitative evaluation research" (Cabinet Office, 2003b, p. 10). It continues that the report was commissioned to "address the need for agreed standards" (p. 10). One wonders who has decided that there is such a need. There are many good reasons why nearly a hundred years of debate about anthropology, ethnography, and the development of qualitative research methodology has not yet produced such agreement. Indeed, it is not at all clear that this is desirable, even if it were possible. Perhaps just as important, the discursive implication of these phrases is that social scientists have been somehow remiss in their lack of attention to standards and quality in qualitative research. Nothing could be further from the truth as library shelves full of methodology texts remind us—the 1,200-page revised edition of Denzin and Lincoln (2005) being one of the most recent additions.

One could argue, as Hammersley (2005) does, that diversity brings fragmentation and is a weakness in current circumstances.

Similarly, not everything that is published is of high quality or informatively presented. Many individual research reports and articles can be found wanting, but over time they disappear and what is left to be debated in the public domain are enduring findings and understandings, often at the level of theory and methodology, rather than particular substantive issues and topics that inevitably change over time. In arguing that some method of quality assurance other than, or in addition to, peer review should be put in place—national standards, systematic review, research governance, or whatever—proponents of such arguments in the end are only arguing for a different group of researchers (or civil servants) to make decisions about quality—there is no ultimate one best disinterested standard.

To return to the Cabinet Office framework, there is not space here to review the full report in detail. Suffice it to say that it reads like an introductory text on qualitative research methods. Paradigms are described and issues rehearsed, but all are resolved in a bloodless, technical, and strangely old-fashioned counsel of perfection. The reality of doing qualitative research and indeed of conducting evaluation, with all the contingencies, political pressures, and decisions that have to be made, is completely absent. Thus, in addition to the obvious need for "Findings/conclusions [to be] supported by data/evidence" (Cabinet Office, 2003b, full report, p. 22), qualitative reports should also include:

> Detailed description of the contexts in which the study was conducted (p. 23); Discussions of how fieldwork methods or settings may have influenced data collected (p. 25);

> Descriptions of background or historical developments and social/organizational characteristics of study sites (p. 25);

> Description and illumination of diversity/multiple perspectives/alternative positions (p. 26);

> Discussion/evidence of the ideological perspectives/values/philosophies of the research team (p. 27).

And so on and so forth across six pages and seventeen quality "appraisal questions."

No one would deny that these are important issues for social researchers to take into account in the design, conduct, and reporting of research studies. However, with government departments being unlikely to fund long-term ethnographic studies (or read 500-page reports), what we have here is a huge hostage to fortune, where short, sharp, potentially flawed studies, which nevertheless come up with findings that the government likes will be acceptable, but where, if the findings are not liked, we now have a framework on which their sponsors can test them to destruction.

To be fair, the authors state that the "framework is designed to aid the informed judgement of quality ... not to be prescriptive or to encourage the mechanistic following of rules" (Cabinet Office, 2003b, full report, p. 7). And the "quality indicators" noted above are defined as "possible features for consideration" (p. 22, ff). Thus, it might be argued that if qualitative social and educational research is going to be commissioned, then a set of standards that can act as a bulwark against commissioning inadequate and/or underfunded studies in the first place ought to be welcomed.

To try, further, to be fair to the authors, it might be also be argued that this document at least demonstrates that qualitative research is being taken seriously enough within government to warrant a guide book being produced for civil servants. This might then be said to confer legitimacy on civil servants who want to commission more exploratory qualitative work, on qualitative social researchers bidding for such work, and indeed on social researchers more generally, who may have to deal with local ethics committees who are predisposed toward a more quantitative natural science model of investigation (especially in health-related studies from where, interestingly, most of the references derive). But should we really welcome such "legitimacy"? The dangers on the other side of the argument, as to whether social scientists need or should accede to criteria of quality endorsed by the state, are legion. Indeed, one of the key quotes used to justify the use of qualitative methods comes not from the epistemological or methodological literature, but from a departmental "research manager":

> I often commission qualitative research when it's about users or stakeholders and ... I want to understand ... how a user is likely to respond.... I want to know how they see the world...it's a wonderful vehicle ... if you want to understand the motives of people. [Cabinet Office, 2003b, full report, p. 34]

Although it can be argued that policy and its evaluation will benefit from being grounded in such data, it is equally the case that such evidence could be used to monitor compliance. Evaluation requires that policy and policymakers are themselves subject to scrutiny, not that (qualitative) social research methods are simply used to provide data for the powerful.

Many more detailed criticisms of the report could be made, but perhaps the most significant is that the authors finally hoist themselves on their own petard when, employing the worst kind of qualitative generalizations, they claim that their framework has "a fair degree of support" (Cabinet Office, 2003b, p. 43) and that "there was a general view that formalised criteria would be of value" (p. 101). Such statements are based on twenty-nine interviews with social researchers and research commissioners (p. 12) out of the thousands who work in the United Kingdom (1,056 in the sociology "unit of assessment" alone, as returned in the last RAE http://www.hero.ac.uk/rae/overview). We do not know how these interviewees were selected, but clearly their views cannot be said to be representative of the social and educational research community as a whole. Were the framework actually to have been used by civil servants in the Cabinet Office to evaluate itself, such statements would not have seen the light of day: early evidence that when a report legitimates policy, it will be published whether it is of high quality or not.

The main point here, however, is that of the seduction or cooption of supposedly independent researchers to the agenda of government, which revolves around centralization of control, establishment of supposedly agreed quality criteria, and the transferring of decision making about what counts as quality in research from the crucible of open, scholarly debate to the closed meeting rooms of the research management group and the ethics committee or institutional review board. Not only are the criteria by which quality might be judged being changed, so, too, are the very social relations of research. How we conceptualize and think about the research process and its relationship to power is being reconstructed.

Discussion and Conclusion

As noted above, implicit and explicit claims about quality in qualitative research are routinely exemplified and interrogated in research methods texts—this is not an argument about there being no criteria or no need for debate—quite the reverse: keeping the debate open is my concern. Likewise, my claims about the unwarranted growth of managerialism in research are not uncontentious. Some would argue that how we conceptualize and think about the research process and its relationship to power should be changed.

Much of the literature of the evidence-based practice movement argues that the interventions of professionals in peoples' lives (students, patients, etc.) should be based on an agreed knowledge base, not simply on enduring taken-for-granted professional practice, or anecdote or fashion (Gough & Elbourne, 2002; NRC, 2005; Oakley, 2003; U.S. Department of Education, 2003). This returns us to the Thatcherite argument about the self-serving nature of the professions referred to above. Many empowerment theorists would argue similarly, if not on exactly the same grounds or toward exactly the same conclusions (see Tuhiwai Smith, 2005). The ESRC report on identifying quality criteria in applied research (Furlong & Oancea, 2005) draws attention to enduring debates about the role of science in society. It quotes approvingly that Gibbons et al.'s (1994) articulation of "Mode 2 Knowledge" is informed by "a diverse range of intellectual interests, as well as other social, economic or political ones" (p. 8) and is "characterised by a context of application, transdisciplinarity, heterogeneity, social accountability, flexibility and permeability of institutional boundaries" (Furlong & Oancea, 2005, p. 11).

Thus, "quality is determined by a wider set of criteria which reflects the broadening social composition of the review system" (Gibbons et al., 1994, p. 8) and "social robustness does not rely on methodological guarantees only" (Furlong & Oancea, 2005, p. 11). Here we have a sort of quasi-Lyotardian argument for the demotion of methodology and science qua science as the determining arbitrational discourse of knowledge production and legitimation (Lyotard, 1978). This is the seductive element of contemporary debates—the status quo of researchers alone deciding what research is and what researchers should do, is no longer tenable. And yet such critical arguments stand alongside and unwittingly and/or unwillingly have supported the parallel emergence of much narrower positions on what counts as science. Complexity intrigues some, but frightens others (especially, it seems, policymakers) and presently appears to have given rise to a retreat into methodological orthodoxy and centralized, bureaucratic managerialism. Nothing could be further from the innovative, flexible, knowledge-creating research activity that our policymakers supposedly crave; nevertheless, risk-aversion and managerial control seem to be winning out over curiosity and critique.

Thus, there is a trend toward centralization of the control of social research and the defining of quality in terms of governance and management. This has been an emergent tendency over a long period with respect to the agenda of social and educational research—for example, the move toward involving users, including government departments, in determining topics of enquiry in the context of the evidence-based policy and practice movement. Current developments seem to go further than this, however, in trying to fix and standardize particular methods and ensconce them in a quality-assurance system that is predicated on management and compliance. The assumption underpinning different documents produced in different circumstances and, indeed, in different countries, seems to be that researchers cannot be trusted to conduct research without guidelines, frameworks, and management systems produced by the state. Researchers are assumed to be public service employees who must serve, and be managed by, their political masters in the now economically crucial knowledge-production industry.

In some respects, as noted above, this is not surprising and might simply be considered to be a manifestation of the wider development of low-trust accountability-driven public sector management systems. After all, most researchers are, at least indirectly, public servants in that their resources largely derive from public (taxation based) funding. Quality, utility, and accountability are not unimportant issues, but neither can they be resolved by central diktat. New knowledge, new methods, and new ways of thinking are not likely to emerge from closely controlled policy-oriented applied research. A key issue at present, therefore, is whether and in what ways educational researchers should engage with an increasingly narrow discourse on quality in educational and social research. It is now almost axiomatic that quality must be improved by control, management, and audit rather than by debate: it must be centrally defined and imposed rather than continually produced and revisited through the juxtaposition and testing of ideas. But quality can never be guaranteed by systems, only pursued through critique and deliberation. The current discourse is about control, not quality, and any engagement with it must hold it to account in these terms.

Notes

1. This chapter is based on a paper originally presented to the First International Congress of Qualitative Inquiry, University of Illinois at Urbana-Champaign, May 5–5, 2005. Correspondence should be addressed to h.torrance@mmu.ac.uk

2. I use the term "state" with respect to its general meaning in political science, rather than with specific reference to states in a federal system such as the United States.

References

Ball, S. (2001). You've been NERFed! Dumbing down the academy: National Educational Research Forum consultation paper: A brief and bilious response. *Journal of Educational Policy, 16*(3), 265–268.

Boaz, A., & Ashby, D. (2003). Fit for purpose? Assessing research quality for evidence-based policy and practice. *ESRC Centre for Evidence-Based Policy and Practice Working Paper 11*, QMC, University of London.

Bridges, D. (2005). The international and the excellent in educational research. Paper prepared for the Challenges of the Knowledge Society for Higher Education conference, Kaunus, Lithuania, December 16.

Brown, S. (2003). Assessment of research quality: What hope of success? Keynote address to European Educational Research Association annual conference, Hamburg, Germany, September 17.

Cabinet Office. (2003a). *Quality in qualitative evaluation: A framework for assessing research evidence. A quality framework* (summary report). London: Cabinet Office.

Cabinet Office (2003b) *Quality in qualitative evaluation: A framework for assessing research evidence* (full report). London, Cabinet Office

Cochran-Smith, M., & Fries, M. (2001). Sticks, stones and ideology: The discourse of reform in teacher education. *Educational Researcher, 30*(8), 3–15.

Commission on the Social Sciences. (2003). *Great expectations: The social sciences in Britain*. London: Academy of Learned Societies for the Social Sciences.

Denzin, N. K., & Lincoln, Y. S. (Eds.). (2005). *Handbook of qualitative research* (3rd ed.). Thousand Oaks, CA: Sage.

Department for Education and Skills (DfES). (2003). *The future of higher education* London: DfES.

Department of Health (DoH). (2001/2005). *Research governance framework for health and social care*. London: Department of Health.

Economic and Social Research Council (ESRC). (2005a). *Research ethics framework*. Swindon, UK: ESRC.

Economic and Social Research Council (ESRC). (2005b). *Postgraduate training guidelines: ESRC recognition of research training programmes* (4th ed.). Swindon, UK: ESRC.

Feuer, M., Towne, L. & Shavelson, R. (2002). Scientific culture and educational research. *Educational Researcher, 31*(8), 4–14.

Foucault, M. (1975). *Discipline and punish*. New York: Vintage Books.

Furlong, J., and Oancea, A. (2005). *Assessing quality in applied and practice-based educational research*. Report of ESRC grant no. RES-618-25-6001. ESRC, Swindon. Report also available from the authors at University of Oxford, Department of Education.

Gibbons, M., Limoges, C., Nowotny, H., Schwartzman, S., Scott, P., & Trow, M. (1994). *The new production of knowledge: The dynamics of science and research in contemporary societies*. Thousand Oaks, CA: Sage.

Gough, D., & Elbourne. D. (2002). Systematic research synthesis to inform policy, practice and democratic debate. *Social Policy and Society, 1*(3), 225–236.

Grayson, L. (2002). Evidence-based policy and the quality of evidence: Rethinking peer review. *ESRC Centre for Evidence-based Policy and Practice Working Paper 7*, QMC, University of London.

Hammersley, M. (2001). On systematic reviews of research literature: A narrative response. *British Educational Research Journal, 27*(4), 543–554.

Hammersley, M. (2005). Countering the "new orthodoxy" in educational research: A response to Phil Hodkinson. *British Educational Research Journal, 31*(2), 139–156.

Hargreaves, D. (1996). Teaching as research-based profession: Possibilities and prospects. TTA Annual Lecture, London: TTA.

Higher Education Funding Councils (HEFC). (2005). *RAE 2008: Guidance to panels.* Retrieved January 2005, from http://www.rae. ac.uk/pubs/2005/01/.

Hillage, J., Pearson, R., Anderson, A., & Tamkin, P. (1998). *Excellence in research on schools.* DfEE Research Report 74, London: DfEE.

Hodkinson, P. (2004). Research as a form of work: Expertise, community and methodological objectivity. *British Educational Research Journal, 30*(1), 9–26.

Lather, P. (2004). Scientific research in education: A critical perspective. *British Educational Research Journal, 30*(6), 759–772.

Lyotard, J. (1978). *The postmodern condition: A report on knowledge.* Manchester, UK: Manchester University Press.

MacLure, M. (2003). *Discourse in educational and social research.* Maidenhead, UK: Open University Press.

MacLure, M. (2005). Clarity bordering on stupidity: Where's the quality in systematic review? *Journal of Educational Policy, 20*(4), 393–416.

Middleton, S. (2005). Disciplining researchers: Teacher educators, professional identity and New Zealand's first research assessment exercise. Paper presented at the annual conference of the British Educational Research Association, University of Glamorgan, UK, September 14–17.

National Educational Research Forum (NERF). (2000). *Research and development for Education.* London: NERF/DfES.

National Research Council (NRC). (2002). *Scientific research in education.* Washington, DC: National Academy Press.

National Research Council (NRC). (2005). *Advancing scientific research in education.* Washington, DC: National Academy Press.

Oakley, A. (2000). *Experiments in knowing.* Cambridge, UK: Polity Press.

Oakley, A. (2003). Research evidence, knowledge management and educational practice: Early lessons from a systematic approach. *London Review of Education, 1*(1), 21–33.

Oancea, A. (2005). Criticisms of educational research: Key topics and levels of analysis. *British Educational Research Journal, 31*(2), 157–184.

Social Care Institute for Excellence (SCIE). (2004). *Improving the use of research in social care practice.* Bristol, UK: Policy Press.

Tooley, J. & Darby, D. (1998). *Educational research: A critique.* London: OfSTED.

Tuhiwai Smith, L. (2005). On tricky ground: Researching the native in the age of uncertainty. In N. K. Denzin & Y. S. Lincoln (Eds), *Handbook of qualitative research* (3rd ed., pp. 85–108). Thousand Oaks, CA: Sage.

U.S. Department of Education. (2003). *Identifying and implementing educational practices supported by rigorous evidence: A user-friendly guide.* Washington, DC: U.S. Department of Education.

Welsh Assembly. (2003). *A review of the nature of action research.* Cardiff: Welsh Assembly.

Woodhead, C. (1998). Academia gone to seed. *New Statesman*, March 20, pp. 51–52.

Yates, L. (2004). *What is quality in educational research?* Maidenhead, UK: Open University Press.

Yates, L. (2005). Is impact a measure of quality? Producing quality research and producing quality indicators of research in Australia. Keynote address for AARE conference on Quality in Educational Research: Directions for Policy and Practice, Cairns, Australia, July.

Part Two
Decolonizing Methodologies

Chapter 8 | Choosing the Margins

The Role of Research in Indigenous Struggles for Social Justice

Linda Tuhiwai Smith
University of Auckland

Introduction

Ka whawhai tonu matou, ake, ake, ake—
We will fight on for ever and ever.
—Rewi Maniapoto, 1864

A nineteenth-century prophecy by a Maori leader predicted that the struggle of Maori people against colonialism would go on forever and therefore the need to resist will be without end. This may appear to be a message without hope, but it has become an exhortation to Maori people that our survival, our humanity, our world-view and language, our imagination and spirit, our very place in the world depends on our capacity to act for ourselves, to speak for ourselves, to engage in the world and the actions of our colonizers, to face them head on. Maori struggles for social justice in New Zealand are messy, noisy, simultaneously celebratory and demoralizing, hopeful and desperate. Although there have been incremental gains, they have often been made from the depths of despair, accepted reluctantly as the crumbs of compromise.

The demands on scholars and intellectuals in similar contexts have been discussed in the revolutionary texts by writers such as Gramsci and Fanon, in feminist and indigenist literature, and in research texts. In the research literature, the issues are often discussed in terms of the methodologies, ethics, theoretical and discursive representations, emancipatory possibilities, and power relations associated with studying marginalized and vulnerable communities, the outsider Other, or within specific populations and communities such as urban youth.

Qualitative researchers are trained to "see things." Researchers working in the field of social injustice witness or see things that may impact directly on their own relationships, identities, safety, and freedom. Speaking for, and speaking out, can land a researcher in considerable trouble; being "named" as a leftist researcher or native sympathizer is likewise a risk that is carried even in societies that value freedom of speech and of academic discovery. In these conservative times, the role of an indigenous researcher and of other researchers committed to producing research knowledge that documents social injustice, recovers subjugated knowledges, helps create spaces for the voices of the silenced to be expressed and "listened to," and challenges racism, colonialism, and oppression is a risky business.

This chapter is written from that messy intersection, from the borders of the vast and expanding territory that is the margin, that exists "outside" the security zone, outside the gated and fortified community. The first part of the chapter revisits Chandra Mohanty's (1991) cartography of struggles, as faced by indigenous and marginalized communities. The purpose is to provide a sense of the landscape that researchers negotiate and seek to understand. In this first part, the chapter emphasizes the notion of struggle and what it means to live a life in struggle. The second part examines some of the implications for indigenous researchers who choose to work in indigenous and marginalized communities, communities that are in engaged struggle. These researchers work the borders, betwixt and between institutions and communities, systems of power and systemic injustice, cultures of dominance and cultures in survival mode, politics and theory, theory and practice.

Revisiting the Concept of Struggle

Struggle, as many social activists have identified, is an important tool in the overthrow of oppression and colonialism. Struggle is a dynamic, powerful, and important tool that is embedded in what at first glance often seems to be just part of the apparatus of Marxist rhetoric and radical discourse. In its Marxist revolutionary sense, the concept of struggle can also be associated with forms of psychological torture and political haranguing, as individuals are coerced into losing their memories of a past regime or into informing on their family and friends.

In its broader sense, struggle is simply what life feels like when people are trying to survive in the margins, to seek freedom and better conditions, to seek social justice. Struggle is a tool of both social activism and theory. It has the potential to enable oppressed groups to embrace and mobilize agency and to turn the consciousness of injustice into strategies for change. Struggle can be mobilized as resistance and as transformation. It can provide the means for working things out "on the ground," for identifying and solving problems of practice, for identifying strengths and weaknesses, for refining tactics and uncovering deeper challenges.

But struggle can also be a blunt tool. As a blunt tool, it has often privileged patriarchy and sexism in indigenous activist groups or been used to commit groups to modes of operation that undermine the very values they espouse and expect of others. As a blunt instrument, struggle can also promote actions that simply reinforce hegemony and that have no chance of delivering significant social change.

Paolo Freire's model of change argues that conscientization leads to action or struggle; when people learn to read the word (of injustice) and read the world (of injustice) they will act against injustice. However, Graham Smith (2004) has argued that in the Maori context, participation in struggle can, and often does, come before a raised consciousness. Smith's research has shown that people often participated in struggles more to show solidarity with friends and family, or some other pragmatic motivation, than as a personal commitment to or knowledge about historical oppression, colonialism, and the survival of Maori people. Along the way, many of those people become more conscious of the politics of struggle in which they are engaged. As Smith points out, "Maori experience tends to suggest that these elements, [conscientisation, resistance, transformative action], may occur in any order and indeed may occur simultaneously" (p. 51).

Struggle, then, can be viewed as group or collective agency rather than as individual consciousness. The political leaders of struggle need some form of collective consent or mandate to act and to sustain action over time. The story of struggle is also a story about activist leadership and collective consent and the tension between these two processes (leading and consenting). It is in this area that much revolutionary literature tends to focus on the hegemonic role of intellectuals who occupy the establishment and their power to influence others and command over what counts as legitimate knowledge.

Struggle is also a theoretical tool for understanding agency and social change, for making sense of power relations, and for interpreting the tension between academic views of political actions and activist views of the academy. Theorizing the politics, psychology, and pedagogy of struggle is the role of activist scholars and the organic intellectuals who work in that intersection between the community and the academy. It often presents itself as a phenomenon that researchers "see" when they see communities living on the edge and in crisis; when they attempt to interpret or make ethnographic sense of life in the margin; when they attempt to account for behaviors, attitudes, value systems; and when they attempt comparisons with their own communities and social class. People, families, and organizations in marginalized communities struggle every day; it is a way of life that is necessary for survival and, when theorized and mobilized, can become a powerful strategy for transformation.

Multiple Layers of Struggle

The Maori struggle for decolonization is multilayered and multidimensional and has occurred across multiple sites simultaneously. Graham Smith (2004) has argued that theorizing this struggle from a Maori framework of Kaupapa Maori has provided important insights about transformation, about how transformation works and can be made to work for indigenous communities. Similarly, Leonie Pihama (2005) writes that, "Kaupapa Maori is a transformative power. To think and act in terms of Kaupapa Maori while experiencing colonisation is to resist dominance." In this section, I focus more on the conditions that intersect or are external to this transformative process and that, at times, can work for or against change, can destabilize the struggle or can present opportunities to be exploited, can provide creative resources, or can unleash a counterhegemonic and narrow agenda of change.

I conceptualize five conditions or dimensions that have framed the struggle for decolonization. I define the first as a critical consciousness, an awakening from the slumber of hegemony and the realization that action has to occur. I define the second condition as a way of reimagining the world and our position as Maori within the world, drawing on a different epistemology and unleashing the creative spirit. This condition is what enables an alternative vision, it fuels the dreams of alternative possibilities. The third is concerned with ways in which different ideas, social categories, and tendencies intersect, the coming together of disparate ideas, the events, the historical moment. This condition creates opportunities, it provides the moments where tactics can be deployed. The fourth I have defined simply as movement or disturbance, the distracting counterhegemonic movements or tendencies, the competing movements that transverse sites of struggle, the unstable movements that occur when the status quo is disturbed. The fifth is the concept of structure, the underlying code of imperialism, of power relations. This condition is grounded in reproducing material realities and legitimating inequalities and marginality.

What I am suggesting by privileging these layers over others is that separately, together, and in combination with other ideas, these five dimensions help map the conceptual terrain of struggle. The categorical terms being used are not of the same type and have not been motivated by a particular "model." Rather, they reflect the multiple positions, spaces, discourses, languages, histories, textures, and world-views that are being contested, struggled over, resisted, and reformulated by Maori.

In writing a "cartography" of the struggles facing Third World women, Chandra Mohanty (1991) has said that "the world (is) transversed with intersecting lines." Along such intersecting lines are ideas, categories, or tensions that often connect with each other in different ways. They are not necessarily oppositions or dualisms. They create and are created by conditions that are inherently unstable, arbitrary and uncontrollable. She also argued that one of the key features of struggle is the "simultaneity" of oppressions that are fundamental to the experience of social and political marginality. Intersections can be conceptualized as lines that intersect or meet other lines and also as spaces that are created at the points where intersecting lines meet. Spaces created by intersecting ideas, tendencies, or issues are sites of struggle that offer possibilities for people to resist.

Making space within such sites has become a characteristic of many Maori struggles in education, health, research, and social justice. What is slightly different between this notion and the idea of struggles in the margins is that, when attached to a political idea such as *rangatiratanga*, often translated as sovereignty or self-determination, then all space in New Zealand can be regarded as Maori space. This takes the struggle out of specifically "Maori contexts" and into the spaces once regarded as the domain of the "settler" or Pakeha community, such as large institutions like universities, where Maori really are a small minority. Rather than see ourselves as existing in the margins as minorities, resistance initiatives have assumed that Aotearoa New Zealand is "our place," all of it, and that there is little difference, except in the mind, between, for example, a Te Kohanga Reo, where Maori are the majority but the state is there, and a university, where there are Maori are the minority and the state is there.

Whereas we can conceive of space geographically and politically, it is important to claim those spaces that are still taken for granted as being possessed by the West. Such spaces are concerned with intellectual, theoretical, and imaginative spaces. One of these is a space called Kaupapa Maori. This concept has emerged from lessons learned through Te Kohanga Reo and Kura Kaupapa Maori and has been developed as a theory in action by Maori people. Graham Smith (1995) has argued for Kaupapa Maori as an intervention into theoretical spaces, particularly within the sphere of education. Kaupapa Maori research refers to Maori struggles to claim research as a space within which Maori can also operate. Given the history of the Western research gaze of indigenous peoples, it may seem unusual that Maori should take hold of the idea of research and attempt to apply it to our own questions. There are imperatives that have forced that on us, such as the constant need to prove our own history and to prove the worth of our language and values.

Maori and other indigenous peoples, however, also have their own questions and curiosities; they have imaginations and ways of knowing that they seek to expand and apply. Searching for solutions is very much part of a struggle to survive, it is represented within our own traditions, for example, through creation stories, values, and practices. The concept of "searching" is embedded in our world-views. Researching in this sense, then, is not something owned by the West, or by an institution or discipline. Research begins as a social, intellectual, and imaginative activity. It has become disciplined and institutionalized with certain approaches empowered over others and accorded a legitimacy but it begins with human curiosity and a desire to solve problems. It is, at its core, an activity of hope.

One of the criticisms made of educators who have been concerned about the emancipatory potential of schooling is that they have often ignored or diminished the role in social agency of such qualities as hope, optimism, and the need to strive for utopian goals. As summarized by McLaren (1995):

> Some radical educators have, in fact, argued that the notion of hope as the basis of a language of possibility is really nothing more than a "trick of counter hegemony," and that hope is employed for ideological effect rather than for sound theoretical reasons. In other words hope as a vision of possibility contains no immanent political project and as such has to be sacrificed on the altar of empirical reality. [p. 121]

I have stated previously the sense of noisy optimism that has been a characteristic of Maori politics. Here, I argue for the importance in Maori struggles of the imagination and of the capacity shown by Maori to constantly imagine and reimagine, to create and recreate our world. The capacity of colonized peoples to continue to imagine and to create our own worlds was the focus of quite systematic imperial and colonial practices that are encapsulated in the concept of dehumanization. The dehumanizing tendencies within imperial and colonial practices are deeply encoded. They constantly deny that colonized people actually have ideas of our own, can create new ideas, and have a rich knowledge base from which to draw.

I would not claim that, on its own, imagination is a critical tool or contains within it a political project that is connected inherently to emancipation. What I would argue is that if they are to work, to be effective, political projects must also touch on, appeal to, make space for, and release forces that are creative and imaginative. This point is made in Smith's (1995) identification of the significant elements within Kaupapa Maori. He argues that the *kaupapa* has to "grab people" emotionally; it has to excite them and "turn them on" to new possibilities.

The danger in such forces is that they do not necessarily lead to emancipatory outcomes. They are inherently uncontrollable, which is possibly why this aspect is excluded from decolonization type programs and other attempts at planned resistance. However, there is a point in the politics of decolonization where leaps of imagination can connect the disparate, fragmented pieces of a puzzle, ones that have different shadings, different shapes, and different images within them, and say that "these pieces belong together." The imagination allows us to strive for goals that transcend material, empirical realities. For colonized peoples, this is important because the cycle of colonialism is just that: a cycle with no end point, no emancipation. The material locates us within a world of dehumanizing tendencies, one that is constantly reflected back on us. To imagine a different world is to imagine us as different people in the world. To imagine is to believe in different possibilities, ones that we can create.

Decolonization must offer a language of possibility, a way out of colonialism. The writing of Maori, of other indigenous peoples and of anti/postcolonial writers would suggest, quite clearly, that that language of possibility exists within our own alternative, oppositional ways of knowing. Even though these may not be seen to connect with current socioeconomic realities, the fact that we adhere to, that we can imagine a connection suggests a resistance to being classified according to the definitions of a dominant group. Furthermore, the language of possibility, a language that can be controlled by those who have possession of it, allows us to make plans, to make strategic choices, to theorize solutions. Imagining a different world, or reimagining the world, is a way into theorizing why the world as it currently is is unjust and posing alternatives to such a world from within our own world-views.

Implications for Researchers: Choosing the Margins

The metaphor of the margin has been a very powerful metaphor in the social sciences and humanities for understanding social inequality, oppression, disadvantage, and power. It is used alongside other similar concepts such borders, boundaries, bridges, center-periphery, and insider/outsider to demarcate people in spatial terms as well as in socioeconomic, political, and cultural ones. Anthropology uses the term "liminal" to capture some of the elements that are lived by people in the margins. Gloria Ladson-Billings (2000) uses the term in this way, "Thus the work of the liminal perspective is to reveal the ways that dominant perspectives distort the realities of the other in an effort to maintain power relations that continue to disadvantage those who are locked out of the mainstream" (p. 259).

Feminists and minority scholars (such as African American writers) have worked the metaphor of the margin, the hyphen, or the border into social theories of oppression and marginalization and of resistance and possibility (Fine, 1992; hooks, 1984). Gloria Anzaldúa (1987), for example, writes of the border where she grew up literally at the border between the United States and Mexico and figuratively at the border and intersection between languages, between home and school, between having and not having, and as a site for positive identity formation. African American writer bell hooks (1984) wrote of the radical possibility of "choosing the margins" as a site of belonging as much as a site of struggle and resistance.

The critical issue hooks and other writers such as Stuart Hall have identified is that meaningful, rich, diverse, interesting lives are lived in the margins; these are not empty spaces occupied by people whose lives don't matter or people who spend their lives on the margins trying to escape. Many groups who end up there choose the margins, in the sense of creating cultures and identities out of the margins (for example, the deaf community, gay and lesbian communities, minority ethnic groups, and indigenous groups).

There are also researchers, scholars, and academics who actively choose the margins, who choose to study people marginalized by society, who themselves have come from the margins, or who see their intellectual purpose as being scholars who will work for, with, and alongside communities who occupy the margins of society. If one is interested in society, then it is often in the margins that aspects of a society are revealed as microcosms of the larger picture or as examples of a society's underbelly. In a research sense, having a commitment to social justice, to changing the conditions and relations that exists in the margins is understood as being "socially interested" or as having a "standpoint."

For researchers who come from the communities concerned, it may also be understood as "insider" research. Kaupapa Maori research can be understood in this way as an approach to research that is socially interested, that takes a position, for example, that Maori language, knowledge, and culture are valid and legitimate, and has a standpoint from which research is developed, conducted, analyzed, interpreted, and assessed. Some of these approaches are also referred to as critical research, as social justice research and as community action research. There are also specific methodologies that have been developed out of the work these approaches have initiated. Participatory action research, Kaupapa Maori research, oral histories, critical race theory, and *testimonio* are just some examples of methodologies that have been created as research tools that work with marginalized communities, that facilitate the expression of marginalized voices, and that attempt to represent the experience of marginalization in genuine and authentic ways.

Focusing on researching with marginalized groups foregrounds many of the issues that are faced by researchers working in the face of inequality and social injustice. As leading researchers in the social justice area have already established, it is crucial that researchers working in this critical research tradition pay particular attention to matters that impact on the integrity of research and the researcher, are continuously developing their understandings of ethics and community sensibilities, and are critically examining their research practices (Cram, 2001; Denzin & Lincoln, 2000; Fine, 1992; Rigney, 1999).

A third dimension to doing research in the margins is that the researchers who choose to study with and for marginalized communities are often in the margins themselves in their own institutions, disciplines, and research communities. It may be that the researchers come from a minority social group or perhaps their interest in and perceived support for marginalized communities unsettles the status quo or questions both implicitly and explicitly dominant approaches to research. Regardless, there is ample literature from feminist and minority group scholars that shows that doing work with marginalized groups or about their concerns can have a significant negative impact on careers and therefore on the perceived expertise and intellectual authority of the researchers concerned.

Maori researchers and academics have also written of the impact of community needs and institutional demands on their work lives and approaches to work and life as a Maori person (A. Durie, 1995; Irwin, 1988). Although communities may want to work with a Maori researcher, they may be quite unaware of the risks that many academic researchers face when researching in the margins. Thus, communities have expectations that researchers should not be building their careers by studying "them," but researchers feel pressure from the academy to turn research into peer-reviewed publications. Increasingly, research is viewed as an activity that must be measured and assessed for quality as part of a researcher's performance, and an individual's performance is linked directly to a department's and institution's ranking. A researcher working for social justice is likely to be involved in hours of work that does not lead to a "quality" academic publication—they may contribute to major social change but their research ranking will not reflect their contribution to society.

There are also implications and risks for researchers who work within the insider frame. From one perspective, the known methodological risks are about the potential for bias, lack of distance, and lack of objectivity. From another research perspective, they are about the potential to see the trees but not the forest, to underplay the need for rigor and integrity as a researcher, and to mistake the research role with an advocacy role. There are other risks, however, in terms of the relationships and accountabilities to be carried by an insider researcher.

Unlike their colleagues, these extra responsibilities can be heavy, not just because of what people might say directly but because of what researchers imagine the community might be saying. It can be difficult, because of the magnitude and amount of urgent tasks that seem to require action and support. Researchers make strategic decisions to deal with the urgent, while sacrificing the research and ultimately their careers. Mentoring by other indigenous scholars who have made their way through the system can provide some support, although these senior scholars are few and far between and are not always the best exemplars themselves of how to balance a life and maintain research while working with communities to make a positive difference.

Many of the social issues and challenges that confront marginalized communities will also be part of the biography and social network of an insider indigenous researcher. Visiting relatives who are sick, looking after grandchildren or someone's teenage child, writing submissions, being the breadwinner for more than one household, being in constant mourning, having to rush home to deal with emergencies, and being at the constant call of a community are often very normal parts of life for an indigenous researcher who is also trying to make his or her way into a career. Although every researcher may claim to have similar responsibilities and at some point to have taken on similar burdens, there is a qualitative difference between the conditions of people living in marginalized communities and those in middle-class suburbia.

Marginalized Populations, Research, and Ethics

For researchers working with "human subjects or participants," the terms "marginalized and vulnerable peoples" appear in the literature in relation to research ethics. Marginalized populations are often described as groups who have little access to power (for example, women, ethnic minority groups, gay and lesbian communities, children and youth). Vulnerable populations are also marginalized from power but are considered particularly vulnerable because they have even less individual agency to provide informed consent. Vulnerable groups include prisoners, armed forces personnel, people who are mentally ill, children, some groups with disabilities, and groups who can be and are more likely to be vulnerable to coercion. The significant event from which Western sensibilities about research abuses with marginalized and vulnerable populations was heightened was the Holocaust and the research undertaken by Nazi doctors on Jewish, Roma (Gypsies), and other groups imprisoned in the death camps. The Nuremberg Code of Ethics emerged from this momentous legacy. According to David Weisstub (1998):

> The Nuremberg Legacy represents almost a mythic chapter in the history of understanding of research ethics... . Nuremberg is a distant collective memory. For most of us Nuremberg emerged as a code and a symbol both in its principles representing the foundations of civilized medical practice and research and in its symbolization of the triumph of the democratic ideal over fascism. [p. 217]

Code was formed from the ashes of the Holocaust through the Nuremberg Tribunal and was an attempt to ensure that the types of research carried out by Nazi scientists would never happen again. The code recognizes that there are likely to be groups of people who are especially vulnerable when it comes to research and that these groups would also most likely exist in the margins of society. It is also the first acknowledgment that there are some basic moral principles by which researchers must abide.

From an indigenous perspective, the Nuremberg Code came too late, as the history of research as exploitation was already embedded in European imperialism leading into the twentieth century. And for other groups of people such as women, African American males, and many indigenous communities, the existence of the Nuremberg Code has not prevented research abuses from occurring. A series of scandals have highlighted the ways in which marginalized and vulnerable groups continue to be exposed to unethical research. According to Tolich (2001), the Cervical Cancer Inquiry, which looked into New Zealand's "darkest hour" in research, came about primarily because of the efforts of two feminist investigators who persisted in their inquiries despite the blocks and barriers put before them by institutional and professional systems. It was only after the Cervical Cancer Inquiry that academic institutions in New Zealand were required by legislation (Statute 161 of the Education Act 1989) to institute policies and practices for conducting ethical research with human subjects.

The Nuremberg Code was later followed by the World Medical

Association Declaration of Helsinki in 1964 and, in the United States, by the Belmont Report in 1979. These three documents are referred to as landmarks in establishing a history of ethical research conduct (Sugarman, Mastrioni, Kahn, & Jeffrey, 1998). There is a difference, however, between professional ethics codes of practice that are essentially self-monitoring and voluntary, legislated, or officially regulated codes of practice. The Nuremberg Code has rarely been used in legal cases (Weisstub, 1998). The Helsinki Declaration is a professional voluntary code for medical practitioners who belong to the World Medical Association. The Belmont Report was an official report of the U.S. Department of Heath, Education and Welfare. What is known in the United States as The Common Rule is a set of federal policies adopted by the major U.S. agencies that conduct or fund research with human subjects.

In New Zealand, there are several legal instruments that cover aspects of ethical research with human subjects, including the Education Act 1989, the Human Rights Act 1999, the Health and Disability Services Human Rights Code, and the Health Information Privacy Code. The Treaty of Waitangi is also incorporated into research and ethics policies, and consultation with Maori communities is part of some institutions requirements when the research involves Maori participants. New Zealand also has a National Ethics Advisory Committee, a National Bioethics Committee, and other specialized committees that deal with single issues such as reproductive birth technologies.

Why is this background important when discussing issues that relate to indigenous peoples? There is one significant reason and three other contextual purposes. The significant reason is to establish the case history, in a sense, for why Maori as peoples need to be recognized as a marginalized group. The literature uses the word "populations" rather than "peoples," and there is a distinction in international law between these two terms. As a marginalized population, Maori are basically just another group or set of individuals and communities. As peoples, Maori have claims to self-determination. There is a risk that in fragmenting small groups of Maori into categories of marginalization and vulnerability we lose sight of the overall picture of Maori as an indigenous and marginalized people in New Zealand. The risk becomes especially important in discussions about the role of the Treaty of Waitangi in protecting Maori rights to develop as Maori and to be treated as equal citizens.

The contextual issues and history are important because research is an international activity conducted across the globe by researchers from different nations, institutions, disciplines, and approaches. The norms of research conduct are developed in this environment. Furthermore, legal precedents established in other Western jurisdictions such as the United States, Britain, Canada, and Australia have weight in the New Zealand context, especially if the issue is related to indigenous communities. Finally, science and technology are making rapid advances into areas that challenge existing notions of ethics on a broad scale, and Maori attempts to articulate and have recognized a different knowledge and ethical system are in a race against time. In this context, being better informed is an important protection.

On-Going Marginalization of Maori

Recent public discourses on the place of Maori and the Treaty of Waitangi position non-Maori as victims of discrimination because of the perceived extra special rights that Maori have to be consulted, to have our language and culture recognized, and to have Treaty of Waitangi protections built into legislation and policy frameworks. It would be quite fair to say that Maori have struggled a long time to make such inroads as part of making the Treaty of Waitangi "real" as the foundational instrument of the nation. Maori have also seen this process as being necessary to fulfill their visions of self-determination and to fulfill and benefit from the rights of citizenship.

It is this last point about citizenship that brings us back to the question of marginalization. In almost every social index, Maori are disproportionately represented as disadvantaged, even when statistical analyses control for class factors such as income levels. Furthermore, the long-term systemic nature of disadvantage has constituted patterns of participation by Maori people in society that are different from mainstream Pakeha norms and consequently tend to challenge taken-for-granted policies and practices of institutions. One obvious example is the impact of underachievement at secondary school, on adult second-chance learning, and on the average age of Maori in postgraduate education.

Maori participation rates in tertiary education is one of the highest in the Organisation for Economic Co-operation and Development, but the level at which Maori are participating is at a low second-chance level and is a direct consequence of the failure of schooling to deliver achievement to Maori. Many Maori students enter tertiary education through bridging programs, they tend to be older, they are more likely to be women, they tend to be part-time students in comparison to non-Maori, and it takes them much longer to complete a degree qualification. Furthermore, they have a disproportionately higher take-up rate for loans and because they are less likely on completion to move into higher-paying positions, they take longer to repay their loans. In sum, the pattern of participation in society reinforces disadvantage.

Whether one drives through New Zealand literally or as a figurative journey to understand social in/equality, Maori communities are on the margins of the economy and society. In the late 1980s, New Zealand began a significant neoliberal program of structural adjustment, of deregulation and reregulation of the economy and major reforms of education, health, and the welfare system (Kearns & Joseph, 1997; Kelsey, 1997; Moran, 1999).

The neoliberal agenda and the continuous process of reform has had a profound effect on New Zealand society; after two decades, it has produced a generation of young people for whom the neoliberal ideologies are normal and taken for granted. In education, neoliberalism is marked by a discourse of education as a marketplace with parents and students as consumers and clients, teachers and schools as self-managing providers of services, and curriculum knowledge as a commodity that can be traded in or traded up for social goodies such as well-being and social status.

The reform process redesigned the way schools were administered, redesigned the role of the principal government agency that was responsible for education, created a new agency to review and assess school performance, created a new curriculum framework, created a new qualifications framework and a new agency to accredit qualifications and institutions, created a user pays system for postsecondary education, and created a competitive environment through its funding arrangements. Private providers of postsecondary education and training were, until recently, able to compete with public institutions for public funding and aspire to attain degree-granting status.

In the neoliberal concept of the individual, Maori people in the 1980s presented a potential risk to the legitimacy of the new vision because Maori aspirations were deeply located in history, in cultural differences, and in the values of collectivity; even the Maori concept of family or whanau seemed threatening. When the neoliberal agenda was implemented, however, Maori communities were already embarked on their own educational revolution. The forward momentum of Maori development at that time has played a significant role in challenging the reform agenda to accommodate or at least attempt to make space for Maori aspirations. Jane Kelsey has argued that at times Maori were the only group in New Zealand society actually contesting the reforms in any serious way.

The development of Te Kohanga Reo sparked and continues to inspire the development of a range of Maori initiatives in education that have developed as alternative models within and outside the current system from early childhood to postsecondary tertiary education. The alternative models include Kura Kaupapa Maori, Maori language immersion schools that developed outside the state and were included as a separate category of education in the Education Amendment Act 1989 and Wananga or tribal degree-granting institutions that were also included as a category of the Education Amendment Act of 1989.

These alternatives were Maori-initiated institutions based on different conceptions of what education was about. They were community efforts that challenged the taken-for-granted hegemony of schooling and, as argued by Graham Smith (2000), revolutionized Maori thinking by demonstrating that Maori people could free their minds from the colonizer, and exercise agency in a purposeful, tactical, and constructive way. These educational alternatives did not begin with active state support, and even after they were included in legislation there was no supportive infrastructure to assist them. In the case of the Wananga, the three institutions took a claim to the Waitangi Tribunal related to capital expenditure. The tribunal ruled in their favor, and two of the Wananga have now settled their claim with the crown and have resources to develop their capital infrastructure.

I want to emphasize that the Maori development momentum was already in progress when the neoliberal reform process began. This meant that Maori had a platform for challenging those aspects of the reform process that seemed to threaten Maori development and a platform for engaging with the process in order to influence change.

This is not to say that the reform process welcomed Maori participation. On the contrary, Maori had to make serious demands to be included or to be heard. At times, overseas experts were brought in to dismiss Maori concerns or show how those concerns would be addressed by the new structures.

Nor can we say that Maori were particularly well organized or mobilized. In fact, the early reforms that privatized the state industries, such as forestry, created massive Maori unemployment and a high degree of community stress. The significance of the revolutionized thinking created by the development of Te Kohanga Reo was that in the absence of organized resistance, there was enough criticism to provide a counterhegemonic possibility and to have it voiced at every opportunity available. The point is that if Maori had been in disarray without any alternative models, the reform process would have run a different and likely a more devastating course. As it was, the reform process has had a disproportionately negative impact on Maori communities, widening disparities between Maori and non-Maori in educational achievement, health, and economic status.

What has become even clearer in the twenty-first century is the way in which policies aimed at Maori continue to resonate and recycle colonizing narratives. The discourse might change subtly, with terms shifting from Maori to *whanau, hapu, iwi,* to urban Maori and *iwi* Maori, and the unit of problem definition might change from tribes to *whanau,* from Maori women to Maori parents, from Maori providers to Maori consultants, but the underlying racialized tensions remain constant. The subtext is that Maori are responsible for their own predicament as a colonized people and that citizenship for Maori is a "privilege" for which we must be eternally grateful. Marginalization is a consequence of colonization, and the price for social inclusion is still expected to be the abandonment of being "Maori."

The impact of this sustained narrative on Maori is both a growing fragmentation within communities alongside a parallel urgency to redevelop and recenter ourselves around common baseline symbols and aspirations, for example, as in Mason Durie's three conceptualizations of "living as Maori, being a citizen of the world and Maori well-being and good health" (Durie, 2004, p. 66). The tension between fragmentation and coming together is an almost impossible situation and, in many cases, at our most vulnerable points, fractures occur, families fragment, core relationships between parents and children break down, and Maori people become alienated from themselves and from their extended families and communities.

It is neither accidental nor genetic that Maori mental health issues have risen dramatically in the last two decades so that they rank as one of the most important health issues for Maori. Marginalization as a process, as well as a state of affairs, impacts at multiple levels and sites.

Maori people are marginalized from mainstream New Zealand society. Some are able to choose the margins by embracing their Maori identities and participating in Maori society and culture. Some are alienated from Maori society. This occurs through a range of mechanisms or social, economic, and political processes. It may simply be that geographic distance from their home is a barrier to participation or that the loss of Maori language and culture is seen as a barrier. Some, by virtue of being institutionalized or enveloped into a system of care and protection, are removed from their social and cultural supports. Other groups (for example, those who have come together around a special interest) may find themselves excluded or alienated from existing Maori power structures but still function as Maori. Then there are probably those who are alienated from Maori and mainstream society (for example, people who have committed crimes against their own communities may never be welcomed back home; they have, in effect, been excluded from their own society).

Researchers in the Margins

As stated earlier, researchers who choose to do research in the margins are at risk of becoming marginalized themselves in their careers and workplaces. One strategy for overcoming this predicament is to embrace the work and commit to building a career from that place. As writers such as bell hooks and Gloria Anzaldúa have argued, the margins are also sites of possibilities that are exciting and "on the edge." Cultures are created and reshaped, people who are often seen by the mainstream as dangerous, unruly, disrespectful of the status quo, and distrustful of established institutions are also innovative; they are able to design their own solutions, they challenge research and society to find the right solutions.

Those who work in the margins need research strategies that enable them to survive, to do good research, to be active in building community capacities, to maintain their integrity, manage community expectations of them, and mediate their different relationships. Kaupapa Maori research developed out of this challenge. As Graham Smith, Leonie Pihama, and others who write in this tradition have emphasized, Kaupapa Maori research encourages Maori researchers to take being Maori as a given, to think critically and address structural relations of power, to build on cultural values and systems, and to contribute research back to communities that are transformative.

There are strategies that researchers can use that will enable them to build strong research relationships with different communities. There are also skills and principles that Maori researchers have learned through experience work well with Maori if practiced in sensitive and nuanced ways. These might be as simple as focusing on building good relationships and "showing one's face" as the first step in a relationship. But they are also about building networks of people who have stronger links into communities and building community capacities so that people can do the research themselves.

One of the anxieties that researchers may have is that when communities have the power to determine their own research they might not choose a Maori researcher even if they have all the right skills. That is a risk and a challenge. Many communities would want to choose the best researcher available or the researcher from their own community or area. Often their choice is brokered by a funding agency, more precisely a government-funding agency that may not know of Maori researchers or may not prefer a Maori researcher.

Experienced community organizations are also learning what they need from researchers, both Maori and non-Maori. In other indigenous contexts, some tribal nations in North America have protocols for researchers and their tribal structures have specialist research directors who manage all research on their nation. What is possibly very different in Aotearoa New Zealand is the growing capacity of Maori researchers across many different fields and disciplines. In the New Zealand context, Maori scholars can assemble quite large and multidisciplinary research collaborations, there are a growing number of independent Maori researchers working with communities, and there are funding agencies eager to support Maori research capacity development.

In what he calls a "sociology of absences," legal sociologist Boaventura de Sousa Santos (2004) calls for an ecology of knowledge/s that enables alternative ways of knowing and scientific knowledge to coexist and argues that there can be no global social justice without global cognitive justice. At the heart of this engagement in social justice and indigenous research are questions about knowledge, education, participation, and development. There are enduring questions about power relations, agency and structure, ethics and methodologies. Research is simply one site at which these issues intersect. Research is important because it is the process for knowledge production; it is the way we constantly expand knowledge. Research for social justice expands and improves the conditions for justice; it is an intellectual, cognitive, and moral project, often fraught, never complete but worthwhile.

References

Anzaldúa, G. (1987). *Borderlands/La Frontera: The new mestiza*. San Francisco: Aunt Lute.

Cram, F. (2001). Rangahau Maori: Tona tika, tona pono—The validity and integrity of Maori research. In M. Tolich (Ed.), *Research ethics in Aotearoa New Zealand* (pp. 35–52). Auckland: Pearson Education.

de Sousa Santos, B. (2004). World social forum: Toward a counter-hegemonic globalisation. In J. Sen, A. Anand, A. Escobar, & P. Waterman (Eds.), *The world social forum challenges empire* (pp. 235–245). New Delhi, India: Viveka.

Denzin, N. K., & Lincoln, Y. S. 2000. The discipline and practice of qualitative research. In N. Denzin. & Y. S. Lincoln (Eds.), *Handbook of qualitative research* (2nd ed., pp. 1–28). Thousand Oaks, CA: Sage.

Durie, A. (1995). Keeping an open mind: A challenge for Maori academics in a time of political change. Keynote address, Matawhanui Hui, Massey University, Palmerston North, New Zealand.

Durie, M. (2004). *Whaiora Maori health development*. Auckland: Oxford University Press.

Fine, M. (1992). *Disruptive voices*. Ann Arbor: University of Michigan Press.

hooks, b. (1984). *Feminist theory: From margin to center*. Boston: South End Press.

Irwin, K. (1988). Maori, feminist, academic. *Sites, 17*, 30–38.

Kearns, R. A., & Joseph, A. (1997). Restructuring health and rural communities in New Zealand. *Progress in Human Geography, 21*, 18–32.

Kelsey, J. (1997). *The New Zealand experiment*. Auckland: Auckland University Press.

Ladson-Billings, G. (2000). Racialised discourse and ethnic epistemologies. In N. K. Denzin & Y. S. Linclon (Eds.), *Handbook of qualitative research* (2nd ed., pp. 257–278). Thousand Oaks, CA: Sage.

Maniapoto, R. (1864). Retrieved from http://www.treatyofwaitangi.govt.nz/casestudies/waikatotainui.php

McLaren, P. (1995). *Critical pedagogy and predatory culture*. London: Routledge.

Mohanty, C. (1991). Cartographies of struggles: Third World women and the politics of feminism. In C. Mohanty, A. Russo, & L. Torres (Eds.), *Third World women and the politics of feminism* (pp.1–47). Bloomington: Indiana University Press.

Moran, W. (1999). Democracy and geography in the reregulation of New Zealand. In D. B. Knight & A. E. Joseph (Eds.), *Restructuring societies: Insights from the social sciences* (pp. 33-58). Ottawa, Canada: Carleton University Press.

Pihama, L. (2005). Asserting indigenous theories of change. In J. Baker (Ed.), *Sovereignty matters: Locations of contestation and possibility in indigenous struggles for self-determination* (pp. 191–210). Lincoln: University of Nebraska Press.

Rigney, D. (1999). Internationalization of an indigenous anticolonial cultural critique of research methodologies. A guide to indigenist research methodology and its principles. *Wicazo SA Review, Fall*, 109–121.

Smith, G. H. (1995). The cultural politics of making space. Seminar presentation, Winter Seminar Series, Education Department, University of Auckland, New Zealand.

Smith, G. H. (2000). Maori education: Revolution and transformative action. *Canadian Journal of Native Education*, 6, 57–72.

Smith, G. H. (2004). Mai i te maramatanga kit e putanga mai o te tahuritanga: From conscientization to transformation. *Journal of Educational Perspectives* (College of Education, University of Hawaii at Manoa), *37*, 1, 46–52.

Sugarman, J., Mastrioni, A. C., Kahn, C. & Jeffrey, P. (1998). *Ethics of research with human subjects. Selected policies and resources.* Baltimore: University Publishing Group.

Tolich, M. (2001). Beyond an unfortunate experiment: Ethics for small town New Zealand. In M. Tolich (Ed.), *Research ethics in Aotearoa New Zealand* (pp. 2–13). Auckland: Pearson Education.

Weisstub, D. (Ed.). (1998). *Research on human subjects: Ethics, law and social policy.* New York: Pergamon.

Chapter 9

A Postcolonial Critique of the Ethnographic Interview
Research Analyzes Research

Radhika Viruru
Texas A&M University
Gaile S. Cannella
Arizona State University

Postcolonial theory is not easy to define or delimit (Dimitriadis & McCarthy, 2001; Young, 2001). Despite being part of academia for several decades (at least since the publication of "Orientalism" by Edward Said in 1978), and impacting multiple academic fields (Pui-lan, 2005), there appears a curious resistance to "understanding" and a perhaps disingenuous repetition of requests for explanation. This demand for legitimation reifies complex bodies of ideas into neatly labeled categories (Mongia, 1996; Viruru, 2005). Further, the appeal of the theory to academia contributes to both popularity and decline of postcolonial studies.

Critics have suggested that because the term "postcolonial" itself can be applied to so many varied terrains and peoples, spanning vast areas of space as well as time, one must be careful not to obliterate individual histories and stories in an attempt to draw together a field that is clearly defined (Hall, 1996; McClintock, 1990; Pui-lan, 2005; Shohat, 1993). There are those who believe that the "post" in postcolonial renders it inappropriate as physical colonization can by no means be seen as being over, and that other forms of domination (such as economic and Western intellectual imperialism) are certainly widespread (Loomba, 1998; McClintock, 1990).

Increasingly, more scholars and others point out that colonialism is back with vigor, as is seen through attempts to bring "unstable" parts of the world under the so-called liberating umbrella of democracy and order. "In the great cities of Europe and America, where a few years ago these things would only have been whispered, now people are openly talking about the good side of Imperialism and the need for a strong Empire to police an unruly world" (Roy, 2004, p. 195). In an earlier era, colonialism was justified as an attempt to spread Enlightenment, whereas the new justification is that of freedom, a freedom that increasingly refers to the free market. We are within an era of "New Imperialism," which is a "remodeled, streamlined version of what we once knew" (p. 195). Colonialism has certainly not ended, and the use of the term post does not imply its demise.

In our own discussions of postcolonial theory, we (and others) have acknowledged the notion that calling postcolonial thought a theory is a sign that we continue to operate within dominant Western discourses (Cannella & Viruru, 2004). Further, we agree that using terminology that would imply the end of colonial imposition from within academia at a time of increased colonialism is certainly dangerous (Loomba et al., 2005). However, we believe that despite what most would call a conflict-ridden status, postcolonial theory represents vantage points that challenge the center of Western thought and cannot be ignored. Postcolonial studies can create "new forms of critique that will address the ideological and material dimension of contemporary neo-imperialism" (Loomba, 2005, p. 4).

The concept of definitions is just one example of how much academic thought reflects the influence of Eurocentric thinking and ways of viewing the world. Hulme (2005) suggests that one of the tasks of postcolonial studies is to unmask and unthink the Eurocentrism that engulfs all of us. Terms like "colonialism," "imperialism," and "neocolonialism" adopt only a "critical relation to the oppressive regimes and practices that they delineate," whereas postcolonial thought goes further (p. 58). If the post in postcolonial is interpreted as "the historical moment of the theorized introduction of new tricontinental forms (*originating from Africa, Asia, and Latin America*) and strategies of critical analysis and practice," it becomes apparent why postcolonialism continues to be a theory of hope for many (p. 58, emphasis added).

Despite the complexities surrounding definition and continued ties to Western institutions like academia, postcolonial theory(ies) offers a way to seek new possibilities and to resist forms of control, no matter how hidden or subtle. Even in the past, when imperialism altered the lives of millions of people, alternative visions of human life were put forward; these are the countervisions from which postcolonial scholars can learn—visions that challenge those who attempt to dominate our contemporary universe (Loomba et al., 2005). Our chapter reflects this spirit of alternative visions. When one focuses on postcolonialism and the practice of postcolonial critique as much more than theory, as a location from which to adopt an activist position that pursues social transformation, scholarship can be reconceptualized. Such activism can

> emerge on different sites in any region: the academic, the cultural, the ecological, the educational, the industrial, the local center-periphery structure of the city and the rural hinterland, the marketplace, the media, the medical in all its different manifestations, the mainstream political, the rainforest, and the social sphere. [Young, 2001, p. 58]

We would add qualitative research to this list.

Postcolonial Critique and the Research Construct

Postcolonial critique is not a process with predetermined steps or hierarchies, but a disposition that employs particular perspectives from often-disqualified locations. In *Childhood and Postcolonization* (2004), we attempted to describe possibilities for that disposition that we also use in this critique. These possibilities are not rules or guidelines, but forms of awareness that are generated for us from within postcolonial scholarship. This awareness causes us to look with eyes that would attempt to reveal unexamined methods that would reinscribe domination and/or reinforce imperialism and to uncover ways that society produces exclusions. Additionally, because colonialism has continually constructed and labeled an "inferior other," we try to point out ways that lives are oversimplified, made invisible, and coopted through a will to power that assumes that the representation of Others is appropriate.

We are also uneasily aware that while we critique such concepts as research and voice for perpetuating colonizing discourses, much of what we do continues to fit within them. The writing of chapters such as this one is an example. Such academic exercises, even those that function from the margins, remain part of a structure that represents the voices of mostly Euro American males. As Gandhi (1998) points out, in its current mood, even postcolonial theory "principally addresses the needs of the Western academy" (p. ix). Neither of us has the answer to this problem, but it is something with which we continually struggle.

Postcolonial Critique of the Ethnographic Interview

Critiquing Ethnography

Although cognizant of the role of the anthropologist/colonizer's gaze in constructing a relationship between ethnography/anthropology and colonization, contemporary researchers have been less aware of how the performance of anthropology within a colonial context influenced the ways, methods, and philosophies of ethnographic research itself. Dirks (2001) provides insight into the connection between ethnography and colonialism in British India. Once physical power had been created over India, the colonial state faced new challenges that required new technologies of control. In this new climate, political loyalty emerged as an important factor in determining colonial policies, and anthropology became the preferred tool of the state in assessing that loyalty. Thus, according to Dirks, by the late nineteenth century, India could be characterized as the "ethnographic state" in the British Empire. Ethnography, from this perspective, became a method for the reinscription of colonialism.

Dirks's analysis also discusses what might be referred to as a/ the fundamental tenet of ethnographic research (and we would add research in general)—the need to know more. Ethnographic research is often lauded for its inclusion of details and its use of thick description. More is generally considered better in ethnography; more details are associated with more accuracy in representing the lives and perspectives of the participants. However, this desire is far more complicated than would appear. The drive to know more also reflects a "colonial intransitivity" that led the

British to think that the more they knew, the "less the native could know them in return" (Dirks, 2001, p. 44). To further complicate matters, because the drive to know can be accompanied by a feeling that too many facts can spin out of control, the casting of "natives" as different implied a continuous state of mystery. Additionally, the collection of ethnographic knowledge was used to justify the practice of deception (perhaps the natives were not really telling the truth). As a reinscription of colonialism, ethnography has contributed to fictions created about the "other" (Said, 1995; Subba & Som, 2005).

Ethnographic Qualitative Interviews

Qualitative research (including ethnography and the ethnographic interview) has traditionally, among academic disciplines, been open to perspectives from diverse locations and aware of its relationship to colonialism/postcolonialism. For example, in the second paragraph of Denzin and Lincoln's (2000) *Handbook of Qualitative Research* we find the statement that "qualitative research in sociology and anthropology was born out of concern to understand the other," meaning the "exotic other, a primitive non-white person from a foreign culture judged to be less civilized than that of the researcher" (p. 2). Denzin and Lincoln also quote bell hooks's comments on the images evoked by the influential book on ethnography titled *Writing Culture* by Clifford and Marcus (1986), images that reifying people of color, women, and children as the Other:

> Two ideas that are quite fresh in the racist imagination: the white male as writer/authority ... and the idea of the passive brown/ black man (and woman and child) who is doing nothing, merely looking on. [hooks, 1990, p. 127]

Qualitative research scholars are not ignorant of the relationship/complicity with colonialism. What we will look at more specifically in this chapter is the complicity of the ethnographic interview in the maintenance of colonialist thought.

Interviews, in some form or another have been part of human life for a very long time (Fontana & Frey, 2005). Ancient Egyptians, for example, are known to have conducted censuses (Babbie,

1992). The field of anthropology is virtually grounded in various forms of the interview that structure the construction of ethnographies (Spradley, 1979). Most recently, interview traditions have been influenced by two major factors: their widespread use in clinical diagnosis and counseling, and inclusion in psychological testing. We would assert that these traditions, however differently they might be philosophically defined, are part of Western culture. Interpreting, diagnosing, and "naming" conditions are given great importance.

The first person known to have used interviews as part of a social survey was Charles Booth in 1886 in his study of the economic and social conditions of the people of London. His work influenced the study done by W.E.B. DuBois in 1889 of the black population of Philadelphia. Interviewing as a technique also gained importance during World War II as more than half a million American soldiers were interviewed in one manner or the other. Specifically within qualitative research traditions, interviews and the forms of language privileged by them became a mainstay for data collection (Fontana & Frey, 2004).

Definitions of the ethnographic interview.

Tied to the study of "culture" (which may also be defined in differing ways), the most common explanation for the ethnographic qualitative interview is a conversation with a purpose. Various scholars have attempted to clarify this purpose. According to Patton (2001), "The purpose of interviewing, then is to allow us to enter into the other person's perspective. Qualitative interviewing begins with the assumption that the perspective of others is meaningful, knowable and able to be made explicit" (p. 341).

However, researchers do recognize that interviews are always incomplete and can be misleading. Baker (1997) has therefore called for a reconsideration of interviewing, shifting the focus from data gathering to data generation. Recognizing that interviews are at best interactional language events used and understood in defined cultural contexts, that questions are not neutral, and that responses are accounts rather than realities, qualitative research scholars generally acknowledge limits in knowing the perspectives of other people.

The language of interviews.

Interviews are about a language (whether verbal or physical) of self-disclosure. The researcher, either through informal observation or negotiated questions, hopes to facilitate this language. Most commonly, the researcher attempts to illicit this disclosure by using a language of questioning. Qualitative researchers from different disciplines disagree on the kinds of questions that should to be asked and the methods of questioning.

Spradley (1979) lists three kinds of ethnographic questions: descriptive, structural, and contrast questions. Descriptive questions are meant to get informants talking about social scenes with which they are familiar. Structural questions are designed to help informants show how they organize the structures of their lives. Contrast questions are similar in that they, too, try to get at how people organize their worlds, by getting at how they distinguish between objects and events.

Patton (2001) offers yet another way to categorize the kinds of questions that can be asked during qualitative interviews: experience and behavior questions (that ask informants to describe the things they do), opinion and value questions (understanding how informants think about the things they do and experience), feeling questions (how they feel, as opposed to how they think, about experiences), knowledge questions (that require factual information), sensory questions (about things experienced through the senses), and background demographic questions (that identify the characteristics of the person being interviewed).

Criticalists and feminists have argued that interviews are structured to give the interviewer more power than the interviewee. As such, they prefer one or two broad questions that encourage conversation than a more formally developed schedule.

Although interviewing tends to involve disclosure by subjects/participants, disagreements between scholars regarding researcher self-disclosure are also an issue. Fontana and Frey (2005), for example, suggest that researchers should avoid "getting involved in a real conversation in which he or she answers questions asked by the respondent or provides personal opinions on the matters discussed" (p. 660), although they do mention that feminist perspectives on qualitative interviewing have encouraged more of this kind of dialogue. Hatch (2005) acknowledges the tension involved in self-disclosure. On the one hand, the view exists that revealing more information about oneself will improve rapport, whereas, on the other hand, the concern exists that such behavior can manipulate individuals into revealing information they would not normally have talked about under such circumstances (Bogden and Biklen, 2002).

Authors such as Lather (1991) have argued that both sides should be honest for the sharing of both understanding and power. Berg (2003) also discusses the issue of self-disclosure, under the broader umbrella of establishing rapport with informants, acknowledging the feminist perspectives. However, he notes that most interview situations "require the interviewer to maintain a certain amount of intentional control over the interview process—no matter how deferential, open, or self disclosing he or she might choose to be during the course of the interview or when developing rapport" (p. 101).

More commonly, methods of control that can be used by the researcher are provided. Hatch discusses "tips for successful interviews," including rules of polite conversation, planning, and transcribing (2005, pp. 114–116). Berg even titles his section The Ten Commandments of Interviewing. Whether attempting to be specific or more open ended, objective, or self-disclosing, the language and structure of the interview ultimately focuses on participants as expected to reveal themselves and allows the researcher to interpret this disclosure.

Reinscribing Exclusion and Imperialist Codes

The above review of well-known texts on qualitative interviews indicates that the field seems to have some fairly well-established expectations about what interviews are and how they should be conducted. Despite the field's historic openness to new ideas and insistence on the inclusion of marginalized perspectives, these structures continue to reflect mostly Euro Western perspectives: define, categorize, and develop guidelines for how it should be done. Smith (1999) has demonstrated how Western research draws from an "archive" of knowledge and systems, rules and values.

Scientific and academic debate in the West takes place within the boundaries of these rules, bearing the unmistakable imprint of Western ways of looking and categorizing the world. When, for example, interviews are carefully structured as limited spaces where conversations can occur, but only within certain bounds and according to certain rules, they become part of a colonizing apparatus. As Mohanty (1993) explains, within such constructions those from the Third World are heard as "fragmented, inarticulate voices in (and from) the dark" (p. 42).

Limiting and controlling how different voices can be heard continues to control people through modulating their "voices" and avoiding the conflict, struggle, and threat of disruption that real dialogue could bring. What happens to the perspectives that do not fit the informal, the formal, or the standardized interview? Young (2001) further expands on this concern by invoking Foucault's (1978) notion of "enunciative modality." Questions are asked like: Who is allowed to speak? Who controls what can be said? How do institutions influence this language and who may speak it? What cannot be spoken? These questions demonstrate that no form of interview is benign or innocent.

Smith (1999) also comments on the dangers of so-called innocent scholarship. Europeans who wrote about their travels in foreign lands and their experiences with indigenous peoples contributed to the difficult relationships between the two cultures. Some of these accounts were not specifically about colonialism but were accounts of indigenous life and happenings. However, these accounts, when relayed back home, inspired others to set off on their own adventures. Thus, these pieces of writing, though not specifically colonial, still drew from the larger apparatus of colonialism, creating the "right" to tell the stories of "others." Although to some extent naive, this "innocence" is implicated in processes of colonization. We suggest that qualitative research (as well as other forms of research) has been and is complicit in the innocent, yet harmful, construction of the other.

Additionally, research, especially social science research, is based on ideas about the social world, and how the human "self" fits into the world as well as ideas about relationships between individuals and groups (Smith, 1999). Other sources (for example,

Cannella, 1997) have commented that a focus on individuality is a very Western preoccupation. Philosophical constructs—like the belief that every individual has a soul, a psyche, a consciousness—have defined the Western idea of what an individual is and does. Although recognizing the need to sometimes include group interviews (like focus groups), the underlying assumption of the ethnographic interview appears to be that the most meaningful conversations one could have would be between two individuals, sitting down, one on one to "talk things over." Even group interviews are conducted with one individual basically talking (or recorded) at a time.

These notions are, however, cultural constructs. The individual as the basic social unit is a fundamental component of the Western cultural archive. Thus, we are not surprised that qualitative interviews are also built on this belief in the individual knower, focusing on the concept of the individual researcher (aware of his or her own limitations and capacities as a human instrument), talking, with rare exceptions, to an individual informant. The structure of the interview processes that are described also represents the individual informant as at least somewhat aware of his or her own capacities as an individual (reasoning, processes of differentiation, and so on). We suggest, however, that setting up the research situation in these terms not only continues to keep interviews firmly grounded within Western cultural practices, but also limits possibilities. For example, when the issue of self-disclosure is conceived of as an important part of the interview process, collectivist perspectives are made invisible, are essentially silenced.

Postcolonial Activism: Transcending Boundaries and Contesting Domination

Hamza (2004) has commented on the question of how research as a practice can be decolonized and offers some examples from various African contexts that are helpful. She points out that research must open itself it up to ways to include such concepts as the world-view that Tournas (1996) describes as the Tswana soul, which "is the composite of every man, woman, animal and plant—in short of all life of which the Tswana individual was just one bull in a herd that acquired its identity as a collective unit" (p. 129). As Hamza points out, this is an example of a pre-Cartesian worldview in which the emphasis is on interconnectedness. What is also interesting is that Hamza points out that research was a part of this world-view. This view of the world is exemplified through tales, riddles, proverbs, and "apprenticeship and inititation practices" and includes understanding ways in which to do research. We suggest that such perspectives should be taken into account when we think about what a qualitative interview might be.

Morrell and Swart (2005) also support the idea of different world-views that transcend Western boundaries of self and community and that question even common determiners of identity such as gender. Oyewumi (1997) writes about how among some Yoruba, gender ceases to be a major category of analysis. This tradition stresses community, not just in temporal ways but in spiritual ones as well. This understanding stresses that

> humanity is what is common among people and is what unites them ... a complex continuity with the past, with ancestors and spirits, and is distinguished by correlative thinking, cyclical times, the self as communal, the interdependence of people and nature and the conduct of politics via participation. The idea of adhesion, what makes people live together is therefore the starting point. [Morrell & Swart, 2005, p. 99]

Adler's (2004) study of three generations of Asian American families included many mixed-generation group interviews and group responses to literature. Adler comments that she designed the study in these terms as it allowed her study to "be less colonial by providing opportunities for participants to co-create perspectives on various issues" (p. 110). Given the potential for interviews to serve as locations from which disquieting knowledge can emerge, limits and rules should most likely be avoided.

Reinscribing Colonialism through Language: Can There Be Interviews without Language?

Interviews are essentially devoted to the gathering and analyzing of language. Although there are other qualitative methods that focus on various aspects of human behavior and the interpretation of human experience, inherent within the research discourse related to the qualitative interview is the assumption that through language we can determine what people are thinking and fairly accurately understand their perspectives. Furthermore, the privileging of language as if it were the most natural form of human expression is deeply embedded within colonialism.

In earlier work (Cannella & Viruru, 2004; Viruru & Cannella, 2001), we examined how language is implicated in the continuing colonization of the world by Euro Western ways of being and thinking (Gandhi, 1998; Loomba, 1998). For example, Seed (1991) has noted that language has been used as a tool to distinguish between "civilization and barbarism" (p. 8); those civilizations that use written languages are considered superior to those who do not. As Gandhi (1998) suggests, language or text, more than any other social or political product, is one of the most "significant instigators and purveyors of colonial power" (p. 141). Tiffin and Lawson (1994) state that although colonial power was established through such means as "guns, guile and disease" (p. 3), language has been, and continued to be, used to maintain this power.

Gibbon (1999) has suggested that the discourses that privilege language as a superior form of representation ignore the fact that not all parts of the world are named. Dominant discourses speak about those locations that are named and treat the others as invisible or nonexistent (Loomba, 1998). Language is not just a transparent window to the world but rather, "the primary medium through which social identities are constructed" (McLaren & Giroux, 1997, p. 21). Language directs attention and legitimizes forms of thinking. Because the use of language is inevitable, at the very least, one should be aware of the impositions and limitations. Thus, when the discourse of qualitative interviews focuses almost exclusively on language such as what kinds of questions should be asked by the interviewer, one way of thinking is legitimized over another. Language may not be the way in which people express their most complex thoughts. To fail to recognize this contingency is to diminish the possibilities that research has to offer.

Finally, we comment on the missing discourse of silence in

qualitative interviews. Silence has generally been perceived as "less than" language. Silence in public is generally deplored in the West as a symbol of "passivity and powerlessness" (Gal, 1995, p. 171). Those who are silent, it is assumed, cannot influence their own lives or the ways in which they are constructed by history. The construction of silence as the dichotomous Other of speech reflects the "discourse of dichotomies fostered in both the enlightenment and modern periods" (Cannella, 1997, p. 34). Thus, perceiving silence as a lack of something reflects Western ways of thinking and viewing the world. Many works about India, for example, have proposed that silence is a way of knowing (Trawick, 1990; Visweswaran, 1994).

In some cultures, verbal skills are seen as essential for power, but in others the belief is quite the opposite (Gal, 1995). Thus, the link between language and power is not as simple and natural as dichotomous ways of thinking have led us to believe. Silence can be used as a "strategic defence against the powerful," as when used by the Western Apache men to "baffle, disconcert and exclude white outsiders" (Gal, 1995, p. 171). Silence thus conceived becomes the opposite of passivity, even representing a form of political protest. Qualitative interviews, and qualitative research in general, we suggest, have yet to transcend the boundaries that would allow discourses such as silence to be an integral part of research.

Postcolonial Resistance Languages

The interpretation of ethnographic qualitative interviews tends to link speech with particular people. An interview usually makes clear who said what and makes complete documentation available. This form of representation can be contrasted with what Britton (1999) has called the quality of "relayed language" (p. 164), a strategy of diversity (described by Bakhtin) that operates within discourse generally but especially as a principle of narrative by resisting an oppressively singular authority. As Britton elaborates, this form of language is a strategy of resistance against the language-identity equation that assumes that individuals are the origin of their own speech, which is an essential part of their identity. In colonial contexts, power was exercised over others by imposing the idea that oppressors owned the dominant language and that it was through their actions that others were allowed to share in that language (Derrida, 1972). For many in what would be characterized as postcolonial societies, interview structures resonate with these kinds of histories and will not always result in data that are easily interpreted, or even usable at all.

The notion of relayed language, especially as seen in the work and theory of Edouard Glissant, suggests that when one punctures the language-identity equation, over time, the origins of words are lost, so that no one really knows who said what (Britton, 1999). Such continuous attacks on origins eliminate the link between utterance and the individual subject. In Spivak's (1988) comments on the Subaltern Studies project, she analyzes the concept of "rumor" as a linguistic device. Rumors, according to Spivak, are both anonymous and plural and cannot be attributed to individuals and therefore do not signify a particular person's point of view. Rumors can thus become a subaltern weapon against dominance (Britton, 1999). When interviews are conceived as representing truth and individual voices, they limit the ways in which people who are fighting oppression can use them as tools for liberation. Resistance languages from within interview contexts are, then, research necessities.

Cautions in the Use of Ethnographic Interviews

Most researchers have multiple intentions and desires, some of which they are aware of and some of which they are not. The same can be said of the person being interviewed. Thus, the language, intentions, rules, and possibilities are "persistently slippery, unstable and ambiguous from person to person, from situation to situation, from time to time" (Scheurich, 1997, p. 62). Data collected do not represent permanence or fixed meaning, as some commonly accepted procedures for conducting qualitative interviews would imply. Conventional ways of interviewing "vastly underestimate the complexity, uniqueness and indeterminateness" (p. 64) of the lives, experiences, and meaning-making of human beings. Further, research as construct, and the ethnographic interview in particular, must continually be critiqued for the colonialism that is perpetuated through rules, language, and the authority created by attempts to represent the Other.

References

Adler, S. M. (2004). Multiple layers of a researcher's identity: Uncovering Asian American voices. In K. Mutua & B. B. Swadener (Eds.), *Decolonizing research in cross-cultural contexts: Critical personal narratives* (pp. 107–122). Albany: SUNY Press.

Babbie, E. (1992). *The practice of social research* (6th ed.). Belmont, CA: Wadsworth.

Baker, C. D. (1997). Membership categorization and interview accounts. In D. Silverman (Ed.), *Qualitative research: Theory, method and practice* (pp. 130–143). London: Sage.

Berg, B. L. (2003). *Qualitative research methods for the social sciences* (5th ed.). Boston: Allyn and Bacon.

Bogdan, R. C., & Biklen, S. K. (2002). *Qualitative research for education: An introduction to theories and methods* (4th ed.). Boston: Allyn and Bacon.

Britton, C. (1999). *Edouard Glissant and postcolonial theory: Strategies of language and resistance.* Charlottesville: University Press of Virginia.

Cannella, G. S. (1997). *Deconstructing early childhood education: Social justice and revolution.* New York: Peter Lang.

Cannella, G. S., & Viruru, R. (2004). *Childhood and (postcolonization): Power, education and contemporary practice.* London and New York: Routledge

Clifford, J., & Marcus, G. E. (Eds.). 1986. *Writing culture: The poetics and politics of ethnography.* Berkeley: University of California Press.

Denzin, N. K., & Lincoln, Y. S. (Eds.) (2000). *Handbook of qualitative research.* Thousand Oaks, CA: Sage.

Derrida, J. (1972). *Marges de la philosophie.* Paris: Editions de Minuit.

Dimitriadis, G., & McCarthy, C. (2001). *Reading and teaching the postcolonial: From Baldwin to Basquiat and beyond.* New York: Teachers College Press.

Dirks, N. (2001). *Casts of mind: Colonialism and the making of modern India.* Princeton, NJ: Princeton University Press.

Fontana, A., & Frey, J. H. (2005). The interview: From structured questions to negotiated text. In N. K. Denzin & Y. S. Lincoln (Eds.), *Handbook of qualitative research* (3rd ed., pp. 695–728). Thousand Oaks, CA: Sage.

Foucault, M. (1978). *The archeology of knowledge*. New York: Pantheon.

Gal, S. (1995). Language, gender and power. In K. Hall & M. Bucholtz (Eds.), *Gender articulated: Language and the socially constructed self* (pp. 169–182). New York and London: Routledge

Gandhi, L. (1998). *Postcolonial theory: A critical introduction*. New York: Columbia University Press.

Gibbon, M. (1999). *Feminism and language*. London and New York: Longman.

Hall, S. (1996). Cultural identity and diaspora. In P. Mongia (Ed.). *Contemporary postcolonial theory: A reader* (pp. 110–121). London: Arnold.

Hamza, H. A. (2004). Decolonizing research on gender disparity in education in Niger: Complexities of language, culture and homecoming. In K. Mutua & B. B. Swadener (Eds.), *Decolonizing research in cross-cultural contexts: Critical personal narratives* (pp. 123–134). Albany: SUNY Press.

Hatch, J. A. (2005). *Doing qualitative research in education settings*. Albany: SUNY Press.

hooks, b. (1990). *Yearning: race, gender and cultural politics*. Boston: South End.

Hulme, P. (2005). Beyond the straits: Postcolonial allegories of the globe. In A. Loomba, S. Kaul, M. Bunzl, A. Burtin, & J. Esty (Eds.), *Postcolonial studies and beyond* (pp. 41–61). Durham, NC: Duke University Press.

Lather, P. (1991). *Getting smart: Feminist research and pedagogy with/in the postmodern*. New York: Routledge.

Loomba, A. (1998). *Colonialism/Postcolonialism*. London: Routledge.

Loomba, A., Kaul, S., Bunzl, M., Burton, A. & Esty, J. (2005). In A. Loomba, S. Kaul, M. Bunzl, A. Burtin, & J. Esty (Eds.), *Postcolonial studies and beyond* (pp. 1–40). Durham, NC: Duke University Press.

McClintock, A. (1990). The angel of progress: Pitfalls of the term "postcolonialism." *Social Text, 31/32*, 84–98.

McLaren, P., & Giroux, H. (1997). Writing from the margins: Geographies of identity, pedagogy and power In P. McLaren (Ed.), *Revolutionary multiculturalism* (pp. 16–41). Boulder, CO: Westview.

Mohanty, C. T. (1993). On race and voice: Challenges for liberal education in the 1990's. In B. W. Thompson & S. Tyagi (Eds.), *Beyond a dream deferred: Multicultural education and the politics of excellence* (pp. 41–65). Minneapolis: University of Minnesota Press.

Mongia, P. (1996). Introduction. In P. Mongia (Ed.), *Contemporary postcolonial theory: A reader* (pp. 1–19). London: Arnold.

Morrell, R., & Swart, S. (2005). Men in the Third World: Postcolonial perspectives on masculinity. In M. S. Kimmel, J. Hearn, & R. W. Connell (Eds.), *Handbook of studies on men and masculinities* (pp. 90–113). Thousand Oaks, CA: Sage.

Oyewumi, O. (1997). *The invention of women making an African sense of Western gender discourses*. Minneapolis: University of Minnesota Press.

Patton, M. Q. (2001). *Qualitative research and evaluation methods* (3rd ed.). Thousand Oaks, CA: Sage.

Pui-lan, K. (2005). *Postcolonial imagination and feminist theology*. Louisville, KY: Westminister John Knox Press.

Roy, A. (2004). *An ordinary person's guide to empire*. London: South End Press.

Said, E. (1978). *Orientalism*. London and Henley: Routledge and Kegan Paul.

Said, E. (1995). Secular interpretation, the geographical element and the methodology of imperialism. In G. Prakash (Ed.), *After colonialism* (pp. 21–40). Princeton, NJ: Princeton University Press.

Scheurich, J. J. (1997). *Research method in the postmodern*. London: Falmer Press.

Seed, P. (1991). Failing to marvel: Atahualpa's encounter with the word. *Latin American Research Review, 26*, 7–32.

Shohat, E. 1993. Notes on the Postcolonial. *Social Text, 31/32*, 91–113.

Smith, L. T. (1999). *Decolonizing methodologies: Research and indigenous peoples*. London: Zed Books.

Spivak, G. C. (1988). *In other worlds: Essays in cultural politics*. New York: Routledge.

Spradley, S. (1979). *The ethnographic interview*. Fort Worth, TX: Holt, Rinehart and Winston.

Subba, T. B., & Som, S. (2005). *Between ethnography and fiction: Verrier Elwin and the tribal question in India*. New Delhi: Orient Longman.

Tiffin, C., & Lawson, A. (1994). *De-scribing empire, postcolonialism and textuality*. London: Routledge.

Tournas, A. S. (1996). From sacred initiation to bureaucratic apostasy. *Comparative Education, 32*(1), 27–43.

Trawick, M. (1990). *Notes on love in a Tamil family*. Berkeley: University of California Press.

Viruru, R. (2005). The impact of postcolonial theory on early childhood education. *Journal of Education, 35*, 7–30.

Viruru, R., & Cannella, G. S. (2001). Early childhood education and postcolonial possibilities. In R. Viruru (Ed.), *Early childhood education: Postcolonial possibilities from India* (pp. 137–156). New Delhi: Sage.

Visweswaran, K. (1994). *Fictions of feminist ethnography*. Minneapolis: University of Minnesota Press.

Young, R.J.C. (2001). *Postcolonialism: An historical introduction*. Oxford: Blackwell Publishers.

Chapter 10

Decolonizing Qualitative Research

Nontraditional Reporting Forms in the Academy[1]

Elsa M. González y González and
Yvonna S. Lincoln
Texas A & M University

In the past, qualitative researchers have assumed that cross-cultural work required deep understanding of the culture being reported on. Earlier cross-cultural work focused on "receiving contexts," and on end-users who were primarily Western and English speaking. The utility of such studies is severely limited, however, in a globalized world, and studies undertaken now must serve the interests of not only Western and English-speaking scholars, but also the needs of nationals and locals (or indigenous peoples) from whom data were originally gathered. Research conducted in different languages and non-Western contexts and cultures becomes more problematic, and understanding intrinsic issues more urgent, with the increasing number of reports (such as dissertations as well as funded studies and studies by nongovernmental organizations who work worldwide) conducted by scholars outside the United States. It is, however, far more complex a task than researchers have imagined, especially as faculties and students alike become more globalized and transnational and thus bear potential for decolonizing the academy (Finkelstein, Seal, & Schuster, 1998). Conducting and reporting cross-cultural qualitative data focus understanding at least five major ideas.

1. Working Bilingual Data

Researchers in different fields contend that one of the principal methodological issues in cross-cultural studies is the accuracy of translations (Vijver & Leung, 1997). Translation of language is deeply embedded in translation of context and culture, neither of which moves on a one-to-one, isomorphic basis across national borders. Because there is no formula to translate culture, the collection of data in a local language and the presentation of the analyses in a second language become important issues to analyze. Data analysis and findings presentation are huge undertakings for any researcher who hopes to make certain that local readers at each end of the context—sending and receiving—understand and make sense of data from foreign participants.

Context plays an important part in interpreting data. Without understanding the context where the participants live, results could emerge with no clear interpretation of the data. Participants express their ideas, perceptions, and interpretations in a context that surrounds their realities and within which they have learned. Jarvis (1987) said that "learning always occurs within a social context and that the learner is also to some extent a social construct" (p.15).

At one level, the analytic process involves a linguistic translation coupled with a deep understanding of the context that helps both researcher and ultimately reader better understand the phenomenon, while ensuring throughout the process that there is no loss of valuable data. The process involves a translation, not only of the language, but also and mainly of the culture. Spradley (1980) explains:

> A translation discovers the meanings in one culture and communicates them in such a way that people with another cultural tradition can understand them. The ethnographer as translator has a dual task. For one, you must make sense out of the cultural patterns you observe, decoding the messages in cultural behavior, artifacts, and knowledge. Your second task is to communicate the cultural meanings you have discovered to readers who are unfamiliar with that culture or culture scene. [p. 161]

Some authors have started addressing this issue with research that focuses on the role of the translator, the origin of the translator, the repercussions of language difference and its translation, and, in the end, its interpretation (Temple, 1997). Expressing a lack of systematic analyses of these factors and their influence on the text, authors explain the importance of including and explaining these aspects in the methodology section so that the reader can understand the whole meaning of the results, which are influenced by translation issues.

In addition, Temple and Edwards (2002) strongly suggest including translators and interpreters as active partners in the research as "key informants," inviting them to participate in an open dialogue, discussion, and exchange of ideas with the researcher about what the findings mean, how to express them, and how to communicate cultural nuances regarding mores and meanings. Temple (1997) explains that "particular concepts may therefore have a history, that is, they can be temporally as well spatially differentiated; they also carry emotional connotations that direct equivalents in a different language may not have" (p. 611). Further, the figure of the researcher as a translator brings up questions such as: What is the first language of the researcher? Can the research be carried out adequately in the researcher's language or would it be more appropriate to use the language of the research subjects? Are the researcher and translator the same person? If not, what position is the researcher taking toward the research? How does that differ from that of the translator? Including detailed answers and discussions about these and similar issues is suggested as a serious item to be included in the methodological approach followed in the study.

In translation, literal equivalency in wording often conveys meanings that are not parallel across languages and cultures. Using several examples, Finnegan and Matveev (2002) affirm that "a deeper linguistic issue is that words often do not translate because elements in one culture are not found in another. Without intimate knowledge of a target culture, the lack of conceptual or functional equivalencies may elude a researcher" (p. 17). These equivalencies may likewise elude one or more target audiences as well, with multiple untoward results. For instance, subsequent researchers may carry with them minor to severe misunderstandings of cultural meanings, resulting in, at best, a failure of rapport, and, at worst, a refusal to work with the researcher. Travelers and tourists alike (although not the same kinds of people, as Paul Bowles made clear in his famous novel-turned-film, *The Sheltering Sky*), having prepared for trips by reading ethnographic accounts of the original fieldwork, may embark on travel with clear misunderstandings of cultural mores and customs, thereby provoking further cross-cultural misunderstanding. More important, however, is the lost or retarded opportunity to work with cross-cultural sensitivity on a variety of issues: schooling, poverty, health issues, work/employment/industrialization concerns, or environmental concerns, for example) because of cultural missteps.

Following the previous rationale, some authors suggest presenting data in more than one language, including the language in which the data were collected. Anzaldúa (1987), in her social studies about the Mexico-U.S. border, insists on presenting them in Spanish, in English, and, in many cases, as a mix of both languages. This conveys the social phenomenon of two cultures bordering each other and invites the reader to understand the "language of the border," where bilingual texts exhibit great power. The influence that language can have in the analysis of data has to be considered, because "the primary function of human language would be to scaffold human affiliation within cultures and social groups and institutions" (Gee, 1999, p. 1).

In analyzing non-English (Spanish) data, González y González (2004) suggested starting from unitizing data, which is the crucial step in transforming interview data "into the smallest pieces of information that may stand alone as independent thoughts in the absence of additional information other than broad understanding of the context" (Erlandson, Harris, Skipper, & Allen, 1993, p. 117). González y González says:

> First, interview data in Spanish were transcribed from audiotapes into computer files. Second, the transcripts were broken into "units" of data, or the smallest fragment of data from which meaning could be obtained. Third, the units were numbered and coded. Units were kept in Spanish, in order to maintain the original language and continuity in each narrative made by the participants. [pp. 50–51]

This procedure was followed to keep the richness of the data in Spanish. Units were presented in English and Spanish in several cases, supporting the idea that the Spanish-speaking reader understands the exact meaning of the unit and its context, in some cases better than the English-speaking reader.

There are important issues to consider when collecting qualitative data in foreign settings. At the risk of sounding overly simplistic, it is important not to overlook ideas. For instance, when conducting research in a foreign country, a researcher should review the literature from the host country in its local language; otherwise, the researcher may miss important research already conducted, of which he or she wasn't aware because of the language in which it was published. As local, indigenous, and national peoples train their own ethnographers, anthropologists, and other fieldworkers, an increasing number of texts have appeared in native or national languages. Cross-cultural researchers need to conduct diligent searches for this emerging research literature to familiarize themselves thoroughly with local perspectives and indigenous interpretations.

2. Considering Non-Western Cultural Traditions

The creation of research that meets the needs of two vastly different audiences takes into account cultural traditions that may be distinctly non-Western, partially Western/partly indigenous, or a fusion of European culture with other cultures (e.g., Caribbean, Latin American, Mexican, Creole). Ethnographers may be working with strong residues of colonial practices—forms of government, languages, bureaucratic agencies—that interact with, or contradict and resist, colonial practices. Stepping between and among these traditions creates a potential minefield of possibilities for cultural offense. Working cross-culturally is one reason for avoiding the "blitzkrieg ethnography" Ray Rist warned about so long ago. Blitzkrieg ethnography offers no chance to observe and understand cultural traditions that are non-Western. Therefore, it poses multiple chances for offense, for organizational "fronts" to be operative and secure, and for later ethnographic work to be foreclosed to future researchers.

It is no longer enough to present the "monumentalized" (Rosaldo, 1989), static cultural images desired by formerly unitary audiences. The audiences for such work have greatly expanded in the past several decades and they are considerably more sophisticated and culturally informed than previous reports would have us believe. A simple glance at world news will confirm this. From far corners of the Earth, when non-Westerners are interviewed on CNN, more often than not, they are speaking English. The automatic assumption that savvy audiences make is that informants are bilingual—a gift that Western ethnographers who speak only English do not bring to their professional practices. The implications for Western ethnographers and their professional practice is that the acquisition of second (and third) language skills may be but one of many cultural skills necessary to carry out sound fieldwork in other cultures.

One example will illustrate what we mean. Antjie Krog, an internationally recognized Afrikaans poet (who writes in Afrikaans, but does her own translations into English), recently joined the faculty of the University of the Western Cape. Her presence has stimulated Truth and Reconciliation Commission research across the faculty. One of the projects in which Ms. Krog has been involved has been the "re-translation of key TRC testimonies" especially the "[re-]transcri[ption] and [re-]transla[tion] … [of] the testimonies of two of the widows of 'The Craddock Four,' which were originally given in Xhosa and simultaneously interpreted into English." One of the startling findings of this research was that "a comparison of the new translation with that of the official TRC version has revealed a number of significant instances where the original meaning is lost, with implications for the historical record" (see http://www.uwc.ac.za/arts/newns/anti-jiekrog.htm, retrieved April 30, 2005).

Cultural practices appear to demand that our respondents speak English, and whatever else they choose, but that we need to speak only English. As the above example shows, however, failure to know and understand the first languages of respondents can leave us with misunderstandings, inaccuracies, and possibly harmful information. The monumentalized image of an informant entirely conversant with English and an ethnographer who cannot take the time to understand either the significant variations in cultural practices or the languages that frame those practices is likely to produce data that may well have little standing in the non-Western world.

What is necessary is a dynamic, interactive, dialectic set of images, reflecting change, exchange, interchange, and galvanic and sometimes conflict-ridden processes. Perhaps the most powerful images of what such work might look like would be the notion of *interchange*. The fact that respondents have acquired sufficient facility with English to respond in English to Western ethnographers should tell us something about the depth of exchange and interchange that is currently occurring in the world.

We should be searching not only for data of interest around the phenomenon we came to study, but also for places, specific sites, and examples of exchange, of cultural practices in conflict, of contradiction between old and new, of locals' dissatisfaction with the "leakage" between cultures, of resistance to the alteration or withering away of traditional cultural practices and processes.

We ought to be alert to conflict between one generation and the next. Youth frequently ignore the traditions of their elders when confronted with the interesting temptations of an invader culture and are quick to adopt practices, dress, speech, music, and other cultural artifacts from television, film, and other cross-national cultural seam lines. Where this is happening, conflict is almost inevitable between generations.

We need to be on the lookout for sorrow, for instances of cultural shame and loss. The habits of colonial pasts, where the forcible intrusions of colonizing powers were thought to be unmitigated social goods, are recognized as European delusions, not only unuseful, but frequently culturally destructive (Mutua & Swadener, 2004; Smith, 1999). Researchers need to be sensitive to open but also subterranean forms of cultural conflict and the sites of interpenetration between Western and non-Western cultural forms where this conflict is played out.

This assumes, of course, that one gets in at all. Russell Bishop's (2005) extended discussion of the deep and meaningful rituals of entering Maori space to do research—the offering of gifts and money, the sharing of a feast, and the acceptance or nonacceptance of the gifts of good and money—speak not only to *kaupapa* Maori epistemology, but also to cultural traditions that are kept alive and lovingly fostered as both a means of identity preservation and as purposive strategies marking the boundaries of insider and outsider. Thus, this set of cultural traditions serves critical demarcation functions that permit the Maori community to debate the intrusion of an outsider and arrive at a community-driven decision to admit or deny entrance and access.

More importantly, cultural traditions, receiving and sending, need to be shown in contest. The smooth and unproblematic texts of the past, prepared for the consumption of a Western audience, rarely, if ever, displayed the conflicts between cultural expectations of the researchers and cultural practices of residents. (Malinowski, of course, was one of the exceptions, with his journals that exemplify the cross-purposes of cross-cultural work and the daily frustrations and resentments engendered by failure to understand cultural practices, or the endless and rich variety of resistance afforded to native or local informants. Margaret Mead was another, in her *Letters from the Field*. But both anthropologists chronicled the stresses of cross-cultural work not as primary text, but rather as personal journals. The cross-purposes engaged by anthropologists virtually always turned up as "confessional texts" [van Maanen, 1988], published considerably after the primary fieldwork text became available.)

Ethnographers trained to "get the facts" on some phenomenon and report them out in fairly straightforward terms, will be hard pressed to develop the "soft eyes"[2] for conflictual cultural practices that permit a *text of contest* to be developed. Texts of context are always layered (skirted, pleated) texts, texts that fold back on themselves to display dominative forms at war with resistance tactics, colonial usages against local customs, and the stresses of exchange and interpenetration. Texts of contest demonstrate the frayed seams of cultural collision and the torn fabric of colonial vestments. Further, they exemplify what Dudu Jankie (2004) calls problematizing both the positionalities and the constructions of who is insider and who is outsider in postcolonial contexts, for it is clear that the very presence of a researcher in some, many, or all of these contexts is itself a source of cultural stress. This is true even when, as Jankie observes, the researcher is a native, and therefore both insider and outsider. (The advantage of being a native, or local is that even if one is considered an outsider, likely by virtue of education and having lived away from the context for many years, one knows the language, and carries around, in some stored recesses of the mind, cultural knowledge, idiomatic usage, and a sense of the "freight" of meanings, specific usages, and relationships. In some sense, the insider/outsider knows where the bodies are buried, as well as knowing about burial practices. Ethnographers know that there is a world of difference between those two bodies of knowledge.)

Texts of contest must be layered, but so, too, must literary, poetic, and communitarian exemplars of struggle, resistance, and cross-cultural stresses. Saying that, however, is, of course, far easier than doing it. One of the significant means for achieving such texts, particularly the layering of cultures, and the display of places where struggles are ensuing is by utilizing multiple perspectives.

3. Multiple Perspectives

It is clear that the only means for achieving multiple perspectives in texts is by accomplishing research that is not only responsive to social scientists' needs, but more critically, shaped by the needs and questions of local peoples as well as carried out under their direction. In fact, many new statements of indigenous people's rights contain specific direction as to how outsider researchers will conduct themselves vis-à-vis locals, including legislation that demands specific attention to local needs, which directs the kinds of authority researchers will have and not have, and instructions regarding how teams of researchers will be constituted, and who will be in charge of the research (Smith, 1999). These new statements of rights are very clear that researchers do not have unlimited access, and frequently, that they will be accompanied (even "chaperoned") by a knowledgeable and well-educated local whose role it is not only to introduce researchers to local mores and customs, but to guide researchers in framing questions that do not give offense and to warn off researchers from protected, tribal, or gender-proscribed questions.

Researchers might well be advised to assume these secondary roles with all cross-cultural research, whether a specific statement of indigenous rights exists or not. That is, ethnographers who automatically assume they will be working with a local co-researcher, who will pose research questions needing answers that grow from local needs, are likely better positioned to conduct research that truly matters and that can respond to local needs and desires first and foremost, rather than to the dictates of a distant academy.

Research conducted in this way—a close fit with the demands of participatory action research—will display characteristics both *conversational* and *dialectic*. This is work that exemplifies clearly the exchange between cultures, including the struggles for self-determination and the forms and forces of resistance. How is such work done? This kind of work implies the intense collaboration of two or more writer-analysts—perhaps one Western, but always one or more local, indigenous, and/or residents—not only vis-à-vis research questions, methodologies, and analyses, but also in text production and cross-translation. Because, noted earlier, some ideas or concepts are not translatable—that is, no concomitant word or sense exists in both languages—conveying both the local meaning, on which local people will act, and conveying some set of usages that may be (but dimly) understood by another (perhaps Western) audience is a painstaking task, involving empathetic negotiation and conversation between cultural participants. This sense of *conversation*, of authentic listening between team members, should be evident in a text. In the same sense, the points of conflict—the dialectic between cultures—should also be present and obvious to readers. In some instances, this will be that personal sense of being "caught" between cultures. In others, it will be a culture-wide sense of encroachment, the inevitable result of interpenetration of cultures. Whether personal or community-wide, the dialectic should be evident, and often painfully so.

The dialectic forces may not be felt equally on both sides. Consequently, multiple voices and multiple perspectives are necessary in the text. In classical ethnography, it was often the married male ethnographer who provided the field text on cosmology, kinship patterns, political and governance forms, and the like, and his spouse (likewise a trained anthropologist, usually) who provided the field text on women's issues: marriage, childbirth and child-rearing practices, food, and women's rituals.

Sometimes this division of labor was necessitated because local customs prevented women from knowing some things about men's customs, and likewise, prevented men from knowing some things that were considered women's knowledge, or women's province. That particular division of labor is rarely the case any more, although there are still indigenous peoples who reserve some knowledge to women and preserve other domains for males only. As a result, as well as providing evidence of cultural conflict, texts ought to display the perspectives of women as well as men. Because the intrusions of one culture on another may impact men and women differently and differentially, texts cannot be the sole province of male researchers. Issues that impinge particularly on women and children need to be highlighted as strongly as those cross-cultural issues that have a direct bearing on local males. Multiple perspectives does not imply merely males from two cultures; women and children feel impacts that are sometimes unnoticed and unnoted by community males, but are as devastating as the more visible effects of colonialism or cultural exchange on males. If social justice is to be sought via the inclusion of multiple textual perspectives, the voices of women and children need to be there.

One example of the impacts of colonialism, globalization, or the potential intrusion of Western on non-Western cultures, for example, might be in the arena of women's health. In some remote areas of the world, it is still males who receive the first and best access to whatever health care exists, although it might be women who experience the more devastating impacts of a health crisis. AIDS in Africa is a good example. Although males often receive primary access to health care, it is women who give birth to HIV-infected infants and women who provide child care. When mothers have no knowledge of their health status, they are left caring for devastatingly sick children, even while experiencing deteriorating health status themselves.

Another impact that differentially affects males and females is access to educational opportunities. In some communities around the world, girls have far fewer or no opportunities for even rudimentary schooling in basic reading and writing, while boys may study religious texts. The participation of girls and women in even simple decisions about money, health, family planning, or local government is seriously limited by the imposition of fundamental illiteracy on females. As a consequence of the gendering of some issues, women's voices need to be heard as strongly as men's voices. This is also an area where a critical dialectic may be engaged. Illiteracy impoverishes all members of a culture, and some critique of educational practices within a culture might eventually help overturn some practices that a globalized world cannot afford if groups are to float upward on the rising tide of the new economies developing around the world.

4. Multivocal and Multilingual Texts

One of the clearest markers for a globalized but decolonized academic research will be the production of scholarly work (including dissertations) that are not univocal, but multivocal, and that are not English only, but rather bi- and/or multilingual (González y González, 2004). For social scientists to reach across cultures and work democratically with local groups, research results must be available and accessible as well as usable both locally and indigenously. This means that texts must be produced in two or more languages simultaneously. One implication of producing bi- or multilingual texts is that texts will be longer, but, as mentioned before, with the purpose of keeping the richness of the data in their original language.

Some studies suggest that units (for example, quotations or actual pieces of qualitative data) be presented in the original language as well as in the language for presentation—many times in English—supporting the idea that the local or indigenous-speaking reader will have available the complete meaning of the unit and its context. Some meanings, interesting but not useful to nonlocal audiences, may carry enormous significance for local consumers of the research, simply because the words may tie into larger events, circumstances, customs, issues, problems, or relationships. Nonlocal consumers of the research cannot know what kind of action will be triggered via the original language, or what social action may be prompted. Only local users can understand what the words, especially untranslatable, idiomatic terminologies, might mean, or what positive forces might be enabled.

In interviews conducted for research carried out in higher education institutions in Mexico (González y González, 2004),

Spanish-speaking participants with English language proficiency wondered how the researcher would translate some of their comments. The following quotes illustrate these concerns and how the data were presented in both languages to avoid presenting a text without original meanings.

> According to the situation with the public finances, the low tax collection that we have in Mexico, plus the large growing student registration in higher education that we have now and that we will have for many years; it is clear that the public subsidies are not going to be enough, and of course, the money is not going to catch up with what the university has needed to grow. [*Dada la situación de las finanzas públicas, de la bajísima recaudación fiscal que hay en México, y junto al fuerte crecimiento de la matrícula de educación superior que tenemos ahora y tendremos por bastantes años, es claro que los subsidios públicos no serán suficientes, es claro que no va ajustar el dinero para lo que tiene que crecer la universidad.*] [p. 98]

Without the knowledge of the context that private and public universities have in Mexico, phrases such as "*subsidios públicos,*" "*recaudación fiscal,*" and "*finanzas públicas*" would not have the same impact on the reader if the paragraph were presented only in English. For readers with background knowledge of higher education in Mexico, the whole paragraph says much more than even a sound translation/interpretation. The final phrase "*no va ajustar el dinero*" has a special connotation of closeness and understanding between the participant and the researcher, the dynamic of which cannot be expressed with a translation to a Spanish-Mexican speaker/reader. More examples from the same research further demonstrate this:

> Some years ago, licenses were given [which granted] the right to open universities without control ... where the academic level was not as good as could be ... generating, in some ways, more unemployment. [*Hace unos años se dieron licencias para abrir universidades a "ton y son." Donde el nivel académico deja mucho que desear ... generando de una forma mas desempleo.*] [p. 101]

> An executive has to make decisions, be responsible for these decisions, obviously, but in a collegial form, with full understanding by one's colleagues, "considering the consensus of a group," but not just "passing the ball" [passing the buck] to the group. (When you

translate this, it's going to be kind of strange this language.) [*Un directivo tiene que tomar decisiones, ser responsables de esas decisiones evidentemente, pero si las hace de una manera colegiada, y por colegiada entiendo, "es considerar el consenso, un grupo," pero no "echándole la bolita" al grupo. (Cuando lo traduzca va a ser medio extraño este lenguaje.)*] [p. 113]

How to communicate our ideas, as executives.... . I think we don't do this enough, in our institutions, ourselves, we are not right, are we? Having basic competencies does not mean that everybody has them. I want to use another colloquialism ... and that is an "extra," an add-on with new media ... visual media, etc." [*Como comunicar nuestra ideas, como directivos yo creo que a veces nos falta, en otras instituciones, a mi mismo, que nos fallan, ¿no? Que sean básicas estas competencias, no quiere decir que todo mundo las tenemos. Le iba a decir otra coloquialidad ... y de "pilon" con nuevos medios, ¿no? visuales, etc.*] [p. 121]

In these paragraphs, phrases and colloquial words give to the reader a sense of "listening" to what the participant in this research wants to say, having a feeling of understanding of sincerity in the description of the whole picture. The participants in this research were chief executives in public and private universities in Mexico, and their words express how, in a forthright talk, without the formality of their positions, they are willing to express the situation that they face in their institutions. For a Spanish-speaking reader, capturing this whole context would be difficult or impossible with just an English presentation. There are numbers of assumptions here, including assumptions about what is not said, about the extent to which the researcher, a former administrator in a public institution herself, knows and deeply understands both the administrative and fiscal context of public and private universities in Mexico, and about what can be communicated "between the lines" for those who know the context intimately.

In these studies, the researcher has to consider the presence of multiple audiences with different data needs. This creates a need for the researcher to make special arrangements regarding language to ensure that both audiences would be able to understand the data and ultimately be able to use the results of the study.

An extended rationale is the rebellious reaction that authors such as Gloria Anzaldúa (1987) propose, explaining the presence of a "new language," the language of the borderlands, not approved by any society. She explains that Chicanos no longer feel that they need to beg entrance. In her book, she presents an invitation from the "new *mestizas*":

> For many *mexicanos del otro lado*, the choice is to stay in Mexico and starve or move north and live. *Dicen que cada mexicano siempre sueña de la conquista en los brazos de cuatro gringas, la conquista del país poderoso del norte, los Estados Unidos. En cada chicano y mexicano vive el mito del tesoro territorial perdido.* North Americans call this return to the homeland the silent invasion. [p. 10]

Extensive explanations of the context and culture behind the words are needed to transmit the meaning of the words. Ann Wright, editor and translator of one of Rigoberta Menchú's books *Crossing borders* (Menchú, 1998), explains:

> Readers of the first book will be familiar with many of the Spanish words, like *compañero, ladino, compadre*, again left in the original because there is no precise equivalent in English as explained in the Glossary. Many more words have been left in K'iche' and explanations incorporated into the text. Doña Rigoberta explains that *haciendo corridores* at the UN does not literally mean "working the corridors," although that was often what she did, but that she lobbied, networked, hustled and even harassed people so that they took notice of her. What she calls la *unidad nacional* refers to a nation-state confronting ethnic, linguistic or territorial groups pressing for greater autonomy from central government not only in the case of Guatemala, but also of Canada and Quebec, Spain and Euskadi, the United Kingdom and Scotland. America naturally refers to the continent of The Americas, not to the United States. The specific use of some of Doña Rigoberta's Spanish words is not entirely clear and I have chosen the ones that seem the most appropriate in the context. For example, *abuelos* may alternatively mean grandparents or forefathers, or more generally village elders. Pueblo may be people in general, a people as in an indigenous nation, or the people as in the masses. I hope Doña Rigoberta will forgive me if I have not always chosen the right one. Also for any mistakes in the way I have inserted linking text or reorganized the taped testimony where I felt clarification was needed for English-speaking readers. [pp. viii–ix]

Ann Wright is trying to explain the many compromises she and other translators must make to create texts intelligible to multiple audiences. In Wright's case, she apparently worked with not just two languages, but three. When words are untranslatable, or may carry multiple meanings, Wright has chosen—as many others might—to leave in the original Spanish or K'iche' words. In this same way, over the centuries, words have migrated from one language into another, carrying their own linguistic and cultural freight with them; examples might be *savoir faire, coup de grace, compadre, bodega, barrio, Weltanschaung, Weltschmerz, ennui,* and hundreds of others. Gloria Anzaldúa's multilingual, nonstandard-border-language Spanish and English texts may foreshadow the next generation of cross-cultural research.

In many cases, the nonlocal audience may require more data regarding the context of local setting. In that case, the language, its translation, and context issues may also affect the analysis of the data. Erlandson et al. (1993) agree that "in qualitative data gathering and analysis, attention should be given to constructing a comprehensive, holistic portrayal of the social and cultural dimensions of a particular context" (p. 85). In this sense, deeper considerations regarding the clarity of the context should be undertaken in order to have a more precise view of the analysis and results of this study, especially for a U.S./American audience. This consideration may seem superfluous to the local audience, but it is indispensable for the U.S. one.

In addition to previous reflections about culture and context, it is important to consider that "culture is not a single undifferentiated phenomenon; it varies by socio-economic class, by ethnic community, by region, and even by gender" (Jarvis, 1987, p. 13). Consequently, in addition to any quantitative and factual data, the researcher may look to include observations that represent hallmark characteristics—what are now referred to as social locations—of the participants.

Given the importance that context plays during the unfolding of the data, and how language plays an important role in the context, data probably should be analyzed in the language in which it was collected. Consequently, making the results accessible in the multiple languages gives readers the option of the original language of the data along with the "presentation" language.

Indigenous people have different and alternative stories to tell. Those cannot be fully understood with a perfect translation. Presenting text in the language of the storyteller has to be a practice that generates authentic discourses in the eyes of the colonized, a practice increasingly promoted and supported within the Western academic world.

5. Technical Issues to Ensure Accessibility

The premier technical issue for research in the West may be validity. Validity concerns both the issue of fidelity of reports to what occurred, or what is reported alongside some reality at the site, and the utility of findings for application beyond that setting (corresponding roughly to internal and external validity). But validity as understood by Western social science, even validity as reconstructed for use with phenomenological and qualitative research, may have little meaning for local peoples (Smith, 1999). In fact, Western scholars' concerns with validity may be annoying or even culturally offensive to local or indigenous peoples (Lincoln & Denzin, 2005). For example, Western institutions, following the Helsinki Protocol, all require some form of informed consent. This does not mean that local, native, or indigenous peoples recognize the rights of Westerners to impose such a form on them. In fact, in some contexts, informed consent forms are themselves seen as subtle and manipulative forms of colonial practice and are resisted by locals.[3]

Validity, of course, is profoundly implicated in "truth" and in specific regimes of truth interlocked with Western constructions of science, knowledge, and power. Even within the West, validity is now being contested, with social scientists choosing teams and sides—one team supporting randomized field experiments as the "gold standard," and the other team supporting a broader definition of validity that includes not only demonstrable facts/data (e.g., enrollment figures, budgets per pupil), but also research participants' social constructions. When truth is held to be collective wisdom, or group knowledge, or linked inextricably to alternative cosmologies, validity, even in its broadest form, becomes unintelligible to locals or indigenous peoples (Smith, 1999). The larger issue with cross-cultural research is accessibility, both to nonlocal audiences, but also and more importantly, to local and/or indigenous audiences.

There are, as readers will intuit, several other concerns in assuring that research is available and accessible to those who can use it most readily. Those other technical issues include: (a) longer text length, (b) publication in local outlets and languages, and (c) vigilant recognition of collaboration via authorship in all outlets. Although we are not prepared to fully understand or explicate all of these issues at this time, we can amplify them somewhat. For instance, when we speak of longer text length, we are trying to take into account the narrative structure of multivocal texts, the extensive elaboration of issues and concerns in the local context (where little can be taken for granted), the need to present sufficient data for nonresident research audiences to begin to have somewhat of a vicarious experience, and the necessity to create texts that are not only records of deep cultural exchange (and perhaps conflict), but, as pointed out earlier, bi- or multilingual. Such texts will never fit into the usual technical requirements for many journals that they be no longer than twenty to twenty-five pages.

In attempting to show the complexities of context, the problems inherent in positionality of the (usually Western) researcher, the kinds and sources of intercultural conflict, the forms of assimilation and resistance, and the deploying of methods, some perhaps created on site, which are culturally responsive, respectful, and cognizant of cultural mores, and the interplay of languages, chapters and articles, especially, will necessarily be longer, more open ended, and more layered as well as less amenable to closure. Longer text length for such work will—or perhaps should—become the norm for cross- and intercultural work.

Publication will also become both the solution and the problem. The academy's rising interest in evaluating only faculty publications that are in "core," "benchmarked," or high-prestige Western-, English-, or European-language journals will have to give way to recognition of journal articles—and other publications, including e-journals—that are not normally a part of the repertoire of Western universities. The central premise of high-quality cross- and intercultural ethnographic work of the future is that it will grow from local and/or indigenous concerns and will be given back to local peoples in forms that are useful to them. This may mean publication in outlets that are not normally a part of the *U.S. News and World Reports'* highest-prestige institutional publication list. If institutions are interested in assuring that faculty's work is respected, supported, funded, and found useful throughout the world, then the rules for promotion and tenure will have to change to accommodate this responsiveness to local peoples and international contexts. In some instances, this will be absolutely necessity, as indigenous people's declarations of rights have already demanded such collaboration. In other instances, volunteering such co-participation and collaboration will be the best route to social justice.

Coauthorship will also be a necessity. Texts without coauthorship will, in all probability, come to be seen as just more evidence of neocolonial forms of domination. The dialectic, conversational, multilingual, exchange-oriented text that characterizes a decolonized academy will be a text that is negotiated and coauthored by both local peoples and their Western collaborators, with equal space afforded for first authorship, and specific arrangements made for the sharing of accrued royalties. Karen Murphy Brown (1991) described a similar situation in her research on a vodou practitioner in the Bronx, where she made it plain that "Mama Lola," having become her family, shared 50-50 in the royalties from the eponymous book, *Mama Lola*. Similar arrangements, although not mandated anywhere, will naturally flow from coauthorship contracts for books. It may be critical, however, for Western scholars to talk openly about these arrangements and how fiscal arrangements may evolve within the community. Some vigilance in this regard will be demanded of Western researchers.

International research may require a vastly different set of premises to ensure that research proves useful, liberatory, and nonoppressive to locals. Methods must be found, or created in situ, to assure accessibility and to enable locals to pursue nomination of research agendas that foster self-determination. It is not merely whether research should serve only or primarily the interests of Western scholars; in fact, in retrospect, it is unclear just how such research has served Western interests. Some ethnographic work has been seriously ethnocentric. Some has served colonial powers far better than it has served local peoples. And some has done little to foster rights to self-determination of indigenous peoples or to preserve cultural traditions. New agendas for ethnographers might redress this imbalance.

Conclusion

In an effort to decolonize the academy, and in recognition of the increasing internationalization of Western institutions, we have identified five major arenas where specific attention might be given to creating decolonizing and locally useful forms of research. Chief among these is the creation of bilingual texts and the purposeful effort to feed results back into the local context via a variety of strategies, where local users can design locally and culturally specific strategies for addressing their own needs as well as empowering themselves to take action. It is clear that for the present, Western scholars hold more power and resources in academic and community research. This creates great obligations, with the premise that from those to whom much has been given, much will be asked. It is likewise true that many native and indigenous peoples have declared their rights vis-à-vis research efforts in their lands, communities, and territories. It is therefore incumbent on Western scholars to reach out in democratic and liberatory ways, with great humility, to effect research collaborations that help achieve social justice. If we do not, we may find ourselves—quite appropriately—locked out.

Notes

1. A previous version of this article was accepted for publication in *Forum: Qualitative Social Research* [on-line journal], 7(4), Art. 1, September 2006.

2. We are grateful to Susan Lynham for suggesting this term. It is a distinctly African terminology, used to train individuals who are going to spend time in the bush to look for snakes. "Soft eyes" refers to an ability to recognize patterns and to "see" snakes before one is so close as to be in danger. It is a kind of focus that not only sees context, but also sees markers, and that sees peripherally, rather than in hard focus on singular objects.

3. A particularly interesting (and personally amusing) example of this occurs in Australia. Australia has policies and procedures almost precisely like those in the United States regarding informed consent and other research protocols. Australia's aboriginal peoples construct such forms as both colonizing (neocolonial) and, at the same time, disrespectful of the community's traditions of having knowledge be a community property/good. Knowledge, therefore, resides in the tribe, not in individuals, who have no right to sign such forms. Although the federal government in Australia requires them, thousands of research participants—all Aboriginal peoples—cannot, in all good conscience, and will not, in resistance, sign them. What's a researcher to do?

References

Anzaldúa, G. (1987). *Borderlands/La Frontera: The new mestiza.* San Francisco: Aunt Lute Books.

Bishop, R. (2005). Freeing ourselves from neocolonial domination in research: A Kaupapa Māori approach to creating knowledge. In N. K. Denzin & Y. S. Lincoln (Eds.), *Handbook of qualitative research* (3rd ed., pp. 109–138). Thousand Oaks, CA: Sage.

Bowles, P. (1949). *The sheltering sky.* New York: New Directions.

Brown, K. M. (1991). *Mama Lola: A vodou priestess in Brooklyn.* Berkeley: University of California Press.

Erlandson, D., Harris, E., Skipper, B., & Allen, S. (1993). *Doing naturalistic inquiry: A guide to methods.* Newbury Park, CA: Sages.

Finkelstein, M. J., Seal, R. K., & Schuster, J. H. (1998). *The new academic generation: A profession in transformation.* Baltimore: Johns Hopkins University Press.

Finnegan, D., & Matveev, A. (2002). There is no word for... . Translation issues for international and comparative research. *Planning and Changing, 33*(12), 13–28.

Gee, J. P. (1999). *An introduction to discourse analysis: Theory and method.* London: Routledge.

González y González, E. (2004). Perceptions of selected senior administrators of higher education institutions in Mexico regarding needed administrative competencies. Unpublished doctoral dissertation, Texas A&M University, College Station, Texas.

Jankie, D. (2004). "Tell me who you are": Problematizing the construction and positionalities of "insider"/"outsider" of a "native" ethnographer in a postcolonial context. In K. Mutua & B. B. Swadener (Eds.), *Decolonizing* research in cross-cultural contexts: Critical personal narratives (pp. 87–106). Albany: SUNY Press.

Jarvis, P. (1987). *Adult learning in the social context.* New York: Croom Helm Ltd.

Lincoln, Y. S., & Denzin, N. K. (2005). Epilogue. In N. K. Denzin & Y. S. Lincoln (Eds.), *Handbook of qualitative research* (3rd ed., pp. 1115–1126). Thousand Oaks, CA: Sage.

Menchú, R. (1998). *Crossing borders.* London: Verso Ed.

Mutua, K., & Swadener, B. B. (Eds.). (2004). *Decolonizing research in cross-cultural contexts: Critical personal narratives.* Albany: SUNY Press.

Rosaldo, R. (1989). *Culture and truth: The remaking of social analysis.* Boston: Beacon Press.

Smith, L.T. (1999). *Decolonizing methodologies.* London: Zed Books.

Spradley, J. P. (1980). *Participant observation.* Orlando, FL: Harcourt.

Temple, B. (1997). Watch your tongue: Issues in translation and cross-cultural research. *Sociology, 31*(3), 607–618.

Temple, B., & Edwards, R. (2002). Interpreters/translators and cross-language research: Reflexivity and border crossing. *International Journal of Qualitative Methods, 1*(2), article 1. Retrieved April 22, 2005, from http://www.ualberta.ca/~ijqm/

van Maanen, J. (1988). *Tales of the field: On writing ethnography.* Chicago: University of Chicago Press.

Vijver, F. J., & Leung, K. (1997). *Methods and data analysis for cross-cultural research.* Thousand Oaks, CA: Sage.

Chapter 11 | Humble and Humbling Research

A Modest Witnessing

Carolyne J. White
Rutgers University

1. "One must choose words carefully and mean what we say. Words are very powerful, spiritually and practically.... . What if everything we said to each other was similar to prayer?" Speaking primarily in the Dine language, Navajo Council delegate, Thomas Walker, Jr., provides an intervention in the convention of the Eurocentric university environment. Educated through community, not schools, Thomas shares traditional knowledge with the thirteen student participants in the Alchini Ba (For the Children) Navajo Teacher Education Program. He invites them to cling to their cultural heritage, to remember the importance of their relationships with people, with nature and with the divine. He tells them that their participation in Alchini Ba is a high calling, saying: "When I read the grant proposal, I was very moved that this was a project to do teacher education differently, Navajo specific. I stand in moral support of the program."

2. Robert Allen Warrior (1995) writes,

> If our struggle is anything, it is the struggle for sovereignty, and if sovereignty is anything, it is a way of life.... . It is a decision—a decision we make in our minds, in our hearts, and in our bodies—to be sovereign and to find out what that means in the process.... . The value of our work then expresses itself in the constant struggle to understand what we do rather than in telling people what they should do.... . We are inserted into the life of a people, and our work grows out of the same landscape as does theirs. [p. 123]

3. Bobby Robbins, Jr., comes by my office to return a book I lent him, *Escaping Education: Living as Learning within Grassroots Cultures*, written by Madhu Suri Prakash and Gustavo Esteva.

Two summers ago, participants in the Hopi Teachers for Hopi Schools Teacher Education Program took a specially designed graduate course focused on issues of tribal sovereignty. This book was one of our readings. Papers written during the course were polished for presentation at the American Educational Studies Association Annual Conference in Mexico City. After the conference, we traveled to Oaxaca to meet with Gustavo Esteva and learn more about the work engaged in by indigenous peoples in Oaxaca, peoples who share a similar history with institutional forms of schooling designed to "civilize" them out of their culture. These peoples are working to regenerate their traditional places and reclaim, restore, and/or recreate their new commons. Many of these indigenous peoples have moved beyond schooling to community-based forms of education. As Corrine Glesne (2003) writes, this is accomplished through local autonomy, harmony with nature, and a valuing of community over individuality, a community where relationships are woven in webs of responsibilities (p. 202).

We talk with Gustavo about this work. One of the students, Melissa Yazzie, asks him if he thinks our program's purpose—to prepare culturally responsive public schoolteachers—is wrong. Should we avoid being part of Western schooling? His answer, "No, you should become Schindlers, challenge cultural genocide from the inside."

4. A Navajo participant in the Hopi Teachers for Hopi Schools Teacher Education Program I codirect, Bobby is completing his student teaching at a reservation school. He loves teaching. With uncontainable passion, he tells me of the positive relationships he is building with his fourth-grade students. We, too, have created a positive relationship over our two years as co-learners, co-researchers, co-conference presenters.

Like Terri McCarty (2002), "I long ago stepped over the line between researcher-writer and friend—a line that is … artificial and obstructive" (p. 3) to my engagement with applied indigenous praxis.

Together, Bobby and I travel personal, cultural, theoretical, and geographical landscapes. On this day, we speak of an article we are writing and we speak of my plans to relocate. Tears fall across my face as I tell him that I will be moving to New Jersey to accept a university position closer to where my adult children live. Bobby says I am making the right decision to be closer to family. We revisit our initial meeting in a social foundations course, a course that invited Bobby to rethink his understandings of sovereignty and to create his vision for culturally responsive pedagogy. Bobby thanks me for inviting him to join the Hopi Teachers for Hopi Schools Program, saying, "It changed my life, and it changed the life of my daughter." He tells me of his plans to take graduate courses at night during his first year of work as an elementary schoolteacher. He says, "I want to get a Ph.D., like you."

5. "My soul moans that part of me that was destroyed by that callous instrument ... the book" (Rosa Villafane-Sisolak, quoted in Anzaldúa, 1987).

I returned to years of doctoral study and my community of friends, Corrine Glesne and Guy Senese, also engaged in work connected to indigenous communities. I reflect on the dissertation I wrote for my Ph.D., a dissertation (see White, 1991) that explored, collaboratively, the educational journeys of a group of Navajo and Hopi former Upward Bound students. Seeking an interruption of what Scott Richard Lyons (2000) terms rhetorical imperialism, the destructive failure discourse that has framed and dominated research with indigenous communities, I wanted to "change the subject" (Henriques et al., 1984) with counter-course stories from former students who had successfully pursued postsecondary education. Weaving my counter-course story as a student from a working-class Mormon military background, a first-generation college student, a white woman seeking to learn my way into a scholarly Schindler-like space, I wanted our work together to make a positive difference in the world, in the world of scholarship where narrative sickness (see Freire, 1972) persists and contributes to the reduction of life chances in the daily lived worlds of so many children for whom the educational system in this country has not been designed to serve well.

Called collective life story research, it was actually closer to the resistance literature tradition of *testimonio* (see Tierney, 2003); its focus on bearing witness to issues of "social urgency" by those who have been "silenced, excluded, and marginalized" (p. 297). My role as researcher similar to that described by Elisabeth Burgos-Debrary (1984) as being a "listener" and "instrument ... allowing ... the transition from the spoken to the written word" (p. xx). Responsive to many of the concerns and recommended protocols advocated by indigenous scholars today (see Crazy Bull, 1997; Haig-Brown & Archibald, 1996; Hermes, 1998; Kana'iaupuni, 2004; Smith, 1999), I sought to write ethically, therapeutically, vulnerably, and respectfully. I knew co-researchers participated more out of trust and friendship than out of a thorough understanding of the implications of "informed consent." I wanted to honor the gift of their friendship, the gift of their stories. I wanted to honor their lives.

6. Gerald Vizenor (1995a, p. 68) writes

The woodland dream songs and trickster stories

that would bear the humor and tragic wisdom of tribal native experience were superseded in the

literature of dominance.

As carefully as I sought to reflexively clarify the subjectivities that informed my work, to respectfully inhabit and engage borderland (see Anzaldúa, 1987) space, to embrace "methodological humility" and honor the "epistemic privilege" (see Narayan, 1998) of the co-researchers, my vision was clouded. Invested in viewing education as the route to liberation, my liberation and the liberation of my indigenous collaborators, I could not imagine the argument I accept today that it may not be possible to sufficiently reform the American colonial system of McEducation (see Prakash & Stuchul, 2004) to ever legitimately serve the cultural, epistemological, and ontological needs of sovereign, indigenous nations (see Prakash & Esteva, 1998).

As Sandy Grande (2004) writes, I am a whitestream scholar who did not understand what it means to be tribal; nor was I fully cognizant of the multiple ways the deep structures of American democracy have sought to extinguish tribalism (also see Lomawaima & McCarty, 2002; Wilkins & Lomawaima, 2001). Thinking myself radical, I did not imagine myself an agent of cultural invasion driven by messianic ethnocentrism (see Bowers, 2004). I unproblematically advocated for, indeed valorized, the

merits of a Western university education. Blinded by my investment in the Western liberal ideals/myths of linear progress, indi-
vidualism, and emancipation, I was also blind to how my focus on
"individuals making their own histories" is one with the Western
Enlightenment ideal of autonomous, self-creating individuals, the
linchpin of the ideology of global capitalism. I failed to see how
these ideological investments undermine indigenous nationhood
(see Deloria & Lytle, 1984) and peoplehood (see Holm, Pearson,
& Chavis, 2003) and collude with the ongoing assault on indigenous life. Ironically, it is within the context of working to equip
Hopi and Navajo students to become culturally responsive teachers, to honor and embrace critical understandings of tribal sovereignty, that I am able to develop this critique of my own work.

6. Chandra Mohanty (1991, p. 5) asks

> Who produces knowledge about colonized peoples
>
> What are the politics of the production
>
> of this particular knowledge?

As told elsewhere (White, 2005), I have traveled a circuitous
journey in and out of work with indigenous communities, a journey begun in the late 1960s when I worked as the secretary for an
Upward Bound Program serving Navajo and Hopi students, work
that invited me to revision myself as capable of completing a college degree, to work in the 1970s as director of the same program
following my completion of bachelor and master's degrees, to my
dissertation research in the 1980s, and my more recent return
in the 1990s and creation of three indigenous teacher education
programs in collaboration with the Hopi and Navajo nations.
A Hopi woman I knew as a high school student in the 1960s
told me that she had prayed me back to assist with the completion of her doctoral dissertation. Among the student participants
of the Alchini Ba program are two Navajo sisters, Andrea and
Cassandra Singer, daughters of two of the collaborators from my
dissertation research. My life and work has been entwined with
indigenous peoples for nearly forty years. My work toward creating indigenous teacher education programs is a form of reciprocity
(see Glesne, 2006) for what I have been given.

My presence as a non-Native scholar engaged in collaborative praxis with indigenous communities remains unacceptable to some indigenous scholars. Within this debate of who can conduct research within indigenous communities, Sandy Grande (2004) advises that, "By displacing the real sites of struggle (sovereignty and self-determination), the discourse of identity politics ultimately obfuscates the real sources of oppression—colonialism and global capitalism" (p. 92).

Devon Mihesuah (2003) draws a distinction between gatekeepers and those who seek to change the status quo:

> Gatekeepers are concerned about their jobs, promotion, profit, and power. Most scholars are concerned about those things, but the major difference between the camps is that Native and non-Native scholars fighting the status quo are concerned about the welfare of tribes, empowerment for Indigenous peoples, inclusive stories of the past and present, and overturning the colonial structures, including the gatekeepers. Indigenes who do not strive for those goals only help to reinforce the power structure that subsumes all Natives, and so do those "friendly" colleagues who stand by and watch gatekeeping occur. [p. 33]

8. "Do you consider yourself an indigenous person?" This question, asked by my colleague, Elaine Riley-Taylor (2002), invites me to "re-think my relational knowing with the land I inhabit, re-think the relations marking me as who I am, as indigenous to this place as any creature threading the web of the ecological balance" (p. 136).

This rethinking invites another knowing. Caught in the crosshairs of identity politics, incalcitrant tribal bureaucracy born of the brutalizing cultural genocide of Euro American colonization, and victimizing paternalistic governmental policies, the cultural hegemony of Eurocentric knowledge, today I claim a fractured, dynamic, subversive identity as white, non-Native indigenous ally, scholar-collaborator engaged with Navajo and Hopi peoples in praxis: that murky and power-filled intersection of theory, language, and practice. Our praxis seeks to honor tribal sovereignty and self-determination. With my university colleague and Alchini Ba co-principal investigator, Guy Senese, this praxis requires a relentlessly local, more organic approach to research. This is research that de-centers the notion of state knowledge production as privileged university activity and centers on community needs within webs of responsibilities. This is research that deconstructs the obsession with research methods and embraces a more improvisational approach to research (see White & Hermes, 2005). This is research that works toward harmony with Native epistemology and cosmology. This is research that honors the indigenous community as the "university."

Carol Lee Sanchez (1983) speaks to the enormity of this undertaking: "Our [indigenous] science studies living things: how they interact and how they maintain a balanced existence. Your [white] science disregards—even denies—the spirit world; ours believes in it and remains connected to it" (p. 152).

I write, conscious that "words are very powerful, spiritually and practically." I seek "prayerful" decolonizing methodologies. Born into saguaro landscape, I travel many circuitous paths to learn my way into Schindler-like scholarly space, to learn connection to the land I inhabit, to learn relationship with the original inhabitants of this land.

9. Donna Haraway (1997, p. 267) incites me to foreground witnessing over other forms of academic knowing that,

> witnessing is seeing; attesting; standing publicly accountable for, and psychically vulnerable to, one's visions and representations. Witnessing is a collective, limited practice that depends on the constructed and never finished credibility of those who do it, all of whom are mortal, fallible, and fraught with the consequences of unconscious and disowned desires and fears. [p. 267]

References

Anzaldúa, G. (1987). *Borderlands/La Frontera: The new mestiza*. San Francisco: Aunt Lute Books.

Bowers, C. (2004). Revitalizing the commons or an individualized approach to planetary citizenship: The choice before us. *Educational Studies: Journal of the American Education Studies Association, 36*(1), 45–58.

Burgos-Debray, E. (1984). Preface. In R. Menchu, *I, Rugoberta Menchu: An Indian woman in Guatemala* (E. Burgos-Debray, Ed., & Trans.) New York: Verso.

Crazy Bull, C. (1997). A Native conversation about research and scholarship. *Tribal College Journal, 40*(1), 17–23.

Glesne, C. (2003). The will to do: Youth regenerating community in Oaxaca, Mexico. *Educational Studies, 34*(2), 198–212.

Glesne, C. (2006). *Becoming qualitative researchers* (3rd ed.). New York: Pearson Education, Inc.

Grande, S. (2004). *Red pedagogy: Native American social and political thought.* Lanham, MD: Rowman & Littlefield.

Friere, P. (1972). *Pedagogy of the oppressed.* London: Penguin.

Haig-Brown, C., & Archibald, J. (1996). Transforming First Nations research with respect and power. *International Journal of Qualitative Studies in Education, 9*(3), 245–267.

Haraway, D. (1997). *FemaleMan_Meets_OncoMouse: Feminism and technoscience.* New York: Routledge. Available online at Modest_witness@ second_millennium

Henriques, J., Hollway, W., Urwin, C., Venn, C., & Walkerdine, V. (1984). *Changing the subject: Psychology, social regulation, and subjectivity.* London: Methuen.

Hermes, M. (1998). Research methods as a situated response: Towards a First Nation's methodology. *Qualitative Studies in Education, 11*(1), 155–168.

Holm, T., Pearson, J. D., & Chavis, B. (2003). Peoplehood: A model for the extension of sovereignty in American Indian Studies. *Wicazo Sa Review, 18*(1), 7–24.

Kana'iaupuni, S. M. (2004). Ka'akala Ku Kanaka: A call for strength-based approaches from a Native Hawaiian perspective. *Educational Researcher, 33*(6), 26–32.

Lomawaima, K. T., & McCarty, T. L. (2002). When tribal sovereignty challenges democracy: American Indian education and the democratic ideal. *American Educational Research Journal, 39*(2), 279–305.

Lyons, S. R. 2000. Rhetorical sovereignty: What do American Indians want from writing? *College, Composition and Communication, 51*(3), 447–468.

McCarty, T. L. (2002). *A place to be Navajo: Rough Rock and the struggle for self-determination in indigenous schooling.* Mahwah, NJ: Lawrence Erlbaum.

Mihesuah, D. (2003). *Indigenizing the academy: Transforming scholarship and empowering communities.* Lincoln: University of Nebraska Press.

Mohanty, C. (1991). Cartographies of struggle: Third World women and the politics of feminism. In C. Mohanty (Ed.), *Third World women and the politics of feminism* (pp. 1–47). Bloomington: Indiana University Press.

Narayan, U. (1998). Working together across differences: Some considerations on emotions and political practice. *Hypatia, 3*(2), 31–47.

Prakash, M., & Esteva, G. (1998). *Escaping education: Living as learning within grassroots cultures.* New York: Lang.

Prakash, M., & Stuchul, D. (2004). McEducation marginalized: Multiverse of learning-living in grassroots commons. *Educational Studies: Journal of the American Education Studies Association, 36*(1), 58–73.

Riley-Taylor, E. (2002). *Ecology, spirituality, & education: Curriculum for relational knowing.* New York: Peter Lang.

Sanchez, C. L. (1983). Racism: Power, profit, product—and patriarchy. *Women Studies Quarterly, 11*(3), 14–16.

Smith, L. T. (1999). *Decolonizing methodologies: Research and indigenous peoples.* New York: Zed Books.

Tierney, W. G. (2003). Undaunted courage: Life history and the postmodern challenge. In N. K. Denzin & Y. S. Lincoln (Eds.), *Strategies of qualitative inquiry* (2nd ed., pp. 292–318). Thousand Oaks, CA: Sage.

Vizenor, G. (1995a). Measuring my blood. In G. Vizenor (Ed.), *Native American literature: A brief introduction and anthology* (pp. 68–74). New York: HarperCollins College Publishers.

Vizenor, G. (1995b). Ishi and the wood ducks. In G. Vizenor (Ed.), *Native American literature: A brief introduction and anthology* (pp. 299–336). New York: HarperCollins College Publishers.

Warrior, R.A. (1995). *Tribal secrets: Recovering American Indian intellectual traditions.* Minneapolis: University of Minnesota Press.

White, C. J. (1991). Experiencing "Upward Bound": An interrogation of cultural landscapes. Unpublished doctoral dissertation, University of Illinois, Urbana-Champaign.

White, C. J., & Hermes, M. (2005). Learning to play scholarly jazz: An exploration into indigenous methods for a culturally responsive evaluation. In S. Hood, R. Hopson, & H. Frierson (Eds.), *The role of culture and cultural context: A mandate for inclusion, the discovery of truth and understanding in evaluative theory and practice* (pp. 105–128). Greenwich, CT: Information Age Publishing.

Wilkins, D. E., & Lomawaima, K. T. (2001). *Uneven ground: American Indian sovereignty and federal law.* Norman: University of Oklahoma Press.

Part Three
Contesting Regulation

Chapter 12	**Affirming the Will and the Way of the Ancestors**

Black Feminist Consciousness and the Search for "Good"[ness] in Qualitative Science

Cynthia B. Dillard and
Adrienne D. Dixson
The Ohio State University

Introduction

Situated in notions of an endarkened feminist epistemology (Dillard, 2000) and current musings on the art and science of portraiture as qualitative approach (Dixson, 2005; Lawrence-Lightfoot and Davis, 1997), this chapter explores the epistemological and spiritual meanings and the "goodness" of science from Black feminist perspectives. Our intention is to step outside the assumptions of social and identity theories that focus solely on intellectual pursuits and pragmatic concerns in qualitative research to examine research work in the world as having multiple and spiritual "points of affinity" (Appiah, 1992, p. viii).

Although formally trained as qualitative researchers and successful at our science, we recognize that, in terms of sustenance, these spiritual points of affinity have created life-affirming spaces for our intellectual, social, and spiritual work as African American feminist and qualitative researchers, spaces of tension and hope created through choosing to *consciously* engage in deeper relationship with spiritual knowing in our research lives as women of color and spirit (Dillard, Tyson, & Abdur-Rashid, 2000). According to Lawrence-Lightfoot & Davis (1997), "goodness [is] a concept whose expression is best documented through detailed, nuanced narratives placed in context" (p. 142). Thus, as we consider the attempts of regulatory bodies (and our own academies) to more strictly define the goodness of science, it is critical that we engage our ideas at the level of representation, to allow others to see that "goodness is really a search for a generous, balanced, probing perspective" (Lawrence Lightfoot & Davis, 1997, p. 146). The following autobiographical narrative pieces are the ground from which our current notions of Black feminism, goodness, and spirituality arise.

We Are the Goodness We Seek: Becoming Black Feminist Thinkers

Cynthia's Narrative: A Literate Life

I was born
a Black child
in a Black family.
My parents loved me
And I, them.
They introduced me to
four sisters
and a
darling baby brother
who loved me
and I, them.

They all
taught me things,
my older sister especially,
she liked all those books
that people dropped off
at our house
My Mom and Dad
didn't have enough money to buy them
'cuz you know
"you can't eat books... ."

I didn't like books,
they didn't say
nothin to me and
Sally

Dick
and Jane
didn't look anything like me,
and I didn't read too well.
But I could write
and so I did.
I wrote on the sidewalk
with a big piece of rock chalk
C-Y-N-T-H-I-A.
That was
my name
and I knew it
'cuz my Mom told me I
"spelled it right" and
"wrote it good."

My sister kept on reading and
I kept on writing.
I went to school
when I was six
with my sister
and my pencils in my
Barbie lunch box.
I liked Barbie.
She was really pretty and
I wanted pretty hair like hers,
not kinky like mine.

I went to the kindergarten room.
There were lots of kids in there!
Black ones and Chinese ones and
White ones and some that were all mixed up!
And there was Mrs. Jones,
my teacher.
She was Black like me and
that made me happy.
And she liked me
And I, her.
One day,

I wet my dress.
And a little White boy called me
a "stupid nigger."
I remember Mrs. Jones
grabbed his arm really hard
and made him apologize.
He said "sorry"
and we were friends after that.
But when I told Mom about what happened
in school
(she always asked),
she said
"When someone calls you a nigger
you just hold your head up
'cuz that's not what you are.
Niggers can be any color
Black, white, grizzly or grey,
but they're people
who don't care about nobody or themselves.
You get your education and
prove to them you ain't no nigger,
you hear me, girl?

So I did.
I learned how to read pretty good
Mrs. Jones had us readin' to each other everyday.
I left Mrs. Jones class
of different colored kids and went
all the way to middle school and suddenly,
I was the only Black kid in my school!
(Well there were two other Black girls
but one was really bad so
I didn't hang around with her,
And one thought she was one of the white girls
so I didn't really like her either!)
Mom always said
That no matter how hard you tried
"Your skin would always tell on you,"
and my teachers would all say that

"everybody is the same and equal and everything,"
But when I asked if I could write about
Malcolm X and my teacher said no
"because we are writing about Martin Luther King during
Black History Week,
I couldn't understand
Why it was only a week,
I thought my history went on everyday?

Then I went to high school,
and I was real popular,
I went to everybody's parties
'cuz I could fit in with all the groups.
But debate was my favorite thing
because I could choose
who I wanted to read
who I wanted to write
or I could write something myself!
Delivery was easy 'cuz the stuff I was reading
sounded like me,
and I wasn't nervous because of what Mom told me:
"Head up, Cynthia. Hold it way up there!
Girl, I'm so proud of you!"

Then I started college.
KKK tried to run me out.
They scared me,
even as I tried to be brave.
There was this little tiny voice inside me
kept sayin'
"Be strong, like Sojourner,
Martin, Malcolm.
Be strong."
I used to sing spirituals
on my way to campus,
they made me feel better and
reminded me of home,
the place I came from and
the place where I was going.

And now I'm here at OSU.
A Black woman professor
in a white university.
That little voice?
It's still inside me.
"Be strong, Cynthia.
Be strong."
I'm still in a place
where I'm usually
the only Black person
on committees
on commissions
at receptions,
but I'm sharing myself
with the rest of the world.
I'm writing life now
and reading it too.
Through all of these trials and tribulations,
I know I've got something to say.
It sounds like me.
It is me.
And people need
to hear my voice
tell my story. [6/89]

Adrienne's Narrative: "You Are the Queen!"

For as long as I can remember people—family members and friends of the family—have always told me that I was "just like" my paternal grandmother, Alice Lynn-Audrey Rose Bryant. Physically, my grandmother and I looked nothing alike. She, "dark chocolate" and me, "toffee" colored, would never be mistaken for each other by the uninformed eye. However, what I think people meant by saying I was "just like" her, was/is this way of being that exhibits a tenacity and sense of place or belonging that comes from knowing, without question who you are. My grandmother, a native of southern Louisiana, instilled in all of her grandchildren, especially the girls, a belief that as individuals, we were to determine our place in the world and that no one, not even *she*, would be able to direct or deter our paths. A deeply spiritual woman, my grandmother taught me the value of prayer and meditation. She taught me to visualize those things that mattered to me—health, happiness and prosperity.

In kindergarten, I came home from school mortified that a white classmate had called me a "nigger." It was my first real negative encounter with race. Recognizing that I looked differently from him, I had never heard the word and wondered if he knew something about me that I didn't. Until that time, my consciousness of what it meant to be Black was shaped by Black people in all shades speaking a beautiful form of English—creolized southern Louisiana patois—that sounded like they were singing. Each home we visited, be it a blood relative or one my grandmother's "home people" (also transplants to South Central Los Angeles from New Orleans), was filled with wonderful smells of food that formed the staple of my diet for the first ten years of my life—red beans and rice, jambalaya, gumbo, boiled crab, "Aint (Aunt) Emma's" German Chocolate Cake. The family stories of life in Phoenix, Louisiana (recently destroyed by the flooding after Hurricane Katrina) and my grandmother's grandfather, "Papa Isaac," a Creole and the first Black man to work for New Orleans' Sewage and Water Board, affirmed that I came from a long line of strong and proud Black people.

In response to my shock at being called a nigger, my grandmother told me a "nigger" was someone who was stupid and ignorant and that Black people were not "niggers." I grew up in a household where I was forbidden from using "nigger" in reference to Black people. Somewhere in the fifth or sixth grade, I learned that the term was historically used to degrade and demean Black people. Until that time, however, I believed what my grandmother told me and never owned or internalized the term.

As a young woman growing into my womanhood and negotiating relationships with men, my grandmother taught me that it was important that I not look for anyone to "do" for me, but rather that I "do" for myself. That is, she made certain that I (and my other female cousins) understood not only the importance of being financially independent but also my value as a woman. She owned several homes, had an impressive stock market portfolio including savings bonds, and acquired all of this before she married my grandfather, Blyde Bryant, from Shreveport, Louisiana. She believed that as a woman, you entered a relationship being able to contribute and not expecting that someone will take of you. She regularly took me with her to collect the rent on her properties, admonishing me to be responsible with my finances.

My grandmother told me on a number of occasions, and each time rather emphatically, "You are the queen!" This "queen-ness" my grandmother told me that I held, was not about a sense of unearned or undeserving privilege, but rather part of a legacy of strong Louisiana women. In her home, she was the benevolent queen. With her help (both financial and emotional), scores of young women and their children, many of whom were either related to us by marriage or were the children of her "home people," lived with us until they could "get on their feet." My grandmother truly embodied this notion of the "othermother." She raised or helped raise so many children that the line between blood and fictive kinship was blurry and insignificant. I grew up with scores of "cousins" and "aunties," never feeling that I was without someone who "had my back." Armed with this sense of self and a connection to others, I have managed to make my way far from the West Coast and even New Orleans to places that are indeed unfamiliar. But I am never alone.

"To Whom Much Is Given, Much Is Expected"

Centering African Cosmology, Endarkened Feminist Epistemology, and Goodness in Science and Research

Three key concepts of an African-based cosmology undergird this paper and are crucial to understanding the roots of an endarkened feminist epistemological stance and our understanding of the goodness of science. They are: spirituality, community, and praxis (thought and action).

Spirituality, according to Richards (1980), is not a rationalistic concept that can be measured, explained or reduced to neat conceptual categories. Instead, as Vanzant (1996) suggests, it is "the truth of who we are at the core of our being ... the consciously active means by which we can recognize, activate, and live the impartial, nonjudgmental, consistent truth of who we are" (p. xxiii). Spirituality, in African-centered thought is the very essence of African people, regardless where we are in the world.

The second concept is community. Joy James (1993) argues for the theoretical and the pragmatic usefulness of Pan African experiences in her analysis of the concepts of community and praxis. According to James, a community is not bound by temporal or physical limits: Africans belong to the African community, even when not residing in a predominately African community:

> Belonging is not determined by physical proximity... .You may move out of the state or the old neighborhood to "escape" your family or people, but you carry that family, the neighborhood, inside yourself. They remain your family... .You determine not whether you belong *but the nature of the relationship and the meaning of the belonging.* [p. 32, emphasis added]

Utilizing this African understanding of community, this chapter has a common theme of our on-going need to connect the unfamiliar (whether language, traditions, or other cultural ways of knowing) to our "home" communities, communities that continue to be more expansive and generative, given research connections made within the African world and beyond.

Thus, within traditional African cosmology, research and educational practice are not viewed as the luxury of a few or as alienated activity: They are *central* to the community and provide a way to realize the ideals of the community. Any notion of goodness must be judged on the basis of whether it serves or is of service to the community. So, the third concept of an African cosmology is activist praxis, mandating research and educational practice as concrete physical action/service beyond solely "researcher theorizing." In this way, research as service on behalf of the community is indispensable to philosophizing and theorizing from an African epistemological standpoint—and activist praxis becomes essential:

> [Activist praxis] is a necessity, for it embodies active service for the good of the community and individuals within that community... .Theory is done from the standpoint of the individual—in relationship to community. Where you stand when you philosophize and theorize determines who benefits from your thinking. [James, 1993, pp. 33–34]

In what James calls "the wedded complementarity of life struggles," praxis on behalf of freedom, and with particular regard for education and research, is not a luxury from an African worldview: It is *essential*. Thus, we believe there is inherent goodness in the way that we, as African people, order our world. More particularly, we believe there is inherent goodness in the way that we, as African American women, order our thoughts and actions based in Black feminist thought, in an endarkened feminist epistemology (Dillard, 2000).

Endarkened Feminist Epistemology[1]

According to Stanfield (1993), "epistemological concerns in cultural research in the social sciences cannot be divorced from concerns regarding the functions of culturally hegemonic domination in knowledge production and dissemination and in the selections and rewarding of intellectual careers" (p. 26). Additionally, the underlying understanding of the nature of reality and the forms of discourse one employs to construct realities in research (or is encouraged or permitted to employ) significantly impacts not only what can be said and how it is said, but where it is said. Nowhere is this truer than in the interpretation and representation of educational inquiry, in its ontologies, epistemologies, pedagogies, and ethical concerns.

In this chapter, we lean on Dillard's (2000) notions of an endarkened feminist epistemology. In defining an endarkened feminist epistemology, Dillard deliberately sought language that attempts to unmask traditionally held political and cultural constructions/constrictions, language that more accurately organizes, resists, and transforms oppressive descriptions of sociocultural phenomena and relationships. And language has historically served and continues to serve as a powerful tool in the mental, spiritual, and intellectual colonization of African Americans and other marginalized peoples. According to Asante (1988), language itself is *epistemic*: it provides a way for persons to understand their reality. Thus, to transform that reality, the very language we use to define and describe phenomena must possess instrumentality: It must be able to *do* something toward transforming particular ways of knowing and producing knowledge.[2]

In contrast to the common use of the term "enlightened" as a way of expressing the having of new and important feminist insights (arising historically from the well-established canon of White feminist thought), I use the term "endarkened" feminist epistemology to articulate how reality is known when based in the historical roots of Black feminist thought, embodying a distinguishable difference in cultural standpoint, located in the intersection/overlap of the culturally constructed socializations of race, gender, and other identities and the historical and contemporary contexts of oppressions and resistance for African American women.

From an endarkened feminist epistemological space, moving away from the traditional metaphor of research as recipe to fix some "problem" to a metaphor that centers reciprocity and relationship *necessitates* a different relationship between ourselves as the researcher and the researched, between our knowing and the production of knowledge. This is also where Black feminist knowledge[3] provides an angle of vision from which to construct an alternative version of this relationship and a new metaphor in educational research, one that moves us away from detachment with participants and contexts and their use as "ingredients" in our research recipes and toward an epistemological position more appropriate for work within such communities.

Thus, a more useful research metaphor arising from an endark-ened feminist epistemology is *research as a responsibility*, answer-able and obligated to the very persons and communities being engaged in the inquiry. A brief discussion of the assumptions of an endarkened feminist epistemology follows.

Assumption #1: Self-definition forms one's participation and responsibility to one's community.

From an endarkened epistemological ground, all views expressed and actions taken related to educational inquiry arise from a personally and culturally defined set of beliefs that render the researcher *responsible* to the members and the well-being of the community from which their very definition arises. What is sug-gested is that the struggle for a self-defined feminist consciousness for African American women in our roles as scholars seems to require embracing both a culturally centered world-view (in this case African centered) and a feminist sensibility. Through such praxis, an alternative ideology and cultural meaning for research is articulated, one that reflects elements of both traditions, a both/and standpoint (Collins, 1990) deeply rooted in the everyday experiences of African American women. Central to an endark-ened feminist epistemology is the idea that, even with the vari-ability that will inevitably be articulated in the unique individual versions of who we are as Black women researchers, coherence is realized in our collective refusal to be reduced to someone else's terms: to give voice to silenced spaces as an act of resistance.

Assumption #2: Research is both an intellectual and a spiritual pursuit, a pursuit of purpose.

An endarkened feminist epistemology draws on a spiritual tra-dition, where the concern is not solely with the production of knowledge (an intellectual pursuit) but also with uncovering and constructing truth as the fabric of everyday life (a spiritual pur-suit). Thus, the "theories" of knowing that have guided research as a value-free social science are directly challenged when an endark-ened feminist epistemology is articulated, as alternate versions of truth are shared. African American women have historically and contemporarily addressed our multiple oppressions (personal and societal) through versions of spirituality (James, 1993; Lawrence-Lightfoot, 1994; Richards, 1980; Vanzant, 1996; Wade Gayles, 1995). However, the educational research literature by or about African American women researchers/teachers' spiritual concerns, though often unnamed, are pervasive (see exemplars in Foster, 1990; hooks, 1994; Hull, 2001; Ladson Billings, 1994).

Although these works are deeply intellectual, several elements are embedded within their purposes that imply research as a spiritual pursuit. First, there is an explicit, very powerful sense of self in the role of researcher/teacher, directly linked to a sense of purpose for whatever research moves are made. Second, there are often multiple levels of vulnerability in the research endeavor. An endarkened feminist epistemology enacts "stepping out on faith," whether traversing tenure and promotion, publication, unequal power relations or just being present in the academy. Third, there is a relationship of reciprocity and care apparent in the research project: Emotions are considered not only appropriate but also necessary in determining the validity of an argument (Collins, 1990). Finally, developing the capacity for empathy in research is critical for attempting to recognize the value of another's perspective, whether or not one agrees with that perspective. In this way, we are encouraged to welcome the conflict inherent in our diversity (of paradigms, methodology, representation), to live within its sometimes seeming ambiguity, and to develop the purpose in research of not just honoring our own version of the practice, praxis, and politics of research as truth, but to seek to honor the truth that is created and negotiated in and between ourselves, in relationship with one another as researchers.

Assumption #3: Only within the context of community does the individual appear (Palmer, 1983) and, through dialogue, continue to become.

Here, dialogue is key in both conducting research and in assessing knowledge claims: that there is value in the telling, in invading those secret silent moments often unspoken, in order to be understood as both participating in and responsible to one another as researchers. Further, there is value in being connected, in seeking harmony and wholeness as a way to discern "truth."

A number of researchers (Asante, 1988; Morrison, 1993; Ngugi, 1986) point to the importance of instrumentality in the language used to create relationships based on equality, that is, in dialogue that provides a new way to understand our reality and communal responsibility, as women researchers, teachers, and scholars of color. "Dialogue implies talk between two subjects, not the speech of a subject and an object. It is humanizing speech, one that challenges and resists domination" (hooks, 1989, p. 131). Thus, through awareness of an endarkened feminist epistemology, all involved in the conversation can resist and challenge entrenched ways of thinking about their research lives, and provide news ways to "be" researchers.

Assumption #4: Concrete experiences within everyday life form the criterion of meaning, the "matrix of meaning making" (Ephraim-Donker, 1997, p. 8).

Collins (1990) suggests that this underlies two aspects of knowing that are particularly important to this fourth assumption of an endarkened feminist epistemology: Knowledge and wisdom. She further elaborates:

> Women of color cannot afford to be fools of any type, for our objectification as the Other denies us the protection that white skin, maleness, and wealth confer. This distinction between knowledge and wisdom, and the use of experience as the cutting edge dividing them, has been key to [our] survival. In the context of race, gender, and class oppression, the distinction is essential. Knowledge without wisdom is adequate for the powerful, but wisdom is essential to the survival of the subordinate. [p. 208]

Thus, in our research, African American women often invoke our own concrete experiences and those of other women and communities of color in our selection of topics for investigation and for the methodologies that we engage (Collins, 1990). We study the concrete experiences and acts of African American or people of color, while at the same time striving to understand and explicate the wisdom contained in those meanings. As Collins states further: "These forms of knowledge allow for subjectivity between the knower and the known, rest in the women themselves (not in higher authorities), and are experienced directly in the world (not through abstractions)" (p. 211).

Thus, concrete experiences—uniquely individual, while at the same time both collective and connected—lend credibility to the work of African American women engaged in transformative research and inquiry, as well as suggest the presence of an endarkened feminist epistemology that grounds such work.

Assumption #5: Knowing and research are both historical (extending backwards in time) and outward into the world: to approach them otherwise is to diminish their cultural and empirical meaningfulness.

An endarkened feminist epistemology both acknowledges and works against the absent presence of women of color from the shaping of the rules that have historically guided formal educational research, the system of knowledge production within higher education, and the meanings and legitimacy surrounding research processes. In other words, Black feminist thought, although not a part of the original canon of theories, rules, and perspectives that surround what gets perpetuated today as educational research broadly defined, attempts to both highlight what's missing from these definitions as well as to extend these definitions through the inclusion of African women's knowledge. However, important to this assumption of an endarkened feminist epistemology is that such omissions have lead to what Wynter (1992) and others aptly describe as a distorted empirical reality fundamentally based on inclusion and exclusion as a way to maintain white and male superiority and as an organizer for our hierarchical social structures in education and society (Ani, 1994; Appiah, 1992; hooks, 1989; James, 1993; Stanfield, 1994).

We must recognize that the forms of discourse and literatures that have defined the claim of an epistemological universality (that which the talk of theory inevitably implies) inhibits both our ability to examine with necessary clarity (not to mention attention to ethical and moral concerns) and to interpret the complexity of human cultural thought and action that we study in educational research. In short, researchers who accept the relevance of post-structural, postmodern, feminist, and critical race theories have reason to be at least uncomfortable with extending these theories to contexts, peoples, methodology, texts, and work outside this tradition. In other words, one's epistemological basis for research must engage in relevant cultural understanding and theorizing that is informed by the insights of those experiencing the world as the very phenomena being explored.

Assumption #6: Power relations, manifest as racism, sexism, homophobia, etc. structure gender, race, and other identity relations within research.

Although African American women are more present in the academy today, the racist, sexist, and classist structures and belief systems around us remain relatively unchanged. The consequences of such stability are even more extreme when Black women seek to situate ourselves into spaces of feminist discourse only to find that:

> In a racist society like this one, the storytellers are usually white and so "women" turns out to be "white women." Why in the face of the challenges from "different" women and from feminist method itself is feminist essentialism so persistent and pervasive? In my view, as long as feminists, like theorists in the dominant culture, continues to search for gender and racial essences, Black women will not be anything more that a crossroads between two kinds of domination, or at the bottom of a hierarchy of oppressions. We will always be required to choose pieces of ourselves to present as wholeness. [Harris, 1990, p. 589]

Thus, an endarkened feminist epistemology has as its research project the vigilant and consistent desire to "dig up" the nexus of racial/ethnic, gender, and other identity realities: of how we understand and experience the world as Black women. For feminist research to truly embrace such an epistemological stance, gender, race, class, and other constructed identities (what some have despairingly referred to as "personal experiences" versus research texts), as well as their meanings within power asymmetries (Harding, 1987) that have historically constructed and been constructed by unequal access and contexts of power for Black women are positioned at the center of the research project. But, at the same time, an endarkened feminism seeks to resist and transform these social arrangements as well, seeking political and social change on behalf of the communities we represent as the purpose for research versus solely the development of universal laws or theories for human behavior.

Goodness in Science and Research and Black Feminist Consciousness

As in all qualitative work, research methodology is intimately connected to one's epistemological standpoint. And the search for goodness for Lawrence-Lightfoot and Davis (1997) is a crucial part of their articulation of a methodology called portraiture. As a methodology, portraiture serves as "counterpoint to the dominant chorus of social scientists whose focus has largely centered on the identification and documentation of social problems" (p. xvi). In addition, given that much of social science research is written for a particular audience, quite often the language is inaccessible for the general lay public. Lawrence-Lightfoot and Davis explain that with portraiture, one must seek to "illuminate the complex dimensions of goodness ... designed to capture the attention of a broad and eclectic audience" (p. xvi). This search for goodness is especially important when we consider the volume of literature (with the exception of some recent research by scholars of color) that focuses a pathological lens on African Americans and other groups of color. Specifically, with respect to Black women teachers, rarely has a positive light been shown on us as women and teachers. Lawrence-Lightfoot and Davis suggest further that the search for goodness

> is an intentionally generous and eclectic process that begins by searching for what is good and healthy and assumes that the expression of goodness will always be laced with imperfections. The researcher who asks first "what is good here?" is likely to absorb a very different reality than the one who is on a mission to discover the sources of failure. [Through the search for goodness], portraits are not documents of idealization or celebration. Rather, the inconsistencies, the vulnerabilities, and the ways in which people negotiate these terrains are central to the expression of goodness. [1997, p. 9]

Similarly for the researcher, the definition of goodness is defined in collaboration with the subject(s) of the research. The examples of goodness are organic. A primary objective for the portraitist is to look for multiple ways the subject expresses what is good and right—about the context, the processes, the structures, the ways of knowing and being.

We embrace this notion the search for goodness as a rather natural outcome of our epistemological and cultural positionalities as African American women, deeply rooted experientially and theoretically in Black feminist thought. Sociologist Patricia Hill Collins (2000) suggests that we can understand Black feminist thought as "facing the complex nexus of relationships among biological classification, the social construction of race and gender as categories of analysis, the material conditions accompanying these changing social constructions and Black women's consciousness about these themes" (p. 22).

Central to our reading of Collins's statement above (and Dillard's notions of an endarkened feminist epistemology discussed earlier in this chapter) is that for Black feminist scholars to engage in the search for goodness is to, at the same time, affirm the synchronous and harmonious relationship between what is "good" within a Black feminist standpoint and what is "good" within African[American] communities. Collins (1990) describes a Black women's standpoint as "those experiences and ideas shared by African-American women that provide a unique angle of vision on self, community, and society—and theories that interpret these experiences ... [Black feminist thought then] "encompasses [the] theoretical interpretations of Black women's reality by those who live it" (p. 22). For Black feminist scholars, embracing and utilizing an endarkened feminist epistemological standpoint and/or Black feminist thought is a fundamental part of a search for goodness, as the primary objective is to look for multiple ways that participants and researcher as participant express what is good and right: about the context, the processes, the structures, the ways of knowing and being. It is a way to center Blackness both as an epistemological standpoint and as a methodological one.

Stirring the Stew, Stirring the Soul:

Searching for Goodness through an Endarkened Feminist Dialogue

With these concepts in mind, the following dialogue both illustrates and illuminates Black feminist and spiritual notions of goodness in science and the ways in which such an alternative vision/version of goodness have the potential to create the sort of activist praxis that we seek. Further, this dialogue is an attempt to create an intellectual and spiritual space that embodies the courage to act collectively in service to our profession and most importantly, to transform our practice of research in service to our world. It is done not only to understand our situated realities as African American feminist scholars, but also to help support the search for goodness in our work and in our consciousness, related to spirituality, community and activist praxis in a space (the academy) that often cannot and does not affirm an endarkened search for goodness in educational research.

> CBD: As we look at our title, what do we mean by affirming the will and the way of the ancestors? To me, it means to recognize the spiritual purpose in everything that is. It means that if you recognize a spiritual purpose in all things, then you have to do what needs to be done in line with that purpose, regardless of the consequences. So, for example, when you affirm the will and the way of the ancestors, you also may choose to center your academic life as we both have, in Black feminist thought, or in African-centered thought, knowing that the consequences may be that we don't publish as much or maybe publish in the top journals. It means you choose to do the things that you do based on knowing it's what you're supposed to do, not necessarily focusing on what the consequences of that work are. That's what the ancestors say to me. I mean, you do it because it's the right thing to do. And the consequences will take care of [laughs] themselves!

> ADD: I think the first thing that pops into my head, and, what I wrote about when I was thinking about this is feeling a responsibility to the people who have shaped me. So, responsibility is probably the most important thing. And, responsibility to the ancestors, both living and not living.

> CBD: Okay.

> ADD: So, that the work that I do is always reflective of the way that I've been "trained." And, not only "trained" academically, but "trained" personally. So, I know that when I go out into the world, in whatever space I'm in, I am representing all the people who have shaped who I am. So, I am responsible in the work: It's

a responsibility that I have to them. It's about responsibility. My work is reflective of that responsibility. But I didn't think of it as a spiritual thing.

CBD: But it is. It's hard for me now not to think of everything that is or that we do as being spiritually guided. Because things happen in these academic lives of ours that I can't explain any other way!

ADD: Right.

CBD: For example, how is it that an article might take six years to find its way to the light of day in a refereed journal? I don't think it's because the article is either good or bad. It's because there are all these places that it has to travel, that have to be influenced before the paper can actually get to that published public place. That's not being guided by me as much as it's being guided by the ancestors saying that these people over here or this editorial board needs to read this and they need to react a particular way. Then they need to go back and fume about it. Or, they need to go back and affirm it or whatever. It needs to travel over here and it needs to travel over there before it actually comes to, a particular journal or a particular place, so that people have their experiences with it along the way. For me, this whole thing that we do is [laughs] always and in all ways about a bigger picture. Bigger work than what any one of us little people are doing! Um, so our work is always affecting people in line with what the ancestors and the Creator want. So [laughs], it doesn't really matter, in some ways, what I'm doing. What I mean is some designated outcome isn't necessarily the point where I try to make my impact. I want to make it in the process, you know? For example, I may have to let go of the idea of getting tenure or promotion, in order to be able to do work that's in line with the will and the way of the ancestors.

ADD: For me, it is always that I represent people who have been responsible for me. And, I am responsible for making sure that I represent them well. That's always in the back of my mind. So, it's my mother, it's my grandmother, it's my aunties. It's Gloria [Ladson-Billings]. It's my colleagues here, so, it'd be you, too, Cynthia. I recognize that I represent all these people when I go out and interact with folks. I have to be responsible and mindful. If people invite me to do things or ask me to do something, I have to think: "Well, what does this mean for all the people I feel I represent?" I know that I don't go out in the world by myself.

CBD: Sure. Actually, in the larger Black scheme of things and for Black women particularly, it is always about affirming Blackness. When you called up all those people who you just named, it's not unlike when I'm in Ghana and we pour libations and we call everybody living and dead to come together. It is this absolute affirmation of Blackness. When we call the ancestors, it's honoring a long lineage of Black folks. It is about saying out loud that Black people, whether here or there, have been doing good things on this Earth for an awful long time. And, in order for us to continue that tradition, we have to call on those who have come before and those who will come after to help us continue. You know, the way is hard. But, the business of affirming Blackness seems really central. We have to choose to *love* Blackness, and do work with spiritual and Black consciousness sorts of aims. We must choose to love Blackness, like bell hooks talks about, and that itself is a radical African-centered thought. To choose to love Blackness.

ADD: Yeah, yeah.

CBD: The next question then is about the search for goodness: What does it mean in our work? Part of what it means to me is that we come to the task in authentic kinds of ways. We attempt to not just write or look for those things that are already "known" in the context of the academy or in the context of research, but also the things that are "known" and need to be talked about again from a grounded perspective, that is, knowing not just intellectually, but also knowing experientially at least some of what it means to be Black. You know?

ADD: Yes. I guess one of the things when we talk about authenticity and about our universal knowing and knowing from particular spaces, the question that I always get is "But where are the perspectives of white teachers?" Now, you know, I don't do comparative work.

CBD: Right (laughs).

CBD: [Laughs]. And I think that's really what you're trying tell people who ask about the White women in your teacher studies. You are *not* studying White women: You *are* studying Black women. And there's no need to compare Black women and White women. This is what Black women's my experience is and it's legitimate on its own. It doesn't have to be compared to something in order to be made legitimate.

ADD: Right. People also have asked me if the goal of research is revisionist. They also want to know if I will only talk about the "good" things that Black women do. My response is that part of why I utilize portraiture is this notion of a search for goodness: It changes the lens that you go in with. For me, part of understanding goodness is recognizing that we *do* indeed stumble. For example, I am less interested that someone stumbles. Rather, I want to know if she gets up and what happens when she gets up. Does she stay down there? Does she stay stuck? Or, if we think about Black women teachers who might have not-so-good things to say around class or race or gender or sexuality, I want to know: Do they recognize their perspectives and what do they do to recover? To frame them differently? To me, that's a good teacher.

CBD: Uh huh.

ADD: Perhaps one teacher might have a particular perspective about all children who are on free/reduced lunch. Or, she might have treated this child who's on free/reduced lunch in this way, but then she recognizes that. What is she going to do about that? Talking about that in our work is the search.

CBD: Go you!

ADD: So to me, when I think about this search for goodness, this moment was a blemish. Now it's not necessarily positive that she has a class bias. That's not necessarily "good." Yet, how does she recover? The recovery, to me, says a lot about her integrity. So that's goodness. I haven't yet written this study because I don't know yet how to talk about these stories. It's not because I don't want to talk about it, but I don't know how people will accept it and it becomes this thing, again, who am I representing? Who am I responsible to? So, I'm responsible to this woman and I know that if I write about her classism, people will misuse it and it won't honor her. And I don't want to dishonor her in that way because other people don't know how to read her story!

CBD: And it seems to me there are two issues going on here. One is the issue of people's responses to your work and the desire to have a "victory" narrative, because we have too few of these about us! The other issue is about what's under the search for goodness.

Part of the response to the question has got to be that the search for goodness does not preclude the recognition of humanity. To be human is to make mistakes. So, the search for goodness is *not* the search for the mistake, which is where many have traditionally stopped in research studies—and Black folks particularly have been pathologized by that. The focus has been to study and talk about what is "bad" in Black communities. However, within a search for goodness is a recognition that to be *human* is to have blemishes. So, as a Black woman scholar, I am telling a particular story of humanity that includes blemishes, strengths and all.

ADD: Yeah.

CBD: That's what it means to search for goodness. I believe human beings are *good*

[ADD says in unison with CBD].

ADD: Right.

CBD: I'm searching for the goodness within that. I will always have the blemishes. I will have the vulnerability. In other words, this is a very spiritual way of looking at human beings and approaching research. And although Lawrence-Lightfoot doesn't name it as spiritual, it is deeply spiritual approach in my mind. To search for goodness is to search for what is human, not just in body, but in spirit. So, for me, that question asked is a nonquestion: There is another question that it is attempting to mask.

ADD: Or, perhaps, it is the disbelief that Black women could really be good. I see that as the underlying issue, a very deep-seated belief that Black women *cannot* have or do anything of value, that we can't bring anything that's valuable.

CBD: The idea that anybody could consciously or unconsciously believe that Black women cannot be or do not have anything good, is so evil. It is evil. I don't know if evil is the right word, but it's just anti-human.

ADD: It makes sense, though in light of how Black women have historically been framed. Early research described Black teachers as mean and authoritative. Authoritative was a bad thing. Again, it's the researcher's lens. What are they looking for and how do they frame it?

CBD: So part of a search for goodness from a researcher's stand-point has got to be about writing the stories that are counter to that lens. Where is the balance in our literature in teacher education around who good teachers are, what good research is? How do we represent data? Where is the balance? What we still see is one version of what research is, which is why it's so difficult to get our students to think about the ways in which identity, race, class, and gender plays into research and to actually honor those knowings in the context of being a researcher. You don't have to get rid of all of who you are in order to engage in this process called research. For me, part of the search for goodness also has to do with our role as researchers to find and write those stories that are the counter-narratives. Given that we've had decades of research that pathologizes Black communities, then frankly, as a Black feminist scholar, it is my responsibility to write narratives that also provide a sense of strength and goodness and wisdom that is also present in the community.

ADD: In talks I've given and in other presentations, a few graduate students have asked me if have I faced any struggles as a Black woman scholar. And I've had to say that this particular moment in which I am a scholar has been good for me. Quite frankly, there is a body of work from very strong Black women that I am able to stand on: you and Gloria, Jackie Jordan-Irvine, Joyce King, Beverly Gordon, I mean, so many women who have done the so-called legitimate work, but work that has affirmed Black people in that process. That's been my model. So, I stand on good ground. I stand in a good place. I can do the work I do because all of that work has been there. I am fortunate that I haven't had to go search for the work: it's been right there.

CBD: Right.

ADD: Where you all might have had to go and look for a different way to do this... .

CBD: It's been there for you. The question then becomes, as a relatively new scholar, what will be the work that you leave and for whom? As you think about Black feminist theory in its next iteration, what is the work that Adrienne Dixson leaves behind? How do you marshal Black feminist theory to respond to that, whether we're looking at teachers or communities or whatever that you study? Whatever Black feminist theory has been, young sisters are troubling it in all kinds of ways. So what will they find in your work that helps them to do the things that are important for Black people?

ADD: I don't know what my scholarship says, but I try to attend to it in terms of the people who I invoke. I think the research that I do with Black people will have to speak for itself. I don't know if I consciously write about the legacy in my scholarship, but it has to be in the relationships that I develop with them.

CBD: That's the will and the way again. Affirmation of our relationships to one another and to our work, both intellectually and spiritually, huh?

Coming Full Circle:
A Call to Liberating Research

From: "Adrienne D. Dixson" Dixson.1@osu.edu
Subject: Idea for the QI Paper
Date: November 22, 2004, 11:15:50 AM EST
To: dillard.17@osu.edu

Hey, my Sista:

So, I've been letting this QI conference paper marinate. I am still forming my ideas at this point ... but it seems to me that with your idea of an endarkened epistemology and my work on jazz, we are again articulating a way of knowing that takes this idea of being African women in America as a fundamental aspect of our work. I wasn't really conscious of how many people I was calling on or who were speaking through me when I was writing my jazz paper—or any of the other work I do. I was just writin' what made sense to me and how this helps me kind of see the world every day. So, I think there is something in the academy where having to call upon our ancestors helps us make sense of being here. Qualitative research allows us (or we demand it) to kind of do that. To do the work we need to do at this moment, the only tools that make sense to do it are the tools we have from our ancestors. The key is to be able to know how to hear the ancestors and to "use" them in a way that honors them and gets the message out.

I think the other inescapable issue is: Who are we talking to when we do this work? Who do we imagine our audience to be? To look like? I think, when I write, the faces I see are always brown faces—yours, Gloria's [Ladson-Billings], my peers.... I wonder if my work will affirm or shame them? How will what I put out there honor them and help them to work with our people? If I'm honest, I know that in the back of my mind I have to consider how others will respond to my work. But in some respects, I don't care because I don't want to care too much about what "they" think. It stifles the voices and energy of the ancestors who, until you pointed it out to me, I didn't realize were always with me! So, that's what's running through my head....

Harambee!

AD

Adrienne's e-mail—and this chapter—are designed as a call to each of us: *What does goodness mean in our work, particularly as qualitative researchers?* At the 2005 Qualitative Inquiry Congress, Dr. Joyce King reminded us that liberating methodologies are also about recuperating identity, about transforming consciousness. This is the promise of endarkened feminist work for us: it allows us to raise new questions about the goodness in/of our academic lives and work.

Notes

1. This portion of our paper draws heavily on Dillard's publication "The Substance of Things Hoped for, the Evidence of Things Not Seen" (2000, pp. 661–681).

2. Given the epistemic nature and power of language that Asante (1988) suggests, Kohain Hahlevi, a Hebrew Israelite rabbi, uses the term "African ascendant" to describe people of African heritage. In contrast to the commonly used term "descendant," Kohain Hahlevi argues that African ascendant more accurately describes the upward- and forward-moving nature of African people throughout the diaspora as well as on the continent itself. I subscribe to this notion.

3. With early roots in the work of Barbara Smith, Akasha Hull, Audrey Lorde, and more recently from Patricia Bell-Scott, Katie Cannon, Joy James, Ruth Farmer, Barbara Omolade, and Patricia Hill Collins, Black feminist voices argue that the very presence and positionality of Black women scholars and researchers gives us a coherent and distinctive cultural, analytical and ideological location through which a coherent epistemology—and a different metaphor for educational research—can be articulated.

References

Ani, M. (1994). *Yurugu: An African-centered critique of European cultural thought and behavior.* Trenton, NJ: African World Press.

Appiah, K. A. (1992). *In my father's house: Africa in the philosophy of culture.* New York: Oxford University Press.

Asante, M. K. (1988). *Afrocentricity.* Trenton, NJ: Africa World Press.

Collins, P. H. (1990). *Black feminist thought: Knowledge, consciousness, and the politics of empowerment.* New York: Routledge.

Dillard, C. B. (2000). The substance of things hoped for, the evidence of things not seen: Examining an endarkened feminist epistemology in educational research and leadership. *International Journal of Qualitative Studies in Education, 13*(6), 661–681.

Dillard, C. B., Tyson, C. A., & Abdur-Rashid, D. (2000). My soul is a witness: Affirming pedagogies of the spirit. *International Journal of Qualitative Studies in Education, 13*(5), 447–462.

Dixson, A. D. (2005). Extending the metaphor: Notions of jazz in portraiture. *Qualitative Inquiry, 11*(1), 106–137.

Ephirim-Donker, A. (1997). *African spirituality: On becoming ancestors.* Trenton, NJ: Africa World Press.

Foster, M. (1990). The politics of race: Through the eyes of African American teachers. *Journal of Education, 172*(3), 123–141.

Harding, S. (1987). *Feminism and methodology: Social science issues.* Bloomington: Indiana University Press.

Harris, A. (1990). Race and essentialism in feminist legal theory. *Stanford Law Review, 42*(3), 581–616.

hooks, b. (1989). *Talking back: Thinking feminist, thinking black.* Boston: South End Press.

hooks, b. (1994). *Teaching to transgress: Education as the practice of freedom.* New York: Routledge.

Hull, A. G. (2001). *Soul talk: The new spirituality of African American women.* Rochester, VT: Inner Traditions.

James, J. (1993). African philosophy, theory, and "living thinkers." In J. James & R. Farmer (Eds.). (1993). *Spirit, space, and survival: African American women in (White) academe* (pp. 31–46). New York: Routledge.

Ladson-Billings, G. (1994). *The dreamkeepers: Successful teachers of African American children.* San Francisco: Jossey-Bass.

Lawrence-Lightfoot, S. (1994). *I've known rivers: Lives of loss and liberation.* Reading, MA: Addison-Wesley.

Lawrence-Lightfoot, S., & Davis, J. H. (1997). *The art and science of portraiture.* San Francisco: Jossey-Bass.

Morrison, T. (1993). *Playing in the dark: Whiteness and the literary imagination.* New York: Vintage.

Ngugi, W. T. (1986). *Decolonising the mind: The politics of language in African literature.* Portsmouth, NH: Heinemann.

Palmer, P. (1983). *To know as we are known: Education as a spiritual journey.* San Francisco: Harper.

Richards, D. M. (1980). *Let the circle be unbroken: The implications of African spirituality in the diaspora.* Lawrenceville, NJ: The Red Sea Press.

Stanfield, J. H. (1993). Epistemological considerations. In J. H. Stanfield (Ed.), *Race and ethnicity in research methods* (pp. 16–38). Newbury Park, CA: Sage.

Stanfield, J. H. (1994). Ethnic modeling in qualitative research. In N. K. Denzin & Y. S. Lincoln (Eds.), *Handbook of qualitative research* (pp. 175–188). Newbury Park, CA Sage.

Vanzant, I. (1996). *The spirit of a man.* New York: Harper Collins.

Wade-Gayles, G. (Ed.) (1995). *My soul is a witness: African American women's spirituality.* Boston: Beacon Press.

Wynter, S. (1992). *Do not call us Negroes: How multicultural textbooks perpetuate racism.* San Francisco: Aspire Books.

Chapter 13 | Writing Race into the Twenty-First Century

An Autobiographical Perspective on Hybridity, Difference, and the Postcolonial Experience

Cameron McCarthy
University of Illinois

Take him and cut him out in little stars,
And he will make the face of heav'n so fine
That all the world will be in love with Night
And pay no worship to the garish sun ...

—William Shakespeare, Romeo and Juliet, 1972, p. 507

The mind of man is capable of anything—because everything
is in it, all the past as well as all the future.

—Joseph Conrad, Heart of Darkness and Other Tales,
1992, p. 186

Ah! The whole diaspora shakes in my skin.

—Anthony Kellman, "Isle Man," 1991, p. 15

Introduction

Within the past few years, I have come to recognize that my writing about race and identity has been a form of postcolonial therapy, an exercise in opening up and pasting over contradictions of knowledge, place, context, and belonging. Writing for me, as I imagine it is for all intellectuals pursuing these topics, is as much a tortuous act of concealment and reinscription as it is one of transcending disclosure. Consider the vast sea of sociological ink now being spilled on the topics of class, or race, or identity.

Consider the boatloads of paper afloat on these subjects. Can we really argue that this ever-expanding volume of writing has led us to other than a very partial, adumbrated understanding of the operation of these dynamics? Can any of us really claim that we have come to a final or definitive understanding of racial logics or the operation of identity formation?

Here, at the beginning of the twenty-first century—the great information age, the age of hypermodernization that classical social scientists and their disciples had told us would usher in the withering away of encrusted and sedimented atavism—we are faced in human societies with the unleashing of ever more virulent forms of particularism and localism operating in politics and popular culture. As a disturbing instance, nationalism and xenophobia in Europe—in the former Yugoslavia, in Germany, and in France—rip at the heart of the great icons of civilization in the West; a civilization against which everything in the Third World and everything within the underclasses of the metropole are counterposed. In the Middle East and on the continents of Africa, Asia, and South America the politics of identity have been fought out in bloody skirmishes and long nights of horror such as those of Israel versus the Palestinians, Hutus and Tutsis of Rwanda and Somalia, the heartless ethnic cleansing of the African population in Sudan, and the excesses of proto-fascist regimes in Indonesia and in Guatemala—just to mention a few examples of spectacularly gruesome forms of racial/ethnic cruelty. And, in giving this litany of racial horror, I must note that after the purgatorial fires that descended on New York and the Pentagon on 9/11, we now live with the transformed circumstances of the world's major power, the United States, conducting wars in Afghanistan and Iraq, motivated by retributive politics and instinctive xenophobic fears.

As an academic who has sometimes pontificated on matters of race and identity over the last decade, I must admit a sense of bewilderment at the endless stream of racial cruelty that resides in the hearts of human beings in our relations with each other across the globe. Contemplating race relations in this country, I am both enraged and dismayed by the virulence of the hostilities and resentments unleashed in the United States against its disenfranchised Latino and Latina and African American inner-city poor. At the same time, I am revolted by suburban excesses and the salivatory prosecution of suburban will in the politics of both liberal and conservative politicians and policy intellectuals.

In these matters, the contemporary observer on race and identity simply walks in the footsteps laid down in the sands of time. It was, after all, the great colonial novelist Joseph Conrad (1992) who, in *Heart of Darkness*, proffered his own disorientation on identity questions through the narrating persona of Marlow. Reflecting on the exorbitant atrocities perpetrated by imperialism in Africa, Marlow uses a nostrum to effectively distance himself from Europe's project of subjugation of the native: "The mind of man is capable of anything—because everything is in it, all the past as well as all the future" (p. 186). As a writer, Conrad, too, was implicated. He was a product of Europe, a seafarer, whose characters like himself, pursued their imperial fantasies and desires onto the bodies of the native even as they tormented themselves about the "evil in the hearts of men." Like Conrad, every writer has his demons. And, "Like a jig shakes the loom/Like a web is spun the pattern/All of us are involved/All of us are consumed" (Carter, 1979, p. 44). Is it the demons in our hearts that we write to exorcise? As with Conrad's fiction, is, perhaps, the ultimate purpose of our writing the great disavowal of our implication in life's history? In racial matters, is the postcolonial intellectual, indeed, washed in the blood of the lamb?

Perhaps every postcolonial writer is a descendant of the forces that produced Conrad's phosphorescent naturalism, Conrad's blind spots and his all-consuming evasion of the role of the bourgeois self in the trauma of the native. On this matter, "truth will not out." In the bright gleam of the realist fiction of the novelist, the anthropologist, the social scientist, the historian, the educator hides the entrails of the imperialist lie. The author's claim to the vantage point beyond passion, beyond complicity and collusion is not to be trusted. The author writing on race and identity conceals as much as he or she discloses. Intellectual observers, it would turn out, would have their stake in the apprehension and containment of the native. The native, too, would have his own dreaming map of possession and rambunctious ownership. As Wilson Harris (1960) suggests in *The Palace of the Peacock*, "Donne, too, was my brother" (p. 42).

The colonizer would inhabit the body of the colonized. The colonial text would freeze and fix the native in the stillness of eternity. The colonizing text of the anthropologist ethnographer would close and bind the frame of the village. The urban sociologist would "tell it like it is" about underclass fecundity and degeneracy. For years and years, the student of history, of anthropology, of sociology, of education would read and perform these texts of ethnicity, of self, and Other. And then one day, the bright, motivated student, too, would arrive at the place of her or his calling, would become an anthropologist, a sociologist, and a writer of fictions about others. The intellectual had finally reproduced him- or herself. The newborn academic, the living Narcissus, would deploy his or her gaze on the world with the fervor of a brand new Baby Bell.

Postcolonial intellectuals, children of the native and the king, always disavowed their own participation in this hypocrisy of completeness and the hierarchy of the global racial order. They, too, maintained their innocence. Dressed in the hand-me-downs of Prospero, they declared their blamelessness before the world and before their peers in the American academy. But truth be told, in the matter of racial identity formation the postcolonial intellectuals also are creatures of paradox: they have had, for instance, an enormous appetite for the imperial symbolic, fine garments, literature, and haute cuisine while ceaselessly denouncing imperialism's excesses at home and abroad. I am a child of that paradox: the product of the exorbitant British presence in the Caribbean and the African slave who would be put out into the fields to work, and chained and bridled at the door. I, too, am part of that peculiar progeny of British imperialism whom Sidney Greenfield (1968) would call "English rustics in black skin."

In this chapter, I write about race from the perspective of the radical instability with respect to race-based forms of knowing and identification. I write from the point of view of the perishability of the sociological understanding of the race question. I write to seek out racial knowledge in places other than the controlled study, or the omniscient intent to organize the field of race relations theory, or the ethnographic excursion into the colonized life world of the Other. I seek out new understandings in new

places: in the realms of popular culture, in the realms of literature, in the realms of the imagination, in the realms of the filmic
fantasy, and in the quiet agonism of postcolonial self-exploration
and self-understanding. I speak for all those lost souls, who, like
Derek Walcott, are "divided to the vein," and who—may God
grant us the courage—find solace only in the exploration (Walcott, 1986, p. 18). This is the enigma of arrival of the postcolonial
intellectual. In the matter of her or his investigation of the subject
of conflicted racial identity formation, the postcolonial soul can
know no peace.

Uses of Culture

I begin this chapter, then, with this confession: that all along my
writing on race in the United States has been informed by an
attempt to straddle, frantically to stabilize, the conflicted biography of being born and educated in the periphery, Barbados, and
coming into academic practice as an immigrant intellectual operating in the imperial center, the United States. My understanding
of race, my foregrounding of its instabilities, its "nonsynchrony,"
as I called it in earlier work (McCarthy, 1988), is more than a little
propelled by my own autobiographical elopement or displacement
from the Third World to the imperial center, home of "the Great
Satan." I live everyday, like Ishmael in Herman Melville's *Moby
Dick* (1851), in danger of being swallowed up and consumed in
the churning belly of the Whale.

I proceed, then, with the deepest sense that there is a complexity to the story of race that writing merely adumbrates, never
fully discloses. This is the paradox of all postcolonial intellectual
writing on the varied forms of life and the differentiated cultural
and economic realities of the metropole and the periphery alike.
Although I will not continue this chapter in the confessional
mode, it must be understood that everything that follows herein
is, in fact, informed by the postcolonial predicament: the reality
of, perhaps, permanent exile or banishment from any singular or
fixed community and the attendant lost of full understanding of
one' s racial self. The imperial inheritance is finally a bag of gold,
a bag of bones (Morrison, 1977).

The English Book

> There is a scene in the cultural writings of English colonialism that repeats so insistently after the early nineteenth century—and, through that repetition, so triumphantly *inaugurates* a literature of empire—that I am bound to repeat it once more. It is the scenario, played out in the wild and wordless wastes of colonial India, Africa, the Caribbean, of the sudden, fortuitous discovery of the English book. [Bhabha, 1994, p. 102]

One of the limitations in current postcolonial theory and methodology regarding the analysis of racial identity and center-periphery relations—and indeed this is true of other critical minority discourses such as Afrocentrism and multiculturalism—is the failure of proponents to account for the conditions of production of their own intellectual work and their contradictory interests and affiliations. As Ali Behdad (1993) has pointed out, postcolonial theorists often present the analysis of center-periphery relations within a zero-sum framework in which all agency, power, and moral responsibility emanate and flow from the center. The postcolonial theorist, therefore, appoints her- or himself as a stand-in or proxy for the oppressed Third World; third world of the imaginary—a third world that is unstratified, uniformly underdeveloped—and one in which the social field has been completely leveled by the mechanisms of exploitation and cultural domination. Even more critically—in the work of some writers such as Molefi Asante (1993, 2000), Martin Carnoy (1974, 1993), Philip Altbach (1987), Philip Altbach and Hassan (1997), and Michael Parenti (1993, 1995)—the imperial text, the text of colonial education, the text of Euro American canonical literature, tends to deliver reproductive [neo]colonial effects, seemingly untouched by indigenous practices or movements. Within these frameworks, the dwellers of postcolonial societies are, too often, hypothetical subjects, model addressees of colonizing discourses. Absent are the voices, cultural practices, and meaning of style of concrete, historical postcolonial, and indigenous minority subjects. Even more disturbing is the methodological tendency to abrogate the whole field of accommodations, negotiations, and trestles of association, affiliation, feeling that link dominant and dominated political and cultural entities both locally and globally.

In this chapter, I take a different view of the dynamics of culture and race. I point to interconnections and continuities between prima facie racially and ethnically antagonistic groups (for example, the continuities of theme and form between Anglo-colonial novelists like Joseph Conrad and Afro-diasporic and anticolonial writers such as Chinua Achebe or George Lamming). I also call attention to the contradictions within atavistically declared "pure" racial or ethnic communities (for instance, radical class tensions within the Black communities of South Africa or the United States and the class hierarchies within the Third World). One never fully knows with terms such as "race," "identity," or "culture." To study race, identity, or culture and to intervene in their fields of effects, one must be prepared to live with extraordinary complexity and variability.

The texts and performativity of these constructs are always subject to aberrant decodings, aberrant meanings, and the dynamic play of histories and contexts. This is not to deny the often-virulent force of racial dynamics, racial inequality, and racism. But it is to announce and acknowledge the broad, tangled, and knotted human engagements and productivities that attend the racial encounter between different individuals and groups. It is to reference the subtle play of desire and the commingling of cultural and symbolic forms in the registers of commodified and uncommodified practices of group expression, group history, even group ancestry. It is to recognize that racial/ethnic heritage of any particular group always exceeds the memory and purposive grasp of its purported or self-declared bearers.

Three Vignettes

Permit me to relate three brief vignettes that illustrate the dynamic encounter between racially dominant and subaltern cultural forms in which processes of rearticulation constantly subvert the putative stability of center-periphery ethnic relations. The first story is autobiographical, highlighting my encounter with hegemonic English and American literature as an undergraduate student at the Cave Hill campus of the University of the West Indies in Barbados in the late 1970s; the second story highlights an example of the unexpected association between canonical literature and the rise of radical vernacular poetry writing in the Caribbean; and the third story is one told by Manthia Diawara of the subversive impact of African American popular music in 1960s French Africa and the way it functions as an alternative cultural capital. These three stories illustrate the instability of racial meanings and challenge any narrow-minded construct of culture as ethnocentric property. They also emphasize the radical multiplier effects that cultural forms release in everyday human encounters across the divides of nation, locality, and race.

Story I: Anglo American Culture War

One of the contradictions of cultural production in the Third World, even in the postcolonial era, is the multiplicity of surreptitious, and not so surreptitious, lines of connection that link the postcolony to the metropole. The postcolony is not ever simply an original entity unto itself shorn of the imprint and trace of the metropole. It is in many ways an impure copy full of the warp and woof of empire—an alloy of many racial, cultural, and economic metals, so to speak. Formal and informal cultural life in education and society reveal these connections in the everyday existence of the postcolonial subject. I can speak of these matters of cultural hybridity first hand. Growing up as a child in Barbados in the 1960s and the 1970s, one existed in a constant state of negotiation between the cultural form of England and that of the emergent postindependence island. Education was a particularly poignant site of the transaction of the competing needs, desires, and interests of the metropole and the indigene. Curriculum content, school ritual, and the formal history of the school system pointed to England. Every single important examination was either set or marked in the metropole. For instance, my high school "Advanced Level" examinations were the matriculation exams for the University of Cambridge. Examinations in Barbados were truly external and "objective"—we were the subject-objects of British cultural suzerainty.

As a youth, my social fate was in the hands of the markers of the General Certificate of Education of the Cambridge Examination Board. Passes or failures in these exams, which one took at the end of high school, had material social meaning in Barbados. This arrangement continued into university, where again the University of the West Indies followed a practice of requiring all end-of-year examinations to be vetted by outside examiners mainly from England, but occasionally from the United States and elsewhere. Often these outside "monitors," as they were called, demonstrated their eminence by giving lectures to students when they were visiting. On one such occasion, the outside examiner for my American fiction course came to give a lecture on Ernest Hemingway's novels. Here was one of the incredibly ironic, but normally unremarked, moments of the postcolonial situation in Barbados: an American authority on a great American fiction writer giving a presentation to the Caribbean students of an American fiction class normally taught by an "eminent" Englishman. There we were, caught in the cross-fires of the postpartum Anglo American war over culture.

In the University of the West Indies Program in English Studies, all the American writers, ancient or modern, black or white, were stuck in the American Literature course and separated out from a course called "The Moderns." The latter course was reserved for the great British writers, which included one luminous American transplant to England: T. S. Eliot. The "eminent American scholar" gave his lecture on the greatness of Hemingway's fiction. The Barbadian students didn't buy it and the technical flaws of Hemingway's novels were insistently raised. The eminent American scholar floundered on questions that focused on the massively flawed love scene between Jordan and Maria in *For Whom the Bell Tolls*, in which the narrator utters those incredible words: "And the earth moved from under her feet." The eminent American scholar was a bit flustered. The eminent English scholar looked gleeful. A great victory was won that day for Great Britain by the educated troops of "Little England." Remarkably, I got a call a few days after this Anglo American skirmish from the gleeful English lecturer congratulating me for my critical challenges to the "orthodoxy" of the American: "He" (the eminent American lecturer) did not appreciate what "we" were doing down "here." There I was, the child of empire, clumsily serving as the vessel of Englishness and hopelessly thrown into the field of what seemed to me interminable Anglo American cultural hostilities.

Power as exercised in culture takes devious routes. American writers of great prominence in the American school curriculum and in the academy regarded as Eurocentric and canonical here in the United States—in the hands of British imperialist scholars operating overseas in the theater of the empire's Atlantic rim— had suffered a canonical declassification and a technical demotion. Whitman was "potentially a great poet" but lacked "disciplined attention to technique and form"; Eugene O'Neil was "one of the few noteworthy American playwrights"; T. S. Eliot "had given up America for England." Black Americans like Richard Wright, James Baldwin, and Ralph Ellison were emergent writers of the "protest novel" or the "jazz novel." And American women writers? Well, besides Emily Dickinson, no American woman of letters was mentioned at all. In Barbados, we stood in culture not as property owners but as interpreted texts, actors in the shadow of power on the world stage, and pretenders to middle-class status in the postcolony.

Imposed canonical literature, what I call the "imperial symbolic," was and is the cultural capital central to the politics of class formation in postcolonial settings like Barbados. In a matter-of-fact way, imperial cultural form plays a critical role in the elaboration of indigenous aesthetic and social hierarchies and cultural distinctions.

Story II: T. S. Eliot and the Rise of the Postcolonial Vernacular

But metropolitan canonical cultural form can also serve radical purposes and can be subjected to aberrant decoding and rearticulated within new horizons of association and feeling and new fields of possibility. Edward Kamau Brathwaite (1984) tells a different story of the imperial symbolic than the one I told above. His story is one about the felicitous impact of the poetry of the canonical high modernist writer, T. S. Eliot, on the rise of vernacular poetry in the Caribbean. Again, the moment here is one of hybridity; the medium and conduit of this improbable connection is one of the most powerful modernist carriers of hegemonic and counterhegemonic cultural form and wish fulfillment—the phonograph record:

For those who really made the breakthrough, it was Eliot's actual voice—or rather his recorded voice, property of the British Council—reading "Preludes," "The love song of J. Alfred Prufrock," *The Waste Land*, and the *Four Quartets*—not the texts—which turned us on. In that dry deadpan delivery, the riddims of St Louis (though we didn't know the source then) were stark and clear for those of us who at the same time were listening to the dislocations of Bird, Dizzy and Klook. And it is interesting that on the whole, the Establishment couldn't stand Eliot's voice—far less jazz! Eliot himself, in the sleeve note to *Four Quartets* ... says: "What a recording of a poem by its author can and should preserve, is the way that poem sounded to the author when he had finished it. The disposition of the lines on the page, and the punctuation (which includes the *absence of* punctuation marks ...) can never give an exact notation of the author's metric. The chief value of the author's record ... is a guide to the *rhythms*." [pp. 30–31]

The vernacular translations of Eliot's poetry transacted through the powerful medium of the phonograph record connected the canonical with the everyday and spilled over into the dream of autonomy for Caribbean letters. Here, in one striking movement, Brathwaite gives credence to Raymond Williams's thesis in *Culture and Society* (1958) of the semiautonomous role of culture, its essentially communicative, translatory function across the manichean divide of centers and peripheries. The culture of the Third World is, therefore, the polysemic text of contestatory identities. It is also brimful of the flotsam and detritus of the metropolitan culture industry. Like seasoned bricoleurs, emergent Caribbean writers fished Eliot from a sea of historical ruins and breathed new life into the literary landscape and map of twentieth-century Caribbean cultural form and meaning of style. This was, in the language of Derek Walcott (1993), a "felicitous moment" of hybridity!

Story III: Afrokitsch

The play of cultural hybridity in lived and commodified culture not only is produced in the context of Third World encounters with Eurocentric cultural form. It is also released in the encounters between the delegitimated cultural forms of marginalized groups such as African American working classes and their Third World counterparts in the periphery. Manthia Diawara (1992) tells the story of the powerful impact of African American R&B and Soul in late 1960s Africa. In this case, the return of diasporic energies from Black America to the African continent unsettles the hegemonic grip of French high culture in the West African neocolony of Mali. In this context, working-class African American cultural form becomes French African "cultural capital." New centers are created in the world and old ones undermined. According to Diawara:

> In 1965, Radio Mali advertised a concert by Junior Wells and his All-Star-Band at the Omnisport in Bamako. The ads promised the Chicago group would electrify the audience with tunes from such stars as Otis Redding, Wilson Pickett, and James Brown. I was very excited because I had records by Junior Walker, and to me, at the time, with my limited English, Junior Wells and Junior Walker were one and the same. (That still happens to me, by the way.) It was a little disappointing that we couldn't have James Brown in person. I had heard that Anglophone countries like Ghana, Liberia, and Nigeria were luckier. They could see James Brown on television, and they even had concerts with Tyrone Davis, Aretha Franklin, and Wilson Pickett. Sure enough, the concert was electrifying. Junior Wells and his All-Star Band played "My Girl," "I've Been Loving You Too Long," "It's A Man's World," "There Was a Time," "I Can't Stand Myself," "Papa's Got a Brand New Bag," "Respect," "Midnight Hour," and, of course, "Say It Loud (I'm Black and I'm Proud)." During the break, some of us were allowed to talk with the musicians and to ask for autographs. The translator for us was a white guy from the United States Information Services. I remember distinguishing myself by going past the translator and asking one of the musicians the following question: "What is your name?" His eyes lit up, and he told me his name and asked me for mine. I said, "My name is Manthia, but my friends call me J.B." ... I got the nickname J.B. from my James Brown records. The next day the news traveled all over Bamako that I spoke English like an American. This was tremendous in a Francophone country where one acquired subjecthood through recourse to *Francite* (thinking through French grammar and logic). Our master thinker was Jean-Paul Sartre. We were also living in awe, a form of silence, thinking that to be Francophone sub-

jects, we had to master Francite like Leopold Senghor, who spoke French better than French people. Considered as one who spoke English like Americans and who had a fluent conversation with star musicians, I was acquiring a new type of subjecthood that put me perhaps above my comrades who knew by heart their *Les Chemins de la Liberté* by Sartre. I was on the cutting edge—the front line of the revolution. You see, for me, then, and for many of my friends, to be liberated was to be exposed to more R&B songs and to be *au courant* of the latest exploits of Muhammad Ali, George Jackson, Angela Davis, Malcolm X, and Martin Luther King, Jr. These were becoming an alternative cultural capital for African youth—imparting to us new structures of feeling and enabling us to subvert the hegemony of *Francite*. [pp. 287–288]

Here again, the performativity of culture exceeds its origins. Black America meets West Africa through the circulatory force of the culture industry: of records, videos and music concerts of the stars. There is nothing pure about being Black or African. There is nothing original: all is intertextuality, rearticulation, translation. There is no transcendent core: all is epidermis. All is movement in the Black Atlantic (Gilroy, 1993). The sound and fury of race signifies everything and nothing.

The Movement of Culture

Of course, these processes of hybridity are not exclusively articulated in the periphery. Contemporary developments in the new century reveal a return of the subaltern gaze onto "the eye of power itself" (Bhabha, 1994). Huge dually disorganizing and integrative energies are exerted from the periphery to the center. This is particularly articulated in the movement of masses of Third World people to the metropolitan center, bringing new tropes of affiliation and cultural affirmation as well as the new sources of tension and contradiction along the lines of race, class, gender, nation, sexuality, and religion. The metropolises of First World societies now struggle to absorb these subaltern subjectivities. State policy and political economies in Europe, the United States, Australia, and Canada now desperately wrestle with the radical challenges and opulent possibilities that the energetic peoples relocated from Africa, Asia, the Caribbean, Latin America, and the Middle East present to their new-found homes. In *The Tourist* (1989), Dean MacCannell tracks the new energies of globalization that strike at the heart of old imperial powers, transforming them from within:

> Twenty-five years ago the dominant activity shaping world culture was the movement of institutional capital and tourists to the remote regions, and the preparations of the periphery for their arrival.... . Today, the dominant force—if not numerically, at least in terms of its potential to re-shape culture—is the movement of refugees, "boat people," agricultural laborers, displaced peasants, and others from the periphery to centers of power and affluence. Entire villages of Hmong peasants and hunters recently from the highlands of Laos, have been relocated and now live in apartment complexes in Madison, Wisconsin. Refugees from El Salvador work in Manhattan, repackaging cosmetics, removing perfume from Christmas gift boxes, rewrapping it in Valentine gift boxes. Legal and illegal "aliens" weed the agricultural fields of California. The rapid implosion of the "third world" into the first constitutes a reversal and transformation of the structure of tourism. [p. xvii]

This tide of mass movement has striking and provocative effects in the realm of culture and literature. It has led, for example, to a virtual transformation of the canons of literature in the center itself. According to Pico Iyer (1993), a new multiperspectival, heterogeneous cultural force is overwhelming and reshaping canonical cultural forms in England and elsewhere:

> The Empire has struck back, as Britain's former colonies have begun to capture the very heart of English literature, while transforming the language with bright colours and strange cadences and foreign eyes. As Vikram Seth, a leading Indian novelist whose books have been set in Tibet and San Francisco, says, "The English language has been taken over, or taken to heart, or taken to tongue, by people whose original language historically it was not."... The centers of this new frontierless writing are the growing capitals of multicultural life, such as London, Toronto, and to a lesser extent New York, that the form is rising up wherever cultures jangle. [p. 68]

Iyer's observation leads us away from the eruptions of simple-minded nationalisms and the calcified identity politics that rule the political imaginations of our time. For after all, "no race has a monopoly on beauty, on intelligence, on strength/and there is a place for all at the rendezvous of victory" (Aime Cesaire, quoted in Said, 1993, p. 310).

Ultimately, then, who can claim ownership of culture or ethnicity as a final property? The transactions of culture in the modern world forcefully undermine the claim to cultural exceptionalism. Radically underlying the material reality of forces at the center of global capitalism—forces such as colonial domination and racial oppression—are the cultural settlements of what Raymond Williams (1961) calls "The Long Revolution." In the Long Revolution, culture is the alchemy of opposites, the alchemy of classes and races, the point and site of radical hybridity. Culture is also the site of the radical disintegration of biologically derived unities of race, ethnicity, or nation. Culture's polysemic movement constantly challenges the modality of conqueror-conquered or oppressor-oppressed as it undermines, reassembles, and reconfigures long-held traditions, affiliations and meanings of style into whole new "forms of life." Williams describes this movement of culture in socioenvironmental and ecological terms:

> The conquerors may change with the conquered, and even in extreme cases become indistinguishable from them. More usually, a continually varied balance will result. Of the Norman conquest of England, for example, it is impossible to say that it did not change English society, but equally the eventual result was a very complex change, as can be seen most clearly in the history of the language, which emerged neither as Norman French nor as Old English, but as a new language deeply affected by both. [pp. 137–138]

Conclusion

Drawing on Williams's insight, and the insights provided by the vignettes of hybridity presented above, I have tried to write about race through the prism of culture. In so doing, I am trying to promote a rethinking of constructs such as race, identity, and cultural heritage. I argue that the experiences and practices that these concepts seek to summarize are far more dynamic than the ways in which we normally conceptualize them in educational and social science research. I suspect that the dynamism and heterogeneity of the myriad everyday human encounters that produce and reproduce cultures and identities are thwarted in education because even the most radical research continues to be overburdened and weighed down by the legacy of behavioral social science and psychology. Against the latter, much is still measured in the educational field. By contrast, it is in literature, in painting, and in popular culture and popular music that the dynamism and complexity of identity, community, and so forth are restored and foregrounded.

The position I am taking runs up against the current politics of racial identity formation, specifically in the areas of multiculturalism, education, and the politics of curriculum reform. Here, racial understandings underlying the discourses of some multiculturalists and their Eurocentric opponents mark out indelible lines of separation between the culture, literature, and traditions of the West and the culture and traditions of the Third World. These highly ideologically charged understandings of identity treat culture as a distinctive form of property that is indisputably owned or possessed by one or another racial group. This is, indeed, one of the symptoms of the racially corrosive heart of human kind that I alluded to earlier.

In the vignettes in this chapter I refuse this Manichean model of racial identity formation. I challenge the glib opposition of the West to the non-West and the curricular project of content addition that now guides the thinking of many of the proponents of identity politics and multicultural reformist frameworks. I have sought instead to highlight specific examples of the complexity and variability of identity formation within the domains of personal autobiography, dominant and subaltern popular culture, and postcolonial literary aesthetics as well as the so-called canonical traditions of the West. I believe that these sites of popular culture and literary production constitute spaces for the exploration of difference, for interrogating the cultural silence over race and identity in education and society, and for opening up a wide-ranging conversation over curriculum reform in the context of the radically diversifying communities we now serve in the university and in the schools. Throughout this chapter, then, I have adopted a cultural studies approach to the topic of racial identity formation by highlighting historical variability, shifting social contexts and environments, and the inevitable trestles of association between the canon and the quotidian, the empire and the postcolony, and suburban and inner-city "realities."

I noted at the beginning, I speak with at least two voices. The first is as an intellectual whose formative and perhaps most decisive education occurred in a Third World country, the postcolony of Barbados. I am, for better or worse, a child of empire—an "English rustic in black skin." My other voice is that of an Afro Caribbean immigrant intellectual displaced to the putative center of the industrial world. I now live in the belly of the beast, a supplicant to a neurotic Uncle Sam. In pursuing this theme of hybridity and duality, I have partially disclosed the agonistic war that wages within the hearts and minds of postcolonial souls, like myself, who inhabit the firmament of the American academy.

For whom do the postcolonial intellectuals speak? Where is their constituency? Where is their theoretical and political warrant? Where is their intellectual and cultural home? I pursue these themes of incompleteness, duality, and discontinuity concerning race, culture, and identity to ward off the costly politics of ethnic and cultural dogmatism and absolutism and the shorted-sighted programs of Eurocentrism and ethnocentrism that now threaten to eviscerate the educational imagination. I argue against the current tendencies to oppose the Western culture against the cultures of the non-West, the First World against the Third World, and so forth.

I want to argue with Edward Said (1993) that any single overmastering or ruling identity at the core of the curriculum—whether African or Asian or European or Latin American—is, in fact, a confinement. Such a closed cultural or intellectual system consolidates a kind of illiteracy about one's racial others that is impractical and dangerous in a society in which the demographics of ethnic diversity have outstripped the meaningfulness of a curriculum founded on nineteenth-century principles of ethnic homogenization and the neutralization of difference. Furthermore, as Aime Cesaire has argued "No one group has a monopoly on intelligence or beauty." I therefore argue for curriculum reform in the area of race relations that is founded on the principle of the heterogeneous basis of all knowledge and the need to find the subtle but abiding links that connect groups across the particularity of ethnic affiliation and geographical and cultural origins and location.

References

Altbach, P. (1987). *The knowledge context*. New York: SUNY Press.

Altbach, P., & Hassan, S. M. (1997). *The muse of modernity: Essays on culture as development in Africa*. Chicago: Africa World Press.

Apple, M. (1993). *Official knowledge*. New York: Routledge.

Asante, M. (1993). *Malcolm X as cultural hero and other essays*. Trenton, NJ: Africa World Press.

Asante, M. (2000). *The painful demise of Eurocentrism*. Chicago: Africa World Press.

Behdad, A. (1993). Traveling to teach: Postcolonial critics in the American academy. In C. McCarthy & W. Crichlow (Eds.), *Race, identity and representation in education* (pp. 40–49). New York: Routledge.

Bhabha, H. (1994). *The location of culture*. New York: Routledge.

Brathwaite, E. K. (1984). *History of the voice*. London: New Beacon.

Carnoy, M. (1974). *Education as cultural imperialism*. London: Longman.

Carnoy, M. (1993). *The new global economy in the information age*. State College, PA: Penn State University Press.

Carter, M. (1979). You are involved. *Poems of resistance*. Georgetown, Guyana: Guyana Printers Limited.

Conrad, J. (1992). *Heart of darkness and other tales*. New York: Oxford University Press.

Diawara, M. (1992). Afrokitsch. In G. Dent (Ed.), *Black popular culture* (pp. 285–291). Seattle: Bay Press.

Gilroy, P. (1993). *The Black Atlantic: Modernity and double consciousness*. Cambridge, MA: Harvard University Press.

Greenfield, S. (1968) *English rustics in black skin*. New Haven, CT: College University Press.

Hall, S. (1992). Cultural studies and its legacies. In L. Grossberg, C. Nelson, & P. Treichler (Eds.), *Cultural studies* (pp. 277–294). New York: Routledge.

Harris, W. (1960). *Palace of the peacock*. London: Faber.

Herrnstein, R., & Murray, C. (1994). *The bell curve*. New York: Free Press.

Iyer, P. (1993). The empire writes back, *Time*, February 8, pp. 68–73.

Kellman, A. (1991). Isle man. *Graham House Review, Spring*(14), 15.

MacCannell, D. (Ed.). (1989). *The tourist: A theory of the leisure class*. New York: Schocken.

McCarthy, C. (1988). Reconsidering liberal and radical perspectives on racial inequality in schooling: Making the case for nonsynchrony. *Harvard Educational Review, 58*(2), 265–279.

Melville, H. (1851). *Moby Dick: Or the white whale*. New York: Harper.

Morrison, T. (1977). *Song of Solomon*. New York: Signet.

Nietzsche, F. (1967). *On the genealogy of morals* (W. Kaufman, Trans.). New York: Vintage.

Parenti, M. (1993). *Inventing reality*. New York: St. Martin's Press.

Parenti, M. (1995). *Against empire*. San Francisco: City Lights Books.

Preston, R. (1994). *The hot zone*. New York: Random House.

Said, E. (1993) The politics of knowledge. In C. McCarthy & W. Crichlow (Eds.), *Race, identity and representation in education* (pp. 306–314). New York: Routledge.

Shakespeare, W. (1972). *Romeo and Juliet*. In E. Barnet (Ed.), *The Complete Signet Classic Shakespeare* (Act III, Scene II, p. 507). New York: Harcourt Brace and Janovich.

Walcott, D. (1986). A far cry from Africa. *Collected poems: 1948–1984*. New York: Noonday.

Walcott, D. (1993). *The Antilles: Fragments of epic memory*. New York: Farrar, Straus and Giroux.

Williams, R. (1958). *Culture and society*. London: Chatto and Windus.

Williams, R. (1961). *The long revolution*. London: Penguin.

Chapter 14 | Qualitative Inquiry and the War on Terror

H. L. Goodall, Jr.
Arizona State University

Rewind

My father once gave me insight into the paradox of higher education. He said, "You should get the best education you can because it is the one thing our government can't take away from you." Then he paused and added a coda: "But *what you know* is something you can't get away from, either."

My father was not being ironic. He loved his country and believed in the power of education. But he also knew firsthand the clandestine world, wherein the whole point of gaining access to secret information carried with it—in addition to considerable risk—personal duties and professional responsibilities. My father was a war-seasoned patriot who became someone we today call a "cold warrior." For him, knowledge was never neutral because it had political uses, and how it was used politically—how it was communicated, interpreted, and acted on—would, in fact, help determine the fate of the world.

My father was an intelligence officer, or, if you prefer, a spy. He joined what was then an obscure government agency in 1947 and retired from it, officially, in 1969. He had his reasons. His childhood had been defined by his family's economic struggles during the Great Depression and his adolescence and young adulthood had been determined by the great ideological struggles that became World War II. His generation of intelligence officers was often comprised of women and men who shared a very similar past, and who thought there was no higher calling—or steadier work—than a lifetime devoted to government service.

Their enemy—my father's enemy—was communism. Under State Department cover as a vice-consul in Rome and London during the 1950s, my father ran agents and fought the Red menace on both sides of the Iron Curtain. He and his boss in Rome, William Colby, were chiefly responsible for turning the tide of the Italian elections away from the communists in 1956. In London, his counterintelligence work acquired a certain duality of purpose, one part devoted to spreading disinformation and propaganda, the other devoted to uncovering the political truth about a singular man.

It began in the Suez. My father was "our man in the Suez" during the first Middle East crises in 1956, ostensibly there to coordinate the evacuation of American citizens and dependents. There he met, was interviewed by, and got seriously drunk and swapped lies with one Harold Adrian Russell "Kim" Philby, supposedly there to cover the crisis as an independent reporter, but in reality the man who would become known as the longest-serving and certainly the most notorious and damaging Soviet deep penetration spy in the history of British intelligence. Today, discovering a Philby in our CIA would be akin to discovering that George Tennant had been a paid operative of al Qaeda.

My father had instincts about certain people. And he trusted those instincts. His instinct in the Suez in 1956 told him Philby—although already exonerated by the British Secret Service and even by the CIA's own James Jesus Angleton—was "dirty." He didn't yet know how dirty, or for how long, or with what devastating impact. It was just something he felt about the man. It was an instinct.

My father reported this contact with Philby to Angleton back in Washington. Angleton—a poet/genius/paranoid who headed the CIA's Counterintelligence Division and named more than a few of his prize hybrid orchids after men whose careers he had ruined—was a man who hated to admit he made mistakes just a little bit less, or maybe a little bit more, than he hated communism. He instructed my father to cease and desist in "this Philby nonsense."

My father didn't follow those orders. He was considered a "fair-haired boy" and thought he had enough agency cachet built up from his successes thus far to do internal political battle with Angleton. He was still a young man, brash, headstrong, and sure of himself, and he was convinced that what he felt about Philby was worth the personal risk.

As it turned out, he was right about Philby but dead wrong about Angleton. My father's pursuit of Philby became a lesson in the abuses of power as his dossier on the man grew larger and more damning and Angleton's resistance to the allegations grew more determined. My father thought Angleton's friendship with Philby had gotten in the way of his judgment. I have no idea what Angleton thought. He buried my father's reports and later destroyed them.

Nor can I say with any assurance exactly what happened next. The CIA has a strict policy of not releasing operational details about its employees, and what I have been able to piece together from other sources—interviews with other spies of his generation, archival data, novels, histories, and memoirs—wouldn't stand much of a truth test in a court of law. But *something* happened. It happened in East Berlin. And it was in June 1960. My father may or may not have been set up by Angleton to take a fall, but either way, and for whatever reason or treachery, he was caught doing something, implicated in a murder, and declared persona non grata. In this way, every spy story is the same story. In the end, intelligence officers are betrayed either by their friends, their country, or the truth.

We returned to Washington. My father had a meeting with Angleton—it didn't go well—and a few days later we found ourselves living in what my father called our "forced exile" in Cheyenne, Wyoming. Cheyenne was a long way from London, Washington, or Rome. My father's posting there may or may not have been entirely gratuitous. Cheyenne is the capitol of the state as well as home to the Francis E. Warren Air Force base. During the years corresponding to my father's work there, the base served as the command center for the largest number of underground ICBMs in our nation's nuclear arsenal. In the event of war, Cheyenne was a likely first-tier target. Angleton's message couldn't have been clearer.

My father was already dead to him.

When Philby officially announced his defection to the Soviet Union in July 1963, my father felt vindicated. He had spent three years in a godforsaken prairie exile and was more than ready to come in from the cold. But he learned the bitter lesson of the paradox of his own "higher education" in the history of espionage: the truth of what he knew, of what he discovered about Philby, about Angleton, about the agency, and about America wouldn't save him or resurrect his career. Instead, what he knew, what he had learned, would haunt him. In the end, it cost him everything—his ambitions, his health, my mother's health, his connection to me, and his respect for our government.

His demise produced only one new thing in Washington: a hybrid orchid. It was lily white and tinged with a peachy pinkness that became stark red at its core. Angleton always enjoyed a good metaphor.

My father died in 1976 a broken man. He died mysteriously, an old man at the age of fifty-three, either ironically or not during the Church Committee hearings on the illegal activities of the CIA, the hearing where his former boss and then CIA Director William Colby first revealed to the public "the family jewels." My father told my mother that he planned to testify. He knew a lot about those illegal activities, given his firsthand experience conducting them. He also probably had a lot to say about Angleton. But he didn't live long enough to do that. He went to his early grave in a family cemetery in Maryland on a cold gray day in March, buried with what he knew, haunted by it, but still caring in his soul about his country's deepest secrets.

Thus, the paradox he spoke of with me. My father had learned through his own experiences that our government couldn't strip him of what he knew, or of the truth of it, but neither could he forget what he knew. Or get away from it.

Sometimes, as philosophers say, knowledge is power.

Sometimes it is a personal moral burden.

¤ ¤ ¤

It was our shared burden of secrecy about my father's clandestine identity that commanded and eventually corrupted my family's life. It was a secrecy nourished by cold war fears and secured by a protected network of official and unofficial lies.

I grew up blessed and damned by this cultural surround. Blessed, because moving from place to place as a child and living under the imposed rules of absolute secrecy, systematic surveillance on our lives by our own government, in constant fear of nuclear death, I acquired a survivor's set of core values early on. Survivor skills are wholly ethnographic: I learned to observe cultural and social contexts and adapt myself, and my narrative identities, to them. I learned how to gain access to secret information, to fit in with the natives, to make sense of new places and people, to befriend them, cultivate relationships, and interpret their inner meanings. I also learned how to protect myself. You could say that growing up in the cold war as the son of a spy, I learned to be an adept participant-observer as well as a seasoned intercultural communicator.

For all the good this practical education in qualitative methods and fieldwork provided me, it, too, came with an unforgettable life price, or what I call these days "a moral" to my own autoethnographic story. It is a moral that I lately choose to interpret as a moral imperative. It is a moral imperative that connects my story, and my father's story, to the ongoing narrative of my country. Elsewhere, I termed this connection my "narrative inheritance" (Goodall, 2005). The short version of it is that the lessons of my family's own cultural education during the cold war have become, in the context of our post-9/11 world, a source of knowledge not easily forgotten.

But I am getting ahead of my story.

¤ ¤ ¤

By the time I graduated from high school, I wanted nothing more than to get away from home. I wanted no more of my father's conservative Republicanism and secrecy or my mother's diplomatically induced fear, a nervousness that had by that time matured into a barely functional madness. I wanted to escape from the nuclear age culture of fear and emotional labor that enveloped my childhood and early adolescence.

It was Spring 1970 and I, like millions of other children of the cold war American culture, rebelled. For the next few years I, like so many others, engaged in all sorts of counterculture behavior, marched on Washington to protest the Vietnam War, marched for civil rights and women's rights, said outrageous things, wrote poetry, stayed in school, grew long hair, and registered to vote as a Democrat. I have been a Democrat—a proud liberal Democrat—ever since.

I acquired a formal higher education in communication. I studied rhetoric and communication theories, organizational and cultural studies, and, eventually, after my first job and tenure, I became a self-made narrative ethnographer. I have been a narrative ethnographer ever since (Goodall, 2004).

Here is where my story probably intersects with yours. Like you, I know things about communication—about its strategic and ethical uses in relationships and community building, about systematic observation and interviewing, about dealing with the inherent ambiguity of information, about the social construction of meanings, and about the organization and management of successful transdisciplinary qualitative research projects—that most people don't know. For 'lo these many years working hard and playing hard by the rules of academe—well away in every way from politics inside the Beltway—I have honed that knowledge and skill set without ever once thinking that what I knew how to do would be—or even should be—valuable to my country in a time of war.

Play

But my father's paradox is still alive within me and I know I can't get away from *what* I know. Since 9/11, here in America, all the old cold war fears of my childhood have been, by this Republican administration, strategically reapplied. As a result, my long-dormant core survivor values and ethnographer's qualitative tools have been similarly reawakened to a new task at hand. One I was born to.

In our post-9/11 culture, like Yogi Berra put it, "it's déjà vu, all over again."

I *know* I've been here, lived within this cultural storyline, before. If you are like me and grew up during the cold war, and particularly if you grew up as a classified child in a military or intelligence or government family, my guess is you had to. Once again, America has a powerful, evil enemy—not ideologically inspired militarist communism but fundamentalism-inspired nonstate terrorism—and once again, Americans have been instructed to distrust our neighbors, our coworkers, and our friends. Christian patriots (such as Timothy McVeigh), Islamic radicals (such as Osama bin Laden), former dictators' offpsring (such as the sons of Saddam Hussein), Aryan supremacists, suicide bombers, and splinter-faction terrorism sleeper cells are said to be everywhere. There are *hundreds* of groups, and *thousands*, perhaps *tens of thousands*, or even *hundreds of thousands*, of people who make up what experts call "the new global social movement" of terrorists allied against American values, beliefs, and interests. Their weapons of mass destruction ran the gamut from suicide bombers to trucks filled with fertilizer, to poison gases such as Sarin and chemicals such as anthrax, to biological agents such as a pneumonic plague, to dirty bombs to render a city useless for a generation to nuclear bombs that end life as we know it on the planet Earth.

We are supposed to be afraid. *Very* afraid. That is the principal goal of terror as well as the principal message of those in government fighting terror. As we learned in the cold war, widespread fear creates the cultural, social, and political exigencies for action against those we suspect of promoting, supporting, or harboring terrorists worldwide. It also encourages the use of heavy diplomacy, military action, police action, espionage, counterespionage, economic sanctions, and whatever else may be needed or implicated by our hunger for national security, or, in this current iteration, Homeland Security.

So, in the interests of Homeland Security, our constitutional freedoms and supposedly guaranteed rights have been limited by our own attorney general and our Congress, the very people charged with the authority to protect and defend them. Instead of old-fashioned cold war civil defense drills we have color-coded daily terror alerts. We accept increased surveillance and security checks. At airports, we routinely remove our shoes, belts, pocket change, cell phones, and computers for security scanning and submit our bodies to the new technological innovation of being "wanded." We are, here, there, and everywhere strongly cautioned against joking about bombs or making allegations against our government or its leaders.

It's déjà vu all over again.

Once again, we find ourselves enmeshed in what has turned out to be an ill-conceived and deeply divisive war abroad. We entered it, once again, claiming as a nation to be all about bringing freedom and democracy to a repressed region, but clearly over there, once again, without a plan for how to win or even to achieve a peace. Our generals and politicians are still fighting nations on account of dictators in the middle of a global war supposedly about the elimination of nonstate-sponsored terrorism, and if this government logic makes little sense, it no longer matters because—unlike reporters during the cold war—our contemporary media have largely abandoned investigative reporting in favor of protecting their commercial and career interests.

And once again, officials entrusted with protecting our good image abroad and our security at home seem to lack the essential knowledge and skill sets to accomplish those urgent and necessary purposes. For example, Karen Hughes, a former Texas reporter who became President Bush's primary public relations campaign manager and who has no experience whatsoever in diplomacy was, in March 2005, named undersecretary of state for public diplomacy, with ambassadorial rank. Her job is to run the campaign to rebuild our image, reputation, and credibility in the world.

In a world ripe for dialogue, we seem to know only spin.

¤ ¤ ¤

Yes, indeed, I've been here before. So have most of you.

But this time we are adults armed with cultural authority, a sense of history, and some highly developed knowledge and skill sets. As my father's example teaches me, I have inherited knowledge that has, in turn, created within me a moral imperative for action. This global war on terror is not something I can ignore.

Nor should you.

Our democratically elected government, even when we disagree with its policies and disbelieve its spokespersons, is nevertheless a reality we cannot ignore as well as a mediated reflection of ourselves. Whereas even as little as two years ago it was possible to travel abroad and hear distinctions made between the American government and the American people, that distinction is rapidly closing. *We are now as individuals—as we have long as a nation been—globally complicit in the causes and cultural conditions that led to this war on terror.*

This is *our* war, whether we like it or not, or approve of it, or not.

It is—rightly or wrongly—a product of our American way of life, our cultural and religious ignorance, and our affluent national ego. These conditions have inspired hatred against America, which is to say, against all of us. It is a war that has conscripted all of us without our consent because all of us—regardless of where we live or what we value or how we believe—are now potential terrorist targets and will continue to be terrorist targets for the foreseeable future. No one gets out of being implicated. For those of us who share a liberal democratic ideology and who oppose the war in Iraq, we represent to our enemies not sympathetic souls but quite the opposite: we are the apostate intellectuals. We are all marked for death.

Hothouse orchids carry our collective names.

Furthermore, this is a costly enduring war in a global economy that is—and will continue—to drain our national economy, threaten our national welfare, and deprive our own children and their children of the better life that we, as a nation, used to promise them. They will inherit not only our debts and our histories, but also our pervasive culture—and the cultural politics—of terror and fear.

These are the reasons why we have no choice but to engage the war on terror (Goodall, 2006). By "engage it" I do not mean reduce to nil the chances of another terrorist attack, because even our most optimistic government officials agree that will never happen. Instead, I mean find better ways to fight it, both at home and abroad, with the goal of reducing the likelihood that we will continue to spawn new generations of terrorists.

In the final section of this chapter, I will detail my personal efforts to apply what I know, and what I have learned, to the war on terror.

¤ ¤ ¤

During the fall semester of 2004, Steve Corman and I began a conversation about what communication theories and research could contribute to the global war on terror at the Hugh Downs School of Human Communication at Arizona State University. Steve is an organizational communication scholar whose specialty is networks. After 9/11, his research had drawn the attention of some "interesting people" in Washington and, I discovered, he currently is part of a scientific team aiding the Joint Special Operations Command.

Given my research into cold war culture and intelligence organizations crafted out of a decidedly qualitative framework and Professor Corman's first-hand knowledge of netwars and communication technology crafted from a more quantitative perspective, we thought it would be interesting to offer a graduate seminar addressing questions related to communication, terrorism, and national security. The seminar was also attractive because we could learn from it. We could—and did—offer a public lecture series along with the course, inviting to campus a wide variety of individuals with differing points of view—scholarly, military, diplomatic, educational, and media, as well as specialists who have "first responder" duties (please see our website: http://www. asu.edu/clas/communication/events/terrorism/).

Our aim was—and is—is to build a transdisciplinary network of global expertise that can be useful in reducing the negative short- and long-term effects of our global war on terror. We want to bring to this war what we know about communication, as well as what we can learn about deploying more successful communication campaigns and practices from our colleagues in allied fields, such as justice studies, psychology, sociology, and religion. We believe, along with the 9/11 Commission, that failures in communication brought about the problem and that improvements in communication—broadly considered—can go a long way toward lessening them.

We began our conversation, and our seminar, with some healthy doubts about that. For one thing, although communication professors in the academic world believe all that is important in life is either constructed or interpreted as meaningful out of communication practices, we weren't sure those who fighting the war with other weapons and strategies would think so. Or, at least, perhaps not think so in some of the same ways. Furthermore, as Steve's experiences had shown, trying to translate complex academic theories into clear, practical advisories for people who then risk their lives based on our findings is a very sobering dose of reality. Finally, although it is easy to be smug in lectures about intercultural understandings in a college classroom, how would what we claimed to be true ring true with those whose careers have been devoted to diplomacy and fieldwork with disparate others in faraway places?

Our concerns were also tempered with some recent history lessons. During the cold war, academics, principally from the Ivy Leagues, were routinely recruited into government service with some fairly disastrous policy-making results. Social science theories and research methods—still often in their evolutionary infancy—may have been the products of the "best and the brightest," but using them as a foundation for public policy was repeatedly demonstrated to be problematic. We certainly didn't—and don't—want to repeat that particular history lesson.

Nor did we want to repeat the problem experienced by a certain prominent anthropology department in a prominent American university during the 1960s, where it was discovered that faculty research was being routinely appropriated by intelligence organizations to launch illegal campaigns in Third World countries.

Beyond these sources of professional anxiety were additional concerns derived from colleagues who thought what we were doing was potentially "dangerous"; administrators who wanted to see a longer-term financial payoff for the institutional investment in the public lecture series; and even the fear expressed to us by a member of the local news media of the likelihood of our series itself attracting potential terrorists, crazies, and protesters.

Our course was considered by us to be an experiment, a venture into the unknown future of collaboration across unknown borders and for that reason potentially risky, particularly if not in the end productive. But nevertheless, we pressed on. Our anxieties and doubts were always balanced with the stark violent reality unfolding before us: our leaders had made a hash of it, and the hash they made was only becoming more robust by the day. Even if diplomacy is not a popularity contest, we simply could no longer trust our government alone to provide the sort of clear, consistent, and culturally adaptive messages capable of winning the hearts and minds of those we claimed to want to help. Public diplomacy initiatives needed to move away from "elites talking to elites" to include other stakeholders, including those of us in the academy and the private sector, who can join forces and talents that offer something other than the empty, repetitive, and clearly ineffective rhetoric whose key point seems to be "freedom and democracy are beautiful words." Nor could we any longer allow our well-intentioned but communicatively inept government officials to be the dominant voice of Americans without at the very least providing those officials with newer, better, and smarter communication approaches to solving communication problems.

Ours was a public, moral responsibility to act.

¤ ¤ ¤

The results have been interesting, affirming, and surprising.

The results have been interesting because those of us participating in the seminar and public lectures have acquired a far deeper understanding of the history and conduct of terrorism worldwide. Within that general statement is a discourse far more complex than I can elucidate in this chapter, but one that we think should be available to Americans everywhere. Until we understand this history, we will never fully appreciate the threat.

It has been affirming as well. We have learned that contrary to our initial anxieties, everyone we have talked to agrees that *communication is essential to combating terrorism, improving national security, and securing a better, more credible posture for the United States in the world.* Without a single exception, they also agreed that current efforts by our government and by our diplomatic corps have largely failed.

Furthermore, our military and diplomatic leaders are far better informed, well read, and engaged with the scholarship on communication than we had originally suspected. For example, the Department of Defense, in September 2004, conducted its own seminar on Strategic Communication (recently declassified) that reveals a depth of intellectual and pragmatic understanding that would surprise most academics in our field. Unfortunately, there also exists within that beltway trap a variety of consultants, public relations firms, and self-professed communication experts adding some very bad ideas and outdated theories into the mix. Clearly, winning the war of ideas begins at home.

And our experience leading the course has been surprising. Our journey into the nexus of communication and terrorism has taught us many valuable lessons, but chief among them is that terrorism itself is a form of communication. It is a message intended for an audience and wherever it occurs and however it is delivered, how that message is interpreted as meaningful is the point of the exercise. Death, destruction, fear, and disruption are part of the message structure, but they must be understood in relation to the overall message campaign and not as stand-alone icons of grief or suffering.

Second, I have learned that those outside of academe are very much aware of their need to incorporate communication research and qualitative methods into their methods of combating terrorism. It was obvious that these specialists would be interested in technological advances in communication (such as network analysis software or content analysis programs), but what has been most surprising is their enthusiasm for learning more about ethnographic inquiry, counter-attitudinal advocacy, message credibility, and narrative theories. Ethnography represents "boots on the ground" intelligence about disparate cultures, and finding ourselves in global war means that how ethnographers learn to penetrate, access, and make sense of others is highly valuable knowledge. Counter-attitudinal advocacy and message credibility are long-established research traditions that have obvious carryover value to the problems of changing minds without resorting to half-truths and outright deception. Narrative theories are useful in understanding and shaping what our "message" is—or should be—at home and abroad. Clearly, the *story* we offer to others will go a long way toward influencing their expectations, attitudes, and willingness to work with us to identify terrorists and build a more secure future together.

To do that, we need to improve how we understand disparate others as well as how we communicate with them. We need to craft a better storyline, a truer and more credible one, in our campaign for public diplomacy at home and abroad. We need to advance knowledge and practice of intercultural communication from the current "transmission model" to a more contemporary one derived from what we know about dialogue and dialectics (Goodall, Under review).

Finally, I have learned that not only is what we know valuable and potentially useful to building a safer world for ourselves and for our children, but that none of us really has the luxury of time. We must begin *now* to combine the tools of academic critique with practical political action. And our political action should redirect our efforts away from resistance to rhetoric of the global war on terror to full-partner participation in the communication and intercultural work that must be done if we are to be successful in reestablishing the image of America as a good thing, a positive force, in the world.

Pause

My father hated communism. When I left for college, he asked me to promise that I wouldn't become one. It was the *only* thing he asked of me.

I had no difficulty making that promise. Hating an ideology was not part of my world. I had no intention of becoming associated politically with any "ist" or "ism." I have largely kept that promise.

But today, I do understand what it means to hate an ideology, an "ism." My enemy is *fundamentalism*. I hate fundamentalism of any variety because in every variety of it fundamentalism is the enemy of communication. Fundamentalism—whether it be Islamic or Baptist—is a faith-based virus that denies a living place for everything in life I value: grammar, logic, rhetoric, science, dialogue, discourse, difference, and discovery. I think of fundamentalism as a virus because it spreads so easily through noninoculated, often undereducated, populations. It is a message-born illness whose fever-pitched yap spawns fanaticism, intolerance, and hate, and whose violent, authoritative appeal is attributed to the will of God.

I hate fundamentalism. I hate it because of what it denies and because of what it inspires. I have learned that terrorism is the name we call its offspring.

Record

One of the unexpected byproducts of our seminar and public lecture series has been a personal realization that I, too, have been complicit in this war. Because I accept the truth of that sentence, I now share a moral and ethical responsibility for doing everything I can to prevent its spread. For me, that means sharing what I know with people who need to know it.

Here is why I am complicit:

Like most North Americans living in relative affluence in our comfortable cities and suburbs, I hadn't paid much attention to the pronouncements of Osama bin Laden, or to the actions of al Qaeda, or to their first attempt to bring down the World Trade Center Towers in 1993. I, like most of you and like almost everyone I've met in government, hadn't properly understood the cultural and narrative context for interpreting the messages of radical Islamic leaders during the 1990s.

Nor had I paid much attention to the attacks on our embassies in Kenya and Tanzania. The bombing of the U.S.S. *Cole* was merely another terrorist event in a land far away, in a region increasingly marked by news reports of violence. In fact, I am somewhat ashamed to admit it, but when talking heads on various news shows turned their collective attention to troubles in the Middle East, I usually switched channels.

I had better, more important, things to do.

Didn't I have an article to write for *Qualitative Inquiry*, or another ethnographic book to explore? I had students to teach, too many meetings to attend, a career to think about, and a wife and child and many friends with whom to enjoy this particular American life. I was *busy*. I voted. I worked for candidates. I thought I had kept up with world events. I listened every day to NPR. Terrorism, horrible as it was, happened elsewhere. It didn't concern me. Not *directly*. It wasn't my fault, so it was someone else's problem.

But I hadn't connected the dots. I hadn't connected the dots all the way down to me. My guess is, neither did *you*.

I nowadays tell that story. I've written an account of what I experienced and thought about when four commercial jets changed the course of my story, our narrative about American history, and undoubtedly the world's foreseeable future (Goodall, 2002). I'll give only the short version of how it begins here. I'll tell it again because it is my anti-orchid. It is the autoethnographic beginning of how and why and where I learned to use my writing to reveal a different truth.

September 11, 2001 was another busy day, and I thought I was just completing another task on my list of daily tasks when, at 8:46:40 American Airlines 11 ripped into the North Tower of the World Trade Center. I was in a small shop run by two nameless Middle Eastern gentlemen getting my new eyeglasses adjusted.

Without my glasses, I am nearly blind. So I didn't actually see the visuals that accompanied the initial news report. I remember that one of the men in the shop was making the adjustment to my frames when the other man, who had been in the rear of the store where a small television was located, reported to both of us what was happening. At first, it seemed an anomaly, a little weirdness in the morning of an otherwise ordinary day. The first news report indicated it was a small plane that had flown into the tower. How strange! We stood together, three strangers, and, when the man handed back my newly adjusted lens, we watched the news reports revise that story.

It may have been a commercial jet.

We were still standing there when United 175 crashed into the South Tower at 9:03:11. Suddenly, these events were not anomalies. None of us knew exactly what we were witnessing. We had no context to interpret it, no way of applying prior knowledge to it, no logical mechanism to kick in and make sense of what our eyes and ears were processing.

None of us had been connecting the dots.

But we knew this: one event can be an accident, but two like events occurring within minutes of each other in the same relative space creates *a pattern*. Gregory Bateson says all communication is pattern recognition. But knowing there is a pattern, and that the pattern is *communicating* something—in this case that it was a terrorist message—isn't the same thing as knowing what the pattern, or the message, means.

I didn't know what it meant. Neither did the men in the shop.

Nor, apparently, did almost anyone else, at almost every level, of our government. Reading *The 9/11 Commission Report* (2004), it is clear that my personal failing to adequately interpret the meaning of these terrorist messages—to even recognize they were messages—was replicated throughout every intelligence agency and political body throughout the land.

We had a failure of message, of message recognition, and of message interpretation. What we had on September 11 was clear evidence of our failures to communicate.

Since that fateful day, and since that particular adjustment to my lenses, I have resolved to learn to see more clearly my personal relationship to history and to accept my professional responsibility for national narratives crafted to tell particular stories about this ill-named global war on terror.

It is, as I said earlier, work I was born to do.

I grew up during the cold war. I know how to apply communication to cultural problems and narrative mysteries. I have skills as a qualitative researcher. I can be, and I want to be, useful to my country. Like my father before me, this unusual repertoire is knowledge I can neither deny nor get away from.

I have connected the dots all the way down to me.

I know I have ways of combating not only terrorism, but fundamentalism.

It is my moral imperative to act. It has been my cold war childhood, my father's life, and my seemingly nomadic autoethnographic academic life that has prepared me, that has equipped me, for a new way of thinking about what my future work should be.

References

Goodall, Jr., H. L. (2002). Fieldnotes from our war zone: Living in America during the aftermath of September Eleventh. *Qualitative Inquiry, 8,* 74–89.

Goodall, Jr., H. L. (2004). Narrative ethnography and applied communication research. *Journal of Applied Communication Research, 32,* 185–194.

Goodall, Jr., H. L. (2005). Narrative inheritance: A nuclear family with toxic secrets. *Qualitative Inquiry, 11,* 492–513.

Goodall, Jr., H. L. (2006). Why we must win the war on terror: Communication, narrative, and the future of national security. *Qualitative Inquiry, 12,* forthcoming.

Goodall, Jr., H. L. (Under review). A question of message: Finding narrative coherence through dialogue in a post-9/11 world.

The 9/11 Commission Report: Final Report of the National Commission on Terrorist *Attacks upon the United States* (2004). New York: W. W. Norton.

About the Authors

Gaile S. Cannella is professor of education at Arizona State University. She is the author of *Deconstructing Early Childhood Education: Social Justice and Revolution* (Peter Lang, 1997), coauthor (with Radhika Viruru) of *Childhood and Post–Colonization: Power, Education, and Contemporary Practice* (Routledge Falmer, 2004), and coeditor of *Kidworld: Childhood Studies, Global Perspectives, and Education* (Peter Lang, 2002). She is also the section editor for Childhood and Cultural Studies in the *Journal of Curriculum Theorizing*.

Julianne Cheek is a professor in the Division of Health Sciences and director of the Early Career Researcher Development program at the University of South Australia. She is the author of *Postmodern and Poststructural Approaches to Nursing Research* (Sage, 2000) and coauthor of *Finding Out: Information Literacy for the 21ˢᵗ Century* (Macmillan, 1995) and *Society and Health: Social Theory for Health Workers* (Longman Chesire, 1996), which won the prize for the best Tertiary Single Book (Wholly Australian) in the prestigious Australian Awards for Excellence in Educational Publishing for 1996.

Norman K. Denzin is Distinguished Professor of Communications, College of Communications Scholar, and Research Professor of Communications, Sociology, and Humanities at the University of Illinois, Urbana–Champaign. One of the world's foremost authorities on qualitative research and cultural criticism, Denzin is the author or editor of more than two dozen books, including *Reading Race, Interpretive Ethnography, The Cinematic Society, The Voyeur's Gaze, Images of Postmodern Society, The Recovering Alcoholic,* and *The Alcoholic Self.* He is past editor of *The Sociological Quarterly,* coeditor (with Yvonna S. Lincoln) of the landmark *Handbook of Qualitative Research* (1st, 2nd, and 3rd editions, Sage), editor of *Contesting Empire/Globalizing Dissent: Cultural Studies after 9/11* (Paradigm, 2006, with Michael D. Giardina), coeditor of the journal *Qualitative Inquiry,* founding editor of *Cultural Studies/Critical Methodologies,* series editor of *Studies in Symbolic Interaction,* and *Cultural Critique* series editor for Peter Lang Publishing.

Cynthia B. Dillard is associate professor of education at The Ohio State University in Columbus, Ohio. She has authored numerous articles and publications, including her latest book *On Spiritual Striving: Transforming an African American Woman's Academic Life* (SUNY Press, forthcoming). She is currently working on her next book, *Living Africa: A Book of Meditations.*

Greg Dimitriadis is associate professor of education at State University of New York, Buffalo. He is the author of *Performing Identity/Performing Culture: Hip Hop as Text, Pedagogy, and Lived Practice* (Peter Lang, 2001) and *Friendship, Cliques, and Gangs: Young Black Men Coming of Age in Urban America* (Teachers College Press, 2003), coauthor of *Reading and Teaching the Postcolonial: From Baldwin to Basquiat and Beyond* (Teachers College Press, 2001) and *On Qualitative Inquiry* (Teachers College Press, 2004), and coeditor of *Promises to Keep: Cultural Studies, Democratic Education, and Public Life* (Routledge Falmer, 2003), *Learning to Labor in New Times* (Routledge Falmer, 2004), and *Race, Identity, and Representation in Education* (2nd edition) (Routledge Falmer, 2005).

Adrienne Dixson is assistant professor of education at The Ohio State University. Dr. Dixson's research focuses on race and racial and gender identities in urban schooling contexts. She situates her work theoretically within critical race theory, Black feminist theories, and culturally relevant pedagogy. Methodologically, she is interested in ethnic epistemologies and qualitative research methodologies.

Michael D. Giardina is visiting assistant professor in Advertising & Cultural Studies at the University of Illinois, Urbana–Champaign. He is the author of *From Soccer Moms to NASCAR Dads: Sport, Culture, and Politics in a Nation Divided* (Paradigm, 2006) and *Sporting Pedagogies: Performing Culture & Identity in the Global Arena* (Peter Lang, 2005) and editor of *Contesting Empire/Globalizing Dissent: Cultural Studies after 9/11* (Paradigm, 2006, with Norman K. Denzin) and *Youth Culture & Sport: Identity, Power, and Politics* (Routledge, Forthcoming, with Michele K. Donnelly). His work on globalization, cultural studies, qualitative inquiry, and the racial logics of late capitalism has also appeared in journals such as *Harvard Educational Review, Cultural Studies/Critical Methodologies, Journal of Sport & Social Issues*, and *Qualitative Inquiry*.

Elsa M. González y González is a research fellow in higher education at Texas A&M University.

H. L. Goodall, Jr., is professor and director of the Hugh Downs School of Human Communication at Arizona State University. He is the author of *Writing the New Ethnography* (AltaMira, 2000) and *A Need to Know: The Clandestine History of a CIA Family* (Left Coast Press, 2006).

Lisa K. Hood is a doctoral/graduate student in educational psychology at the University of Illinois at Urbana–Champaign. Her interests include evaluation, qualitative research, and career and technical education in high schools and community colleges.

Ernest R. House is Emeritus Professor in the School of Education at the University of Colorado at Boulder. Previously, he was at the Center for Instructional Research and Curriculum Evaluation (CIRCE) at the University of Illinois, Urbana–Champaign. He has been a visiting scholar at UCLA, Harvard, and New Mexico, as well as in England, Australia, Spain, Sweden, Austria, and Chile. His primary interests are evaluation and policy analysis. Books authored include *Evaluating with Validity* (Sage, 1980), *Jesse Jackson and the Politics of Charisma* (Westview Press, 1988), *Professional Evaluation: Social Impact and Political Consequences* (Sage, 1993), and Schools for Sale: Why Free

Market Policies Won't Improve America's Schools, and What Will (Teachers College Press, 1998). He was the 1989 recipient of the Harold E. Lasswell Prize presented by Policy Sciences and the 1990 recipient of the Paul F. Lazarsfeld Award for Evaluation Theory, presented by the American Evaluation Association.

George Kamberelis is associate professor in the Department of Reading, School of Education, at State University of New York, Albany. He has conducted research on children's emerging and developing literacies, children's writing development, discourse and identity, language and cultural diversity, critical media literacy, and interpretive research methods. Among his many works, he is coauthor (with Greg Dimitriadis) of *On Qualitative Inquiry: Approaches to Language and Literacy Research* (Teachers College Press, 2004).

Patti Lather is professor of cultural studies in education in the School of Educational Policy and Leadership, College of Education, at the Ohio State University. She is the author of *Getting Smart: Feminist Research and Pedagogy with/in the Postmodern* (Routledge, 1991) and *Troubling the Angels: Women Living with HIV/AIDS* (Westview, 1997, with Chris Smithies), which was a CHOICE Outstanding Book of the Year for 1998. In addition, she published extensively in journals, including articles in the *Journal of Curriculum Theorizing*, *Qualitative Studies in Education*, *Review of Educational Research*, *Educational Theory*, and *Harvard Educational Review*.

Yvonna S. Lincoln is professor of higher education and human resource development at Texas A&M University, where she holds the Ruth Harrington Chair of Educational Leadership and University Distinguished Professor of Higher Education. She is the coauthor of *Effective Evaluation, Naturalistic Inquiry, and Fourth Generation Evaluation*, the editor of *Organizational Theory and Inquiry*, and coeditor (with Norman K. Denzin) of *The Handbook of Qualitative Research* (1st, 2nd, and 3rd editions, Sage) and the journal *Qualitative Inquiry*.

Cameron McCarthy is Research Professor, Communications Scholar, and University Scholar in the Institute of Communication Research at the University of Illinois, Urbana–Champaign. He is the author, coauthor, or editor of dozens of books, including: *Race Identity and Representation in Education* (1st and 2nd editions, Routledge, 1993/2005), *The Uses of Culture* (Routledge, 1998), and *Foucault, Cultural Studies and Governmentality* (SUNY Press, 2003).

Janice M. Morse is professor of nursing and director of the International Institute for Qualitative Methodology at the University of Alberta, Canada. Presently funded by the Medical Research Council of Canada, she is the author or editor of eighteen books, including *Nursing Research: The Application of Qualitative Approaches* (Stanley Thorne, 2003), *The Nature of Qualitative Evidence* (Sage, 2001), and *Preventing Patient Falls* (Sage, 2001). She is also the editor of the journal *Qualitative Health Research* (Sage), two methods series for Left Coast Press, Inc., and the Qual Institute Press.

Katherine E. Ryan is an associate professor in the Department of Educational Psychology at the University of Illinois at Urbana–Champaign. She is the editor of *Exploring Evaluator Role in Identity* (with Thomas Schwandt, Information Age Publishing, 2002), *Evaluation as a Democratic Process: Promoting Inclusion, Dialogue, and Deliberation* (with Lizanne DeStefano, Jossey–Bass, 2000), and *Evaluating Teaching in Higher Education: A Vision for the Future* (Jossey–Bass, 2000) Her most recent work addresses issues in educational program evaluation and student evaluation

Harry Torrance is professor of education and director of the Education and Social Research Institute at Manchester Metropolitan University, United Kingdom. He is the author of *Investigating Formative Assessment: Teaching, Learning and Assessment in the Classroom* (Open University Press, 1998, with J. Pryor), and has led several ESRC–funded research projects on the topic of research and teaching assessment. He is also coeditor of the British Educational Research Journal, series editor of Open University Press Series Assessing Assessment and Conducting Educational

Research, and serves on the editorial boards of *Assessment in Education*, *Cambridge Journal of Education*, and *International Journal of Educational Research*.

Linda Tuhiwai Smith is professor of Maori education and director of the International Research Institute for Maori and Indigenous Studies at the University of Auckland, New Zealand. In New Zealand, she has been central to the development of a tribal university, *Te Whare Wananga o Awanuiarangi*, and to the nationwide movement for an alternative schooling system, *Kura Kaupapa Maori*. Her leadership represents the pioneering work of Maori scholars and activists, which inspires indigenous and sovereignty work internationally. She is the author of the widely celebrated *Decolonizing Methodologies: Research and Indigenous Peoples* (Zed, 1999), which explores the intersections of imperialism, knowledge, and research.

Radhika Viruru is clinical associate professor in the Department of Teaching, Learning, and Culture at Texas A&M University. She is the author of *Early Childhood Education: Postcolonial Perspectives from India* (Sage, 2001) and coauthor (with Gaile S. Cannella) of *Revolution and Childhood and Post–Colonization: Power, Education, and Contemporary Practice* (Routledge Falmer, 2004).

Carolyne J. White is professor and chair of Urban Education at Rutgers University, where she honors American Indian educational sovereignty and prepares culturally sensitive educators.

Index